Rebuild and Renew

The Post-Exilic Books
of Ezra, Nehemiah, Haggai, Zechariah, and Malachi

for Personal Devotional Use, Small Groups or
Sunday School Classes, and Sermon Preparation for Pastors and Teachers

JesusWalk® Bible Study Series

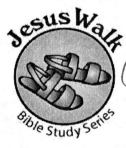

by Dr. Ralph F. Wilson
Director, Joyful Heart Renewal Ministries

Additional books, and reprint licenses are available at:
www.jesuswalk.com/books/rebuild.htm

Free Participant Guide handout sheets are available at:
www.jesuswalk.com/rebuild/rebuild-lesson-handouts.pdf

JesusWalk® Publications
Loomis, California

Paperback

ISBN-13: 978-0-9962025-4-1

ISBN-10: 0-9962025-4-4

Library of Congress subject headings:

> Bible. Old Testament Commentaries.
> Judaism – History – Post-exilic period, 586 B.C.-210 A.D.
> Bible. – Ezra – Commentaries
> Bible. – Nehemiah – Commentaries.
> Bible. – Haggai – Commentaries.
> Bible. – Zechariah – Commentaries.
> Bible. – Malachi – Commentaries.

Suggested Classifications

> Dewey Decimal System: 222.7; 222.8; 224.9
> Library of Congress: BS 1355.3, BS 1655

Published by JesusWalk® Publications, P.O. Box 565, Loomis, CA 95650-0565, USA.

JesusWalk is a registered trademark and Joyful Heart is a trademark of Joyful Heart Renewal Ministries.

Unless otherwise noted, all the Bible verses quoted are from the New International Version (International Bible Society, 1973, 1978), used by permission. A portion of Lesson 6 is adapted from my book *Great Prayers of the Bible* (JesusWalk Publications, 2005, 2011).

8/26/2017 3:35 PM

Preface

Old Testament history has two primary "watersheds," by which events are date "before" and "after." The first of these is the Exodus from Egypt. The second is the Exile to Babylon as judgment for the apostasy of God's people. Amazingly, however, God brings a remnant of his people back from exile. It is this "post-exilic" period that we're concentrating on here.

The Post-Exilic Books of Ezra, Nehemiah, Haggai, Zechariah, and Malachi are written about the period between 537 and perhaps 430 BC. Themes include returning to Jerusalem after the Exile, rebuilding the temple, restoring the wall, and then learning to walk before the Lord with sincerity and purity.

Of course, these books seem pretty obscure to the average believer. As a boy I was impressed by a Sunday school illustration of people celebrating the restoration of the wall of Jerusalem under Nehemiah – thousands of people marching *on top* of the new wall! You've probably heard some tithing sermons from Malachi – "God will open the windows of heaven." But perhaps your familiarity ends there.

These five books have been revered as the inspired Word of God for more than two thousand years and contain vital nuggets of truth that God has for you and me. As I've been pouring over these books for the past twelve months, I'm beginning to see how important they are. Jesus himself quotes from Zechariah and Malachi.

The books include:

- How God **changes the heart** of kings to bless His people (Ezra, Nehemiah).
- How to **handle the enemies** – both physical and spiritual – who hinder the rebuilding of the Temple of God in Jerusalem and in our hearts (Ezra).
- Why God **withholds his blessing**, and why he restores it (Haggai).
- **Messianic promises** of Christ's glory in the temple (Haggai).
- How **God uses prophets** to encourage, motivate, and correct his people (Haggai, Zechariah, Malachi).
- Why we shouldn't despise the **day of small beginnings** (Zechariah).
- **Messianic prophecies of Jesus** entering Jerusalem on a donkey, "the one they have pierced," the 30 pieces of silver, the "cleansing fountain," and striking the shepherd that the sheep are scattered (Zechariah).

- **Nehemiah's faith**, managerial wisdom, and spiritual toughness to complete God's assignment (Nehemiah).
- The outstanding feat of **restoring the broken wall in only 52 days** – amidst heavy opposition – and the importance of building protective walls in our lives to guard God's work in us (Nehemiah).
- The **amazing spiritual revival** of Ezra's day, and why it waned (Ezra).
- What happens when **believers marry unbelievers** (Ezra, Nehemiah, Malachi).
- Finding the **joy of the Lord** as our strength (Nehemiah).
- Spiritual lessons on purity of heart in **worship** and **giving to God** (Malachi).
- Prophecies about **John the Baptist** – the Messenger of Yahweh (Elijah who is to come) – and **Jesus, the Messenger of the Covenant**, and the Son of Righteousness who rises with healing in his wings (Malachi).
- And much, much more....

I'm particularly interested in **spiritual lessons that we disciples of Jesus can apply to our lives** to help us grow. These books are chock full of lessons for disciples, which I'll summarize at the end of each lesson, as well as highlight in the discussion questions interspersed in each lesson.

Zechariah, especially, contains a number of symbolic images. I won't try to interpret them all, but will concentrate on what the prophet says to the people that relates to their current task of rebuilding, so don't expect an End Times timeline here.

Unlike some of my studies of New Testament books, where we cover only a few verses per lesson, in this study of the post-exilic books we'll often cover several chapters per lesson. I feel a little apologetic that some of the chapters are so long. I've cut them down as far as I can and moved some into footnotes, but I want to leave enough so that someone doing a careful study has helpful material to guide them. If you must, skip some material to get to the material directly referred to in the Discussion Questions, for those contain the most important applications.

I invite you to join me as we take a JesusWalk through these important books. The Spirit has much to teach us here, as we're open to His voice. May God bless us as we study together.

> Dr. Ralph F. Wilson
> Loomis, California
> September 1, 2017

Table of Contents

References and Abbreviations

Baldwin Joyce Baldwin, *Haggai, Zechariah, Malachi: An Introduction and Commentary* (Tyndale Old Testament Commentaries; Tyndale Press, 1972)

BDAG Walter Bauer and Frederick William Danker, *A Greek-English Lexicon of the New Testament and Other Early Christian Literature*, (Third Edition; based on previous English editions by W.F. Arndt, F.W. Gingrich, and F.W. Danker; University of Chicago Press, 1957, 1979, 2000)

BDB Francis Brown, S.R. Driver, and Charles A. Briggs, *A Hebrew and English Lexicon of the Old Testament* (Clarendon Press, 1907)

DOTHB Bill T. Arnold and H.G.M. Williamson, *Dictionary of the Old Testament Historical Books* (InterVarsity Press, 2005)

DOTP Mark J. Boda and J. Gordon McConville, *Dictionary of the Old Testament Prophets* (InterVarsity Press, 2012)

ESV English Standard Version (Crossway, 2001)

Fensham F. Charles Fensham, *The Books of Ezra and Nehemiah* (New International Commentary on the Old Testament; Eerdmans, 1982)

Harrison R.K. Harrison, *Introduction to the Old Testament* (Eerdmans, 1969)

Holladay William L. Holladay, *A Concise Hebrew and Aramaic Lexicon of the Old Testament*, based on the Lexical work of Ludwig Koehler and Walter Baumgartner (Grand Rapids: Eerdmans / Leiden: E. J. Brill, 1988)

ISBE Geoffrey W. Bromiley (general editor), *The International Standard Bible Encyclopedia* (Eerdmans, 1979-1988; fully revised from the 1915 edition)

Kidner Derek Kidner, *Ezra and Nehemiah: An Introduction and Commentary* (Tyndale Old Testament Commentaries; Tyndale Press, 1979).

Kitchen K.A. Kitchen, *On the Reliability of the Old Testament* (Eerdmans, 2003)

KJV King James Version (Authorized Version, 1611)

Macmillan   Yohann Aharoni and Michael Avi-Yonah (completely revised by Anson F. Rainey and Ze'ev Safrai), *The Macmillan Bible Atlas* (Third Edition, Macmillan, 1993)

NASB   New American Standard Bible (The Lockman Foundation, 1960-1988)

NIV   New International Version (International Bible Society, 1973, 1978)

NJB   New Jerusalem Bible (Darton, Longman & Todd Ltd, 1985)

NRSV   New Revised Standard Version (Division of Christian Education of the National Council of Churches of Christ, USA, 1989)

Phillips   Richard D. Phillips, Zechariah (Reformed Expository Commentary; P&R Publishing, 2007)

TWOT   R. Laird Harris, Gleason L. Archer, Jr., and Bruce K. Waltke, (editors), *Theological Wordbook of the Old Testament*, (2 volumes, Moody Press, 1980)

Reprint Guidelines

Copying the Handouts. In some cases, small groups or Sunday school classes would like to use these notes to study this material. That's great. An appendix provides copies of handouts designed for classes and small groups. There is no charge whatsoever to print out as many copies of the handouts as you need for participants.

Free Participant Guide handout sheets are available at:

www.jesuswalk.com/return/return-lesson-handouts.pdf

All charts and notes are copyrighted and must bear the line:

"Copyright © 2017, Ralph F. Wilson. All rights reserved. Reprinted by permission."

You may not resell these notes to other groups or individuals outside your congregation. You may, however, charge people in your group enough to cover your copying costs.

If you copy the book (or the majority of it) for your congregation or group, you are requested to purchase a reprint license for each book. A Reprint License, $2.50 for each copy is available for purchase at

www.jesuswalk.com/books/return.htm

Or you may send a check to:

Dr. Ralph F. Wilson
JesusWalk Publications
PO Box 565
Loomis, CA 95650, USA

The Scripture says,

"The laborer is worthy of his hire" (Luke 10:7) and "Anyone who receives instruction in the word must share all good things with his instructor." (Galatians 6:6)

However, if you are from a third world country or an area where it is difficult to transmit money, please make a small contribution instead to help the poor in your community.

Introduction to the Post-Exilic Period

As mentioned in the preface, Old Testament history clusters around two "watersheds," the Exodus from Egypt and the Exile to Babylon.

All five of the books we are studying were written in Judah during what is known as the Post-Exilic Period, that is, the hundred years or so that follows the return from exile in Babylon that began about 537 BC.

If you're just getting familiar with the Old Testament, here's a quick glance at where these books fit:

Here's my mental image of what Nehemiah must have looked like. John Singer Sargent, 'Head of an Arab' (1891), oil on canvas, 31.5 x 23.12 inches, Museum of Fine Arts, Boston.

1. Patriarchs (1800-1500 BC) – Abraham, Isaac, and Jacob
2. Exodus (1400 BC) – Moses
3. Conquest and Judges (1400-950 BC) – Joshua, Gideon, etc.
4. Monarchy (950 to 587 BC) – Saul, David, Solomon, and the Divided Kingdom
5. Exile (604 to 537 BC) – the Jewish community lives in Babylon
6. **Post-Exilic Period (537 to 430 BC) – rebuilding the temple and walls of Jerusalem. Malachi, last book of the Old Testament, written about 430 BC.**
7. Intertestamental Period (430 BC to 6 BC) – Greeks desecrate temple, Maccabee Rebellion, Hasmonean Dynasty, Romans conquer, Herod the Great.
8. Life of Jesus of Nazareth (6 BC to 27 AD)
9. The Early Church (27 AD to 95 AD). Last books of New Testament written about 95 AD.

Overview of Post-Exilic Books

We're studying five books in this series – Ezra, Nehemiah, Haggai, Zechariah, and Malachi. Here's a quick overview so you can see where we're going. Instead of progressing in order of the books as they appear in the Bible, I've arranged the lessons in approximate chronological order. Here's what we'll cover in the 10 lessons.

1. **Returning to Rebuild the Temple (Ezra 1-6).** This historical passage covers the period from Cyrus's proclamation, and includes the return of the first group from Babylon about 537 BC, the rebuilding of the temple, work stoppages due to enemies, and the completion and dedication of the temple about 515 BC.

2. **Realigning Priorities (Haggai 1-2).** This is a short prophetic book of four prophecies given about 520 BC designed to encourage the Jewish leaders to get started again on rebuilding the temple.

3. **Encouragement for the Builders (Zechariah 1-6).** Zechariah is a longer prophetic book that I've broken up into two lessons. The first lesson contains prophecies given about 520 BC designed to encourage the Jews to complete the temple project. Zechariah's prophecies come with some rather bizarre images to interpret.

4. **Prophecies of the Messiah (Zechariah 7-14).** The second half of Zechariah contains four prophecies without a specific date. These point to the coming Messiah, a call to righteousness, an indictment of false shepherds, the final battle, and the New Jerusalem.

5. **Confession and Repentance (Ezra 7-10).** After studying the prophecies leading up to the completion of the temple, we return to Ezra's narrative. Ezra leads a new caravan of Jews from Babylon to Jerusalem about 458 BC. Then we see how Ezra deals with the people's sins of intermarrying with non-believers.

6. **Nehemiah's Prayer (Nehemiah 1:1-2:8).** Nehemiah hears of the plight of Jerusalem and offers a prayer to God that can serve as a model for us of a prayer of confession and intercession. We see a tough, spiritual leader in action.

7. **Restoring the Wall (Nehemiah 2:9-7:73).** Jerusalem's wall has been broken down. Nehemiah organizes resources and teams, then completes the task in 52 days – all amidst stiff opposition from Judah's enemies. But Nehemiah has to deal with intermarriage with non-Jews – again.

8. **Repentance and Revival (Nehemiah 8-13).** Now Ezra takes center stage again by reading and explaining God's law to the entire nation. The result is a genuine spiritual revival, and a final celebration of the completion of the wall.

9. **Love, Worship, and Marriage (Malachi 1-2).** Now we move to the Prophet Malachi, who writes sometime between 460 and 430 BC. His first three prophecies concern the need for sincere worship, and faithfulness to a covenant of marriage, rather than easy divorces.

10. **Justice, Tithing, Purifying, and Judgment (Malachi 3-4).** We conclude with Malachi's last three prophecies concerning purifying God's people, faithfulness in tithing, and the future Day of Judgment when the wicked are punished and the righteous vindicated. A final promise looks forward to John the Baptist and Jesus the Messiah.

A Quick Guide to the Exiles of Israel and Judah

The super-powers that conquered Israel and Judah – both the Assyrians and the Babylonians – responded to rebellious kings by destroying their cities and deporting thousands of their leaders and leading families to other places in the empire, leaving the local populations poor and leaderless. Let's look at these exiles.

Assyrian Captivity (began 740 to 722 BC). Assyria conquers many cities in both Judah and Israel, though not Jerusalem. They begin to deport people from the Northern Kingdom of Israel into exile about 740 BC (1 Chronicles 5:26; 2 Kings 15:29). When Samaria the capital falls after a three-year siege, thousands more are deported (2 Kings 17:3-6; 18:11-12). Most of these exiled Jews assimilate into the peoples of the lands where they are taken, and never return in any large numbers. The Assyrians go a step further and bring displaced peoples from other regions to settle in Israel. Those Israelites that remain retain a kind of Yahweh worship that mixes with worship of pagan gods of the land and of the displaced persons

James J. Tissot, 'The Flight of the Prisoners' (1898-1902), gouache on board, The Jewish Museum, New York.

brought by the Assyrians. This group is known as the Samaritans, and opposed the Jews who return from exile from Babylon. They were still rejected by the Jews in Jesus' day.

Babylonian Captivity (began 604-587 BC). The Babylonians, who succeed the Assyrians as a superpower, conquer rebellious Judah and seek to subdue it by three deportations in 604 BC, 597 BC, and finally in 587 BC, when Jerusalem is destroyed and all the leaders exiled, leaving only the poorest in the land. The Jewish faith, however, experiences a renewal while in exile, a return to observance of the Mosaic Law. Though many Jews eventually prosper in Babylon and have no desire to return, many long to return to Jerusalem and rebuild their temple, the center of their faith and the locus of the sacrificial system that remits their sins.

Rise of the Medo-Persian Empire

Cyrus, King of Persia (Cyrus II to historians), is known as Cyrus the Great because he is the founder of the Achaemenid Empire. In 559 BC, he receives from his father reign over the minor Persian kingdom of Anshan, in what is now southwest Iran. Cyrus is ambitious. His kingdom is a vassal of the overlord Astyages who rules the vast Median empire. But Cyrus rebels. By 550 BC he has captured the capital at Ectabana and overthrown Astyages, taking control of all the vassal kingdoms of the Medes, uniting them with the Persian kingdoms, and forging the great Medo-Persian empire that lasts for more than 200 years. Next, he turns his attention to putting down a rebellion in Assyria. Finally, he turns to Babylon. (For more details see Appendix 4. The Medo-Persian Empire.)

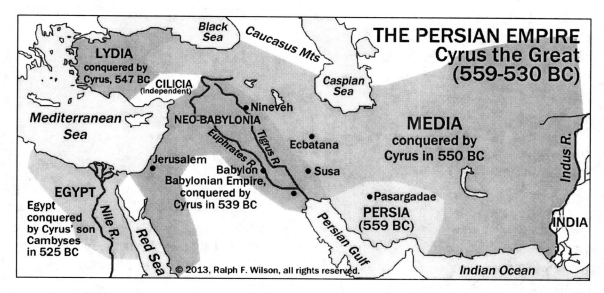

The Fall of Babylon

Babylon is ruled by Nabonidus (556–539 BC). He isn't much interested in governing or commanding the army. Instead, he spends years at a time away from the capital city pursuing his hobbies. He leaves his son Belshazzar to command the army and rule in Babylon as co-regent. The Babylonian Empire, strong under Nebuchadnezzar, is now growing old and weak.

Moreover, there are rumors of the rising power of the neighboring Medo-Persians, united 549 to 546 BC under Cyrus the Great (559–530 BC). After putting down a rebellion in Assyria, Cyrus now turns his attentions to the once-great Babylonian Empire.

In October, 539 BC, a great battle occurs at Opis, a regional capital located at a crossing of the Tigris river, 47 miles (76 km.) north of the city of Babylon. The Babylonian army is attacked by Cyrus's Medo-Persian army of overwhelming numbers, delivering the Babylonians a crushing defeat. Almost immediately, the nearby city of Sippar – less than 40 miles (about 60 km.) north of Babylon – surrenders. And in a short period of time, the Medo-Persian army is at the gates of Babylon.

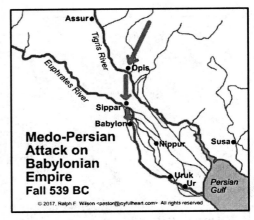

Medo-Persian Attack on Babylonian Empire Fall 539 BC

Though accounts differ, it seems that Babylon fell to the Medo-Persians without a fight.[1] Daniel's account of the handwriting on the wall of the royal palace describes the swiftness of Babylon's fall. Daniel the Prophet is summoned to interpret the cryptic words on the wall. He declares

"This is what these words mean:

Mene: God has numbered the days of your reign and brought it to an end.

Tekel: You have been weighed on the scales and found wanting.

Peres: Your kingdom is divided and given to the Medes and Persians."
(Daniel 5:26-28)

God's execution of this sentence is swift:

"That very night Belshazzar, king of the Babylonians, was slain, and Darius the Mede took over the kingdom, at the age of sixty-two." (Daniel 5:30-31)

Overnight, the vast Babylonian Empire is under the control of Cyrus the Great – and things change rapidly for the Jewish exiles.

---

[1] Both the Babylonian Chronicle and the Cyrus Cylinder describe Babylon being taken "without battle." The Greek historians Herodotus and Zenophon report a siege of the city. Daniel's account implies that Babylon was taken in one night.

The Province of Judah (Yehud)

A remnant of the Jewish community in Babylon returns in several migrations, beginning about 537 BC (Ezra 1-6) led by Zerubbabel (grandson of Jehoiachin, a former king of Judah) and Jeshua, the high priest. We're told that another company comes with Ezra about 458 BC (Ezra 7-8).

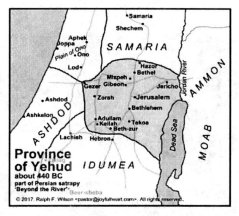

After building homes in various towns in Judah, the Jews seek to rebuild the temple in Jerusalem. Due to opposition from the surrounding provinces – the Amorites, the Samaritans, and the Arabs – they are hindered and finally have to stop. God sends two prophets about 520 BC – Haggai and Zechariah – who inspire the people to complete the temple about 515 BC.

Rebuilding the Walls under Nehemiah

However, Jerusalem's walls are still broken down, making the city defenseless. Any attempts to restore the walls are met by sharp opposition from enemies that obtain restraining orders from various kings of Persia – including Artaxerxes (464-424 BC). But Nehemiah is cupbearer to Artaxerxes, who appoints him to be governor of Judah and complete the walls – trumping previous anti-Jewish policies (445 BC). After developing building teams and assembling the needed materials, Nehemiah leads them to complete the walls in 52 days and later leads in a great celebration as the Jews march around the city on the top of the newly repaired walls.

Revival

While Nehemiah is primarily the civil governor during this time, Ezra, a priest and scribe, is the spiritual leader. By means of a Scripture-reading marathon, the people's hearts are touched, and they begin to repent of sins and pledge themselves to serve God faithfully.

Later, however, we see signs of the revival waning. Like Ezra before him, Nehemiah has to deal with the vexing problem of intermarriage with the surrounding non-Jewish people that directly affect the integrity of the Jewish people. Sometime in this period God sends the Prophet Malachi to challenge the people's complacency and spiritual drifting. Malachi is the last Old Testament book to be written, perhaps as late as 430 BC, and closes the Post-Exilic Period that we are studying.

John Singer Sargent, detail of 'The Triumph of Religion: Frieze of the Prophets' (installed 1895, East Wall), Boston Public Library. Left to right: Haggai, Malachi, and Zechariah.

1. Returning to Rebuild the Temple (Ezra 1-6)

It is 539 BC. The nightmare of warfare, slaughter, and deportation to Babylon has faded. Many alive now have never seen the Holy City, but have been born in Babylon, in the area around Nippur, where the Jews had settled after three deportations from Jerusalem between 604 and 587 BC. The last deportation in 587 BC had coincided with the utter destruction of

Zely Smekhov, "Rebuilding the Temple"

their beloved city. As thousands of Jews were marched off to exile in Babylon, their last view may have been the smoldering ruins and broken down walls of their temple and city.

The Jewish Community in Babylon

The exiled Jews are settled together in Babylonia in an area along the Chebar (or Kebar) canal.[2] This seems to be a navigable "great canal," designed for irrigation, flowing southeast for about 60 miles from above Babylon to east of Nippur, rejoining the Euphrates near Uruk (Erech).[3] In our day this watercourse is silted up and dry. The exiled Jews live in a number of towns in this general area.[4]

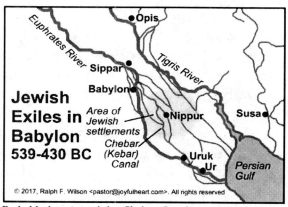

Probable location of the Chebar Canal near Nippur. Since 539 BC, the Persian Gulf has silted up, extending the outlet of the Tigris and Euphrates Rivers into the Gulf by many miles..

[2] Ezekiel 1:1,3; 3:15, 23; 10:15, 20; and 43:3.
[3] W. Ewing, "Chebar," ISBE 1:638. The Arabs refer to it as Shaṭṭ en Nî.
[4] See Ezra 2:59; Nehemiah 7:62.

After the initial shock of radical displacement, the exiled Jews settle down and prosper in their new land. They plant farms in the rich and productive river bottom land between the great Tigris and Euphrates rivers. A strong religious community flourishes here, and for some, the desire for home never leaves/ One psalmist of this period writes:

> "By the rivers of Babylon we sat and wept
> when we remembered Zion....
> If I forget you, O Jerusalem,
> may my right hand forget [its skill].
> May my tongue cling to the roof of my mouth
> if I do not remember you,
> if I do not consider Jerusalem my highest joy."
> (Psalm 137:1-6)

James J. Tissot, 'Waters of Babylon' (1896-1902), gouache on board, The Jewish Museum, New York.

The Jews seem resigned to their fate as exiles far from their homeland. Yes, many years before, Jeremiah had prophesied that the exile would last 70 years (Jeremiah 25:11-12), but most have forgotten.

Then, all of a sudden, Babylon falls to the Medes and Persians in 539 BC. Overnight, the vast Babylonian Empire is under the control of Cyrus the Great – and things change rapidly for the Jewish exiles. (For details see Introduction to the Post-Exilic Period and Appendix 4. The Medo-Persian Empire.)

Cyrus Helps the Exiles to Return (Ezra 1)

The Book of Ezra begins with events that occur many years before Ezra himself is born, with the momentous events of the return to Jerusalem. Let's take a look at the text and the historical events that surround it.

> "In the first year of Cyrus king of Persia, in order to fulfill the word of the LORD spoken by Jeremiah, the LORD moved the heart of Cyrus king of Persia to make a proclamation throughout his realm and to put it in writing" (Ezra 1:1)

The "first year of Cyrus king of Persia" is measured by the writer from the date Cyrus took over Babylon, that is 539 BC. "The word of the Lord spoken by Jeremiah" promised God's intervention to "bring you back" to Jerusalem after 70 years.

> "When seventy years are completed for Babylon, I will come to you and fulfill my gracious promise to bring you back to this place." (Jeremiah 29:10)

The text tells us, "the Lord moved the heart of Cyrus the king of Persia...." Yes, there are historical factors, which we'll consider. But God is the key factor. Through Jeremiah has predicts the return 70 years before it takes place, and now uses these historical factors to "move" or "stir up"[5] Cyrus's heart and restore his people to his homeland.

Cyrus's Proclamation (Ezra 1:2-4)

"[2] This is what Cyrus king of Persia says: 'The LORD, the God of heaven, has given me all the kingdoms of the earth and he has appointed me to build a temple for him at Jerusalem in Judah. [3] Anyone of his people among you – may his God be with him, and let him go up to Jerusalem in Judah and build the temple of the LORD, the God of Israel, the God who is in Jerusalem. [4] And the people of any place where survivors may now be living are to provide him with silver and gold, with goods and livestock, and with freewill offerings for the temple of God in Jerusalem.'" (Ezra 1:2-4)

Religious Policy of the Persian Empire

It is rather remarkable that upon conquering Babylon, Cyrus both frees the Jewish exiles to return to their homeland – and helps fund rebuilding the temple in Jerusalem. How did this come about?

A notable feature of the Persian empire is its integration of a great diversity of peoples into a single administrative system, while at the same time maintaining a tradition of respect for their local customs and beliefs.

The Assyrians, and the Babylonians after them, destroy the temples of their adversaries. But the Persians are different. Though they have their own gods, they are polytheists. Their attitude is that having more gods on their side, who are favorable to them and to their rule, is a good thing.

---

[5] "Moved" (NIV), "stirred up" (NRSV, ESV, KJV) is *ûr*, "rouse oneself, awake, incite" (TWOT #1587).

Indeed, the Jews are not the only recipients of this more liberal view. The Cyrus Cylinder, a clay cylinder dating from the sixth century BC, written in Akkadian cuneiform, chronicling Cyrus's deeds, indicates that Cyrus is responsible for returning a number of peoples to their lands and rebuilding their temples in order to get more gods favorable to him and his family. Does this mean that God isn't the one who brings the exiles back to Judah? No, it is God who raises up a ruler to do just this.

The Cyrus Cylinder (front, written 539-538 BC), Babylon, now in the British Museum, London.

Isaiah prophesies hundreds of years before this era about Cyrus and even refers to him by name (Isaiah 45:13).

> "He is my shepherd and will accomplish all that I please;
> he will say of Jerusalem, 'Let it be rebuilt,'
> and of the temple, 'Let its foundations be laid.'" (Isaiah 44:28)

It turns out just as Isaiah prophesies. Cyrus releases the people and rebuilds Jerusalem (2 Chronicles 36:22-23; Ezra 1:1). Amazing!

We Christians should follow Paul's exhortation to pray for government leaders, no matter what our personal political persuasion or how righteous they are. God is greater than political party or man's policies. God is at work in the affairs of nations (1 Timothy 2:1-4).

God's Preparations (Ezra 1:5-6)

God not only prepares the heart of Cyrus. He also prepares the hearts of the people he has chosen to be part of the first wave of returning exiles.

> "5 Then the family heads of Judah and Benjamin, and the priests and Levites – everyone whose heart God had moved – prepared to go up and build the house of the LORD in Jerusalem. 6 All their neighbors assisted them with articles of silver and gold, with goods and livestock, and with valuable gifts, in addition to all the freewill offerings." (Ezra 1:5-6)

Even though they aren't part of the returnees, "all their neighbors" contribute generously to the cause (Ezra 1:4). They may have decided to remain in their new land, but they aren't so materialistic that they refuse to help those who wish to return.

I wonder about the people who stay in Babylon. Some continue to be part of a vibrant and faithful Jewish community. Some help finance the expedition to Jerusalem, even though they stay behind. But some, I am sure, stay behind because they have become comfortable away from their land. Returning and rebuilding is too much trouble. Are we too tired or complacent or comfortable to become pioneers once again as God leads us?

To help you internalize and apply what you are learning from this study, I have included several Discussion Questions in each lesson. These are designed to help you think about and ponder the most important points. Don't skip these. It is best to write out your answers, whether you post them or not. However, you can post your answers – and read what others have written – by going to the online forum by clicking on the URL below each question. (Before you can post your answer the first time, you will need to register. You can find instructions at http://www.joyfulheart.com/forums/instructions.htm

Q1. (Ezra 1:5-6) Why did only some return to Jerusalem when given the opportunity? What are the likely characteristics of those who return vs. those who stay behind in Babylon? Why do only some answer Jesus' call to follow him on his journey to a radically different kind of lifestyle and mission? What are the characteristics of true disciples?
http://www.joyfulheart.com/forums/topic/1719-q1-motivation-to-return/

Restoration of the Temple Treasure (Ezra 1:7-11)

One sign of God at work is Cyrus's willingness to restore to the Jews the equivalent of many millions of dollars from the Babylonian's hoard of temple treasure stolen from the Jerusalem temple before it was destroyed. For a rich king to part with treasure takes God! Verses 7-11 list all the expensive articles of silver and gold.

Sheshbazzar, called "the prince of Judah" (Ezra 1:8, 11) is designated by Cyrus as the responsible party. The term "prince" refers to a person in authority, not necessarily someone of the royal line.[6] He is mentioned in Ezra 5:14-16 as participating in laying the foundation of the temple.[7]

List of the Exiles Who Returned (Ezra 2)

Chapter 2 consists of a list of the returning Jews by family. The "province" mentioned is that of Yehud (Judah), which was a sub-unit of the larger Persian division (or satrapy) called Abar-Nahara ("Beyond the River"),[8] referring to the Euphrates River.

I draw your attention to a few leaders listed in verse 2. Zerubbabel is of royal blood and becomes governor of the province of Judah (Yehud). Jeshua is the high priest. More on them in Lesson 2. Nehemiah is a relatively common name. This Nehemiah is not the later governor and rebuilder of the walls, featured in the book of Nehemiah. Some of the other names are found elsewhere in Ezra and Nehemiah, but these are common names, and probably not the same people. A similar list in Nehemiah 7:7 includes one further name. (To clear up confusions with names, refer to Appendix 3 – Main Characters of Ezra and Nehemiah).

Note that the people who return are listed according to family or clan (Ezra 2: 3-19 or 20), others according to their ancestral home (verses 20 or 21 to 35). Those whose genealogy cannot be traced are listed separately (verses 50-61).

Several groups stand out: the priests (verses 36-39), the Levites (verses 40-42), the temple servants (verses 43-54), and the sons of Solomon's servants (verses 55-57). Priests who can't be certified according to their genealogy aren't allowed to partake of the priests' portion of the sacrifices until their status can be determined by a high priest consulting the Urim and Thummim, holy lots, by which God's will can be determined (verses 61-63).[9]

---

[6] *Nāśî*, "prince, captain, leader, chief, ruler" (TWOT #1421b).

[7] Some identify Sheshbazzar as Shenazzar (1 Chronicles 3:18), which would make him a son of Jehoiachin, and uncle of Zerubbabel, who emerges as a more prominent leader of this period. R.L. Pratt, Jr., "Sheshbazzar," ISBE 4:475. Fensham sees this identification as "not acceptable" (*Ezra and Nehemiah*, p. 46). See also a discussion of the issues in Kidner, *Ezra and Nehemiah*, Appendix 2.

[8] Ezra 4:10, 11, 17, 20; 5:3, 6; 6:6, 8, 13; 7:21, 25; 8:36; Nehemiah 2:7; 3:7.

[9] According to Numbers 3:10; 16:40, only the descendants of Aaron should serve at the altar. Presumably, the Urim and Thummim had been lost at the destruction of the temple, or the current high priest has no practice in using them to determine God's will. Scripture doesn't mention the use of the Urim and Thummim after the exile.

Ezra 2:64 gives the total number of Israelites as 42,360, with an additional "male and female servants" or slaves totaling 7,337, as well as 200 male and female singers. In other words, one sixth of the returnees are slaves! This gives some indication of the

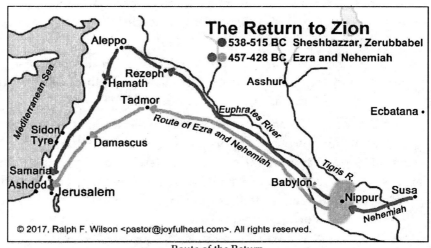

Route of the Return

wealth of some of the company. This acceptance of slavery comes back to hurt the community later during a famine, when Jews who can't pay for food are sold into slavery by wealthier Jews (Nehemiah 5:5). The number of horses, mules, camels, and donkeys indicates that most of the returnees walked the entire way from Babylon to Jerusalem. Only the wealthy rode animals; the rest of the animals were to carry the goods they brought with them.

Ezra 2:68-69 indicates that when they arrive, the wealthy give generous gifts to help rebuild the temple, as well as money for priests' garments.

Once the company arrives in Jerusalem, they return to the towns and villages that their families had lived in prior to the exile. The priests and Levites have assigned villages, as well as the other Israelites. A list of these villages is found in Nehemiah 11:25-36. Few people lived in Jerusalem itself (Nehemiah 11:1-2).

Rebuilding the Altar (Ezra 3:1-6)

When Noah's family come out of the ark, the first thing he does is to build an altar to the Lord and make a sacrifice (Genesis 8:20). Abraham, too, when he comes to a new place, would build an altar (Genesis 12:7-8; 13:4, 18; 22:9), as did Isaac and Jacob after him (Genesis 26:25; 33:20; 35:1, 3, 7).

So far as we know, the Jews built no altars for sacrifice in Babylon.[10] So in the seventh month after they arrive in Jerusalem, they clear away a space on the site of Solomon's temple, and build an altar.

"They set the altar in its place, for fear was on them because of the peoples of the lands, and they offered burnt offerings on it to the LORD, burnt offerings morning and evening." (Ezra 3:3)

There is considerable fear among the Israelites as they gather in Jerusalem. For one, no one is at home in their towns to protect their families. Since the Israelites displaced some other peoples when they settled, there is lots of tension. Nor do the people of the land want the Israelites to establish themselves by rebuilding the Jerusalem and their temple. But their fear leads them to God. If they can reestablish the sacrifices, then God will look with favor upon them.

So they "set the altar in its place" and begin the prescribed sacrifices that they had conducted in the old temple. These consisted of morning and evening sacrifices, as defined in the Pentateuch (Exodus 29:38-43; also Numbers 28:3-8). In addition these, they begin to offer the special sacrifices prescribed for the Feast of Tabernacles (Numbers 29:12-40), Sabbath sacrifices (Numbers 28:9-10), New Moon sacrifices (Numbers 28:11-15), for the other prescribed festivals (Numbers 28-29), and for families that bring "freewill offerings" (Numbers 15:3).

Offering sacrifice before the temple is rebuilt. Artist unknown.

What was the altar like that was built on the temple site by the returning exiles?[11] It was likely made of unhewn stones. We read in 1 Maccabees, after the temple was defiled

---

[10] A Jewish community on the island of Elephantine, on the Upper Nile opposite Aswan (6th through 4th centuries BC) built a temple where sacrifices were offered. It was destroyed by Egyptian insurgents in 410 BC. Apparently worship there was polytheistic (R.K. Harrison, "Elephantine Papyri," ISBE 2:61).

[11] The tabernacle and temple had seen various altars over time, from the portable bronze altar that accompanied the tabernacle, to the simple altar David built on the threshing floor of Arunah (2 Samuel 24:18-25). We don't have a description of the original altar in Solomon's temple, except that it was bronze

by Antiochus Epiphanes, that they took the defiled stones away and built the altar with "unhewn stones" (1 Maccabees 4:47).[12]

Beginning the Restoration of the Temple (Ezra 3:6-13)

"[6b] But the foundation of the temple of the LORD was not yet laid. [7] So they gave money to the masons and the carpenters, and food, drink, and oil to the Sidonians and the Tyrians to bring cedar trees from Lebanon to the sea, to Joppa, according to the grant that they had from Cyrus king of Persia.... [8b] They appointed the Levites, from twenty years old and upward, to supervise the work[13] of the house of the LORD." (Ezra 3:6-7, 8b)

Sidon and Tyre are ancient Phoenician trading cities on the coast of present-day Lebanon. These cities were ports for the export of timber from the "cedars of Lebanon" that supply beams and lumber for roofs and gates in the public buildings of the region.

Rather than seeing the *foundation* completed here, it's probably more accurate to see the work of restoration begun, in the sense of "to build."[14] Ezra 3:6ff describes the *beginning* of the work in 537 BC, which quickly fell into activity. In Haggai 2:18, 17 years later in 520 BC, the same word is used to describe the *resumption* of building, not recompleting the foundation. We'll revisit this issue in Lesson 2.

The Babylonians had destroyed Solomon's temple in 587 BC by fire (2 Kings 25:9). You can't burn stone, though heat will crack some stones. But as the roof timbers burn,

---

(1 Kings 8:64; 2 Kings 16:14). For a while it was supplanted with a copy of a pagan altar from Damascus (2 Kings 16:10-15).

[12] They apparently follow instructions in Deuteronomy 27:5-7, which directs construction of the altar built by Joshua at Mount Ebal (Joshua 8:30-31).

[13] "Building" (NIV), "work" (NRSV, ESV, KJV) at the end of verse 8 is *melāʾkâ*, "work, business." It can refer either to the activity of working, the requisite skills of work, or to the results of work. In contrast to terms like *ʿāmal* and *yāgaʿ* which emphasized the toilsome, laborious side of work, this term emphasized work as involving skill and benefits (Andrew Bowling, TWOT #1068b).

[14] "Foundation" in verses 6, 10, 11, and 12 is not a noun, but a verb, the Pual stem of *yāsad*, "to found, to fix firmly," from which the major nominal meanings derive, i.e. "foundation," especially of a building (TWOT #875). Sometimes the word is probably used more generally, as here, in the sense of "to build." Joyce Baldwin (*Haggai, Zechariah, Malachi*, pp. 52-53) notes that "the Hebrew employs no noun corresponding to the English 'foundations.' Two sentences in which the Chronicler uses this verb are particularly instructive: 'Now concerning ... the rebuilding of the house of God...' (2 Chronicles 24:27, RF), and, speaking of the collection of tithes, 'In the third month they began to lay the foundation of the heaps' (2 Chronicles 31:7, RF), or 'they began to pile up the heaps' (RSV). These examples show that the word 'foundation' is not essential; in fact it has been a very misleading translation. In both sentences quoted, *yasad* could have been adequately translated by the simple verb 'build'."

the entire structure, walls and all, come tumbling down, breaking many of the stones and making them unusable. Only rubble is left. So eventually, the ruins of the temple will have to be completely cleared from the site. Foundations, however, typically consist of large cut blocks of stone. You can see some of the foundations of the Second Temple at the present-day Wailing Wall.[15]

Celebration and Mourning (Ezra 3:10-13)

Beginning construction of the temple is a huge accomplishment, a big step towards the goal of completing of the temple. And this step merited a great celebration with singers, instruments, trumpets, and shouting.

> "[11b] And all the people shouted with a great shout when they praised the LORD, because the foundation of the house of the LORD was laid. [12] But many of the priests and Levites and heads of fathers' houses, old men who had seen the first house, wept with a loud voice when they saw the foundation of this house being laid, though many shouted aloud for joy, [13] so that the people could not distinguish the sound of the joyful shout from the sound of the people's weeping, for the people shouted with a great shout, and the sound was heard far away." (Ezra 3:11b-13)

Those who had seen the previous temple aren't weeping tears of joy. Rather they "wept with a loud voice," words that describe mourning that the Second Temple isn't as grand as Solomon's. As we'll see in Lesson 2, Haggai rebukes this attitude (Haggai 2:3) and in Lesson 3, Zechariah warns against despising "the day of small things" (Zechariah 4:10). Faith looks to God, not just to what we can now see with our eyes, "for we walk by faith, not by sight" (2 Corinthians 5:7).

> **Q2. (Ezra 3) Rebuilding the temple in order to restore worship is the point of all this work. Is your personal worship what it should be? What foundations do you need to lay again in your personal restoration and revival of faith?**
> **http://www.joyfulheart.com/forums/topic/1720-q2-restoring-worship/**

---

[15] The new structure is less grand than Solomon's, which had been built when the nation was rich and powerful. Many who had seen Solomon's temple weep when they see the foundation of its replacement (Ezra 3:12). The large façade at the front of the Second Temple seems different from the design of Solomon's Temple. The Second Temple is 60 cubits high and 60 cubits wide (Ezra 6:3). A cubit was the length of a man's forearm, from the elbow to the finger tips, typically about 18 inches (0.5 meter) So the size is 90 feet (27 meters) high and wide. The weight of that stone edifice is tremendous, so the foundation stones underlying that area must be sound and strong. It is quite possible that entirely new foundations are needed to bear the weight of the differently-positioned walls of the Second Temple.

Opposition to the Rebuilding (Ezra 4:1-5, 24)

Any time people are led to a great thing for God, there is opposition. Sometimes opposition to God's work seems almost reasonable.

> "¹ When the enemies of Judah and Benjamin heard that the exiles were building a temple for the LORD, the God of Israel,² they came to Zerubbabel and to the heads of the families and said, 'Let us help you build because, like you, we seek your God and have been sacrificing to him since the time of Esarhaddon king of Assyria, who brought us here.'
>
> ³ But Zerubbabel, Jeshua and the rest of the heads of the families of Israel answered, 'You have no part with us in building a temple to our God. We alone will build it for the LORD, the God of Israel, as King Cyrus, the king of Persia, commanded us.'" (Ezra 4:1-3)

When you read the offer of the surrounding peoples to help with the construction of the temple, it appears generous. In contrast, Zerubbabel 's answer might appear narrow and dogmatic. But to understand the situation accurately, we need to read between the lines.

Those who make this "generous offer" are "enemies of Judah and Benjamin," the two tribes that have returned from exile. The word "enemies," "adversaries" is the noun *tsar*, from the verb *tsor*, "oppress, press" someone hard.[16] Prior to the Jews returning from exile, they had been the dominant rulers and people of the area and they resent losing power over the region.[17]

Samaritan Syncretism

The Jews know that the worship of the "peoples of the land" is not pure Yahweh worship, but syncretism, a mixture of the pagan worship and Yahweh worship. Nor are the enemies Jewish by parentage. Notice their claim:

> "We worship your God as you do, and we have been sacrificing to him ever since the days of Esarhaddon king of Assyria who brought us here." (Ezra 4:2)

---

[16] Holladay, *Hebrew Lexicon*, p. 305.

[17] The province of Judah (Yehud) is in the satrapy Abar-Nahara ("Beyond the River"). Yehud had been formed by the Babylonians to replace the Kingdom of Judah after the fall of Jerusalem, with an appointed governor over it. However, rebels assassinated the governor and then fled with the remaining people to Egypt (2 Kings 25:22-26; Jeremiah 40-41). So the Babylonian Province of Judah was really only a province on paper until the new Persian king Cyrus appointed Sheshbazzar, and later Zerubbabel, governor of Judah (Ezra 1:8, 11). As we'll see, the enemies included governors of other Persian provinces in the area.

These are Samaritans, primarily foreigners brought in by the Assyrians from another area to subdue the rebellious kingdom of Israel after 723 BC. They build their own temple at Mt. Gerizim in the fifth century BC, which is later destroyed by the Jews. Even in Jesus' day, the Samaritans contend that the proper place of worship was on Mt. Gerizim (John 4:20-24).

The Samaritans' "generous offer" to help with construction is a thinly veiled plot to retain control and influence. If the Jewish leaders accept their help, worship of Yahweh will be corrupted by mixture with pagan practices – and likely, the Jews would be absorbed into the people of the land, rather than retain their distinctive identity as the people of Yahweh. The offer is refused.

But their decision to reject Samaritan help comes with a cost.

> "⁴ Then the people of the land discouraged the people of Judah and made them afraid to build ⁵ and bribed counselors against them to frustrate their purpose, all the days of Cyrus king of Persia, even until the reign of Darius king of Persia." (Ezra 4:4-5)

Q3. (Ezra 4:1-3) Sometimes uncommitted people try to co-opt true worship for their own ends, as did the enemies of the Jews. What is the danger of letting people without a deep heart commitment and close walk with God redesign the church's image in the community? Redesign worship? Redesign the preaching? How can we be innovative and still be faithful to God's heart?
http://www.joyfulheart.com/forums/topic/1721-q3-redesigning-worship/

Let's skip down to verse 24 to see the conclusion. As a result of the constant harassment and discouragement of enemies putting barriers in their way, the sounds of workmen on the temple site eventually cease.[18]

> "Thus the work on the house of God in Jerusalem came to a standstill[19] until the second year of the reign of Darius king of Persia." (Ezra 4:24)

---

[18] Work on the temple began shortly after 537 BC following Cyrus's decree, and then lagged for perhaps a decade or more. It didn't resume until about 520 BC, the second year of Darius, the new Persian emperor. Some of the details of restarting the project are found in Ezra 5 and 6, as well as Haggai and Zechariah.

[19] "Came to a standstill" (NIV), "stopped and was discontinued" (NRSV), "stopped and it ceased" (ESV), "ceased … ceased"(KJV) indicate the use of the Aramaic verb *beṭal* ("stop, be discontinued") twice (Holladay, Hebrew Lexicon, p. 399).

Later Opposition under Xerxes and Artaxerxes (Ezra 4:6-24)

Now let's return briefly to the passage we skipped. Verses 6-23 are letters added here parenthetically, though they belong to a later period (486-459 BC). We'll discuss the content of these letters in Lesson 6, where they shed light on the historical period of Ezra and Nehemiah.

Tattenai's Letter to Darius (Ezra 5)

As you recall, the opposition of the steady opposition of the Samaritans and others, results in work stoppage on the temple site. God responds by raising up two prophets.

"¹ Now Haggai the prophet and Zechariah the prophet, a descendant of Iddo, prophesied to the Jews in Judah and Jerusalem in the name of the God of Israel, who was over them. ² Then Zerubbabel son of Shealtiel and Jeshua son of Jozadak set to work to rebuild the house of God in Jerusalem. And the prophets of God were with them, helping them." (Ezra 5:1-2)

As a result of prophetic urging, the rebuilding recommences. In Lesson 2 we'll explore Haggai's prophecy. In Lessons 3 and 4 we'll explore Zechariah's prophecies. We'll wait until then to fill in some of the details of how God reenergizes his people.

However, here we see the details of a bureaucratic attempt to frustrate the building of the temple.

"³ At that time Tattenai, governor of Trans-Euphrates, and Shethar-Bozenai and their associates went to them and asked, 'Who authorized you to rebuild this temple and restore this structure?' ⁴ They also asked, 'What are the names of the men constructing this building?'" (Ezra 5:3-4)

This time, the opposition comes not from local enemies (though they probably instigated this official investigation). Tattenai is the current satrap, the governor of the satrapy of Abar-Nahara ("Beyond the River"). He is the highest Persian authority in the whole region, and his authority extends over the province of Judah (Yehud).

When you read his letter, the satrap doesn't sound like an enemy, per se, but a bureaucrat who is trying to cover himself. He has received a complaint and feels it necessary to conduct an official investigation.

Notice that in his report to King Darius, he includes the Jews' testimony. They tell of "the God of heaven and earth." They also recount their sins, God's judgment, and then his gracious faithfulness (Ezra 5:11-16). Tattenai dutifully records the Jews' answers to his questioning, and then asks for a records search.

"Now if it pleases the king, let a search be made in the royal archives of Babylon to see if King Cyrus did in fact issue a decree to rebuild this house of God in Jerusalem. Then let the king send us his decision in this matter." (Ezra 5:17)

Tattenai is the consummate bureaucrat. He is unwilling to make the decision Jerusalem's enemies are pressing him to make. Rather he passes the decision up the hierarchy to the king's court for a determination.

But notice God's protection, even during this time of opposition.

"The eye of their God was watching over the elders of the Jews, and they were not stopped until a report could go to Darius and his written reply be received." (Ezra 5:5)

What a praise! Followers of God often must work and minister under threats and pressure. But God is faithful. The bureaucrat refused to stop work until he got word from his superiors! Sometimes even bureaucracy can further God's work.

The Decree of Darius (Ezra 6:1-12)

And so the wheels of government grind on, taking many months, perhaps years. But finally they find Cyrus's original decree among the government archives.

Notice the reminder, "Let the cost be paid from the royal treasury" (Ezra 6:4). This probably doesn't please Tattenai, the satrap, since the money will have to come out of his accounts. But the proclamation of Darius is clear and explicit. He acknowledges Cyrus's decree and reissues it under his own authority.

1. The Jewish governor has authority to rebuild the temple.
2. The workmen are to be paid from the royal revenue.
3. They are to be given animals for sacrifice.
4. Anyone who opposes the edict is cursed.
5. Darius, the current king commands, "Let it be done with all diligence." (Ezra 6:12)

What had begun as a serious threat to building the temple has now become an answer from God – full authority and full funding! Praise the Lord! Tattenai and his court carry out the orders with no further foot-dragging. The temple now has official government sanction and funding.

Completion and Dedication of the Temple (Ezra 6:13-18)

And so the temple is completed.

"[14] So the elders of the Jews continued to build and prosper under the preaching of Haggai the prophet and Zechariah, a descendant of Iddo.... The temple was completed on the third day of the month Adar, in the sixth year of the reign of King Darius." (Ezra 6:14, 15)

The completion can be rather precisely dated to March 515 BC.

> **Q4. (Ezra 6:1-12) When faced with "insurmountable odds," why do we give up so easily? What are the characteristics of a disciple who retains a robust faith in the God of amazing breakthroughs and impossible solutions?**
> **http://www.joyfulheart.com/forums/topic/1722-q4-never-give-up/**

The Passover (Ezra 6:19, 22)

Passover is the celebration of God's deliverance of the Israelites from slavery in Egypt. Each household sacrifices a lamb, daubs the blood over their door so that the angel of the Lord would "pass over" them, and then eats a festive meal together (Exodus 12). The Feast of Unleavened Bread begins the next day and lasts seven days, celebrating the haste with which the Israelites left Egypt, without time enough for their bread to rise (Exodus 13).

> "[19] On the fourteenth day of the first month, the exiles celebrated the Passover....
> [22] For seven days they celebrated with joy the Feast of Unleavened Bread, because the LORD had filled them with joy by changing the attitude[20] of the king of Assyria,[21] so that he assisted them in the work on the house of God, the God of Israel." (Ezra 6:19, 22)

---

[20] "Changing the attitude" (NIV) is literally, "turned the heart" (NRSV, ESV, KJV).

[21] The reference to "the king of Assyria" is unexpected. The Persians, not the Assyrians, are the current rulers. Perhaps the reference is designed to remind the reader of the traditional oppressor (see Nehemiah 9:32). Of course, the reference points to Cyrus who issued a decree to return, and then the current king Darius, who has recently dramatically underscored the Persian policy to subsidize the temple at Jerusalem.

Purification and Separation (Ezra 6:20-21)

There's a clear emphasis on purification[22] and separation that precedes celebration of the Passover.

> "20 The priests and Levites had **purified themselves** and were all **ceremonially clean**.... 21 So the Israelites who had returned from the exile ate it, together with all who had **separated themselves from the unclean practices** of their Gentile neighbors **in order to seek the LORD**, the God of Israel." (Ezra 6:20-21)

Ezra's Passover involves repentance from sin – and inward action rather than just outward purity. The "Israelites who return from the exile" eat the Passover, but they are joined by people living in the land who have converted to faith in Yahweh, "the God of Israel." These converts "separated themselves from the unclean practices of their Gentile neighbors in order to seek Yahweh."

The pagans in the land would practice idol worship, eat foods forbidden to the Jews, and engage in sexual immorality. Those who want to "seek Yahweh" repent of the immorality of their culture and separate themselves from its sins. Jewish exclusivism in Ezra and Nehemiah may seem offensive to us until we realize that theirs is not a closed society, but one which a Gentile can join as a proselyte through faith and repentance.

There are lessons for us today. A lot of Christians are merely believers in a religious position. They might gather to worship, but do they – do you – come to "seek the Lord"? To know him? To love him? To find his way for your life? To surrender your heart afresh to him? We Christians are instructed to prepare our hearts prior to taking the Lord's Supper, a continuation of the Passover tradition. Paul tells us,

> "A person ought to examine himself before he eats of the bread and drinks of the cup." (1 Corinthians 11:28)

For believers, this is not outward purification, but a time of reflection before God, a confession of sin, and a repentance from the areas of our lives that reflect "the unclean practices of our Gentile neighbors."

> "If we walk in the light, as he is in the light, we have fellowship with one another, and the blood of Jesus, his Son, purifies us from all sin.... If we confess our sins, he is faithful and just and will forgive us our sins and purify us from all unrighteousness." (1 John 1:7, 9)

---

[22] Purification of oneself for the Passover continues to Jesus' day (John 11:55). Purification is largely through outward acts. In Jesus' day this involves ceremonial baths, purging the house of any leaven, and avoidance of contact with anything (or anyone) ritually unclean.

Q5. (Ezra 6:20-21) What do repentance and separation from the sins of our culture look like for a disciple today? How should we prepare ourselves to worship Jesus in the Lord's Supper? How should we prepare to serve him with purity day by day? http://www.joyfulheart.com/forums/topic/1723-q5-purity/

Lessons for Disciples

Ezra 1-6 provides a number of lessons for disciples to ponder.

1. God can raise up rulers, even non-Christian rulers, and then "stir their spirit" to carry out his plans. Cyrus was one of these God had chosen long before (Isaiah 45:13; 2 Chronicles 36:22-23; Ezra 1:1). We need to pray for our civil leaders (1 Timothy 2:1-4).

2. The many Jews who remained in Babylon symbolize perhaps a tendency in us to become too comfortable to radically serve God any longer. We must never become too comfortable, or too tired, or too complacent to follow Jesus wherever he leads us, at whatever personal cost may be required.

3. Rebuilding the altar and laying again the foundation (Ezra 3) speak of a strong desire on the part of the Israelites to restore worship to what it should be. Is your personal worship what it should be? What foundations do you need to lay again in your personal restoration and revival of faith?

4. Whenever you seek to do Kingdom work, you can expect opposition from enemies, who are ultimately motivated and energized by Satan (Ezra 4). Sometimes we experience temporary setbacks in our spiritual warfare. This shouldn't surprise us.

5. Sometimes uncommitted people try to co-opt true worship for their own ends, as did the enemies of the Jews (Ezra 4:1-3) There is a desire for us to make church "attractive" to our community and accessible to seekers. This can be good. However, what can happen is that "the show" and "feel-good" preaching, replace authentic worship and careful teaching of the Word. If we allow the uncommitted to "build with us," it may not result in something that is God-centered any longer.

6. God uses gifted men and women to stir up his people and call them to return to the central tasks of our faith, as God used the prophets Haggai and Zechariah to energize the people to complete the temple (Ezra 5:1-2)

7. We should not give up when times are hard. God is well-able to bring amazing break-throughs, such as Darius's reinforcement of Cyrus's original decree, resulting in full funding and renewed energy to complete the task of rebuilding God's house (Ezra 6:1-12).

8. God calls us to repentance and separation from the sins of our culture (Ezra 6:20-21), both to prepare ourselves to worship him in the Lord's Supper, and to serve him with purity day by day.

Prayer

Father, put in us the kind of faith-pioneer spirit that those who returned from exile possessed. Help us to remain separate from the sins of our culture that would compromise our integrity. Help us not to give up when the going gets hard, but to continue to believe in the paradigm-changing power of the Almighty God, our Father. In Jesus' name, we pray. Amen.

Key Verses

"Anyone of his people among you – may his God be with him, and let him go up to Jerusalem in Judah and build the temple of the LORD, the God of Israel, the God who is in Jerusalem." (Ezra 1:3)

"Then the peoples around them set out to discourage the people of Judah and make them afraid to go on building." (Ezra 4:4)

"Now Haggai the prophet and Zechariah the prophet, a descendant of Iddo, prophesied to the Jews in Judah and Jerusalem in the name of the God of Israel, who was over them. Then Zerubbabel son of Shealtiel and Jeshua son of Jozadak set to work to rebuild the house of God in Jerusalem. And the prophets of God were with them, helping them." (Ezra 5:1-2)

"So the elders of the Jews continued to build and prosper under the preaching of Haggai the prophet and Zechariah, a descendant of Iddo. They finished building the temple according to the command of the God of Israel and the decrees of Cyrus, Darius and Artaxerxes, kings of Persia. The temple was completed on the third day of the month Adar, in the sixth year of the reign of King Darius." (Ezra 6:14-15)

2. Realigning Priorities (Haggai 1-2)

By the time Haggai the prophet appears on the scene about 520 AD [BC], discouragement has set in.

James J. Tissot, detail of 'Haggai' (1898-1902), gouache on board, The Jewish Museum, New York.

Sixteen or seventeen years before this, a band of hopeful exiles had come to Jerusalem ready to rebuild the temple, armed with the king's edict, laden with temple treasure, and empowered by contributions from the Jewish community in Babylon.

They have made a hopeful start. An altar has been built on its ancient site (Ezra 3:2). Some of the rubble of the collapsed buildings has been cleared, and some work has begun to rebuild the temple. But then it becomes bogged down due to opposition from the Samaritans and others who don't want to see the Jews established and become strong in a land that they wanted for themselves. Ezra 4 concludes:

> "The work on the house of God that is in Jerusalem stopped, and it ceased until the second year of the reign of Darius king of Persia." (Ezra 4:24)

The Jews have failed. But God intervenes again, this time in the person of a prophet.

Haggai the Prophet (Haggai 1:1a)

The short book of Haggai begins with the words:

> "In the second year of King Darius, on the first day of the sixth month, the word of the LORD came through the prophet Haggai...." (Haggai 1:1a)

We know nothing about Haggai except his name, which means "festal," from *ḥag*, "feast, festival." Perhaps he was born during a major Jewish festival, such as Passover, Feast of

Weeks, or Feast of Tabernacles.[23] Whatever his background, when Haggai speaks, the people obey his words as from God himself (Haggai 1:12).

Zerubbabel and Joshua (Haggai 1:1b)

"The word of the LORD" is directed toward the Jewish colony's leaders:

> "… to Zerubbabel son of Shealtiel, governor of Judah, and to Joshua son of Jehozadak, the high priest." (Haggai 1:1b)

We met them previously in Ezra 2:2 among the first group of exiles that return to Jerusalem from Babylon, and in Ezra 3-5 as leaders of the people. Both are descended from famous ancestors. Zerubbabel is the civil leader and Jeshua is the religious leader, the high priest. Now let's look at them further.

Zerubbabel and Jeshua celebrate beginning the rebuilding of the temple. (Artist unknown)

Zerubbabel is of royal blood: a descendant of David, son of Shealtiel,[24] and grandson of Jehoiachin, one of Judah's last kings.[25] He is governor of Yehud (post-exilic Judah). In addition to references in Ezra and Nehemiah, he is also mentioned in both Haggai 1:1-2:9 and Zechariah 4:6-10. Zerubbabel name means "seed of Babylon" or "descendant of Babylon."

Jeshua (or Joshua), son of Jozadak, is high priest in the early days of the return. He is mentioned in Ezra, Nehemiah, as well as by the prophets in Haggai and Zechariah. His sons are also prominent, though two of his sons are censured later for marrying foreign women (Ezra 10:18). Jeshua's name means "Yah(weh) saves." He is named after Joshua, Moses' successor. In the New Testament, Jesus bears this name also (Matthew 1:21). Jesus is the Greek form of Hebrew Joshua.

---

[23] Horace J. Wolf, "Haggai," ISBE 2:595.

[24] Zerubbabel's father is given as Shealtiel in Ezra, Nehemiah, Matthew, and Luke, but in 1 Chronicles 3:19 he appears as the son of Pedaiah, Jehoiachin's third son. Perhaps he is the literal son of Pedaiah and linked with Shealtiel by some legal device as levirate marriage (H.G.M. Williamson, "Zerubbabel," ISBE 4:1194).

[25] Zerubbabel had two sons, Meshullam and Hananiah (1 Chronicles 3:19). Although both these names occur in Ezra and Nehemiah, they are so common that we're not sure what role Zerubbabel's sons played, if any.

The Word of the Lord – Prophecy

"The word of the LORD came through the prophet Haggai...." (Haggai 1:1a)

This phrase, "the word of the Lord came..." is a standard formula that identifies a prophetic revelation by the Holy Spirit.[26]

Let's pause for a moment to consider whether prophecy is the same as inspired preaching. Though some contend that they are one and the same, I disagree. When you look at the New Testament, you see that prophets are differentiated from evangelists and teachers (Ephesians 4:11). The examples of prophets we have are John the Baptist, Agabus (Acts 11:27; 21:10-11), members of the Jerusalem church (Acts 11:27; 13:1), and the daughters of Philip the Evangelist (Acts 21:9). In addition, people who have just received the Holy Spirit might prophesy (Acts 2; 19:6), as well as members of the congregation (1 Corinthians 14).[27]

However, the prophetic word of the Lord was rare in post-exilic Judah. We don't know of any prophet who had ministered there since Jeremiah and Ezekiel many decades previously. Nor did Jeshua the high priest seem to be able to receive revelation from God during this time (Ezra 2:63). So when Haggai spoke as a prophet by the "word of the Lord," people listened. Hearing prophecy was a new phenomenon for all but the oldest among them.

Dating the Prophecies

This prophecy (and all Haggai's prophecies) are precisely dated, so we know that Haggai brought his first prophecy on August 29, 520 BC. The first of the month would have occurred on a new moon, a feast day when many of the Jews would have gathered in Jerusalem for the festival. Many of them would have heard the word of the Lord that day.

Haggai brought his prophecies over a period of 15 weeks. Two or three months after Haggai's ministry started, Zechariah began to prophesy. For the next few years, several prophecies came to this people, both concerning their immediate situation and events far in the future. The final prophet is Malachi, though his prophecies are not precisely dated.

---

[26] We see this phrase with regard to appearances or revelations to Abraham (Genesis 15:1, 4), the prophet Samuel (1 Samuel 15:10); the prophet Nathan (2 Samuel 7:4), Solomon (1 Kings 6:11), the prophet Isaiah (Isaiah 38:4), the Prophet Jeremiah (Jeremiah 1:2, 4, 11), and most other prophets.

[27] To pursue this further, read my article, "Understanding the Gift of Prophecy: I. Is Prophecy Preaching?" www.joyfulheart.com/scholar/preach.htm

Year[28]		Reign of Darius	Text	Synopsis
520 BC	Aug 29	Day 1, month 6	Hag 1:1-11	Haggai's Prophecies 1 and 2
520	Sep 21	Day 24, month 6	Hag 1:12-15	Restoration of the temple resumes 23 days later
520	Oct 17	Day 21, month 7	Hag 2:1-9	Haggai's Prophecy 3
520	Nov	month 8	Zech 1:1-6	Zechariah begins to prophecy
520	Dec 18	Day 24, month 9	Hag 2:10	Haggai's Prophecy 4
520	Dec 18	Day 24, month 9	Hag 2:20	Haggai's Prophecy 5 (later the same day)
519	Feb 15	Day 24, month 11	Zech 1:7	Zechariah's Prophecy 2
518	Dec 7	4th year, month 9, day 4	Zech 7:1	Zechariah's Later visions.
515	Mar 12	6th year, month of Adar, day 3	Ezra 6:15	Temple completed
c. 460 – 430	undated		Malachi	Malachi's prophecies

Prophecy 1. A Call to Build the House of the Lord (Haggai 1)

Now that we've looked at the date and the named targets of the prophecy – Zerubbabel and Joshua – let's consider the prophecy itself.

"This is what the LORD Almighty says...." (Haggai 1:2a)

The word is not Haggai's, but that of "the LORD Almighty" (NIV), "the LORD of hosts" (NRSV, ESV, KJV). It is an exalted title. LORD when it appears in caps in English Bibles refers to the divine name "Yahweh." (Jehovah in the KJV). "Hosts" translates ṣebā'ôt, "armies." The Hebrew word is found in the hymn, "A Mighty Fortress Is Our God," in the line, "Lord *Sabaoth* his name...." It is one of God's most exalted titles – the One who commands armies of angels, who has authority over all creation, and we see it often in the prophets of this period – Haggai, Zechariah, and Malachi.

God first cites people's justification for neglecting to finish the temple.

---

[28] John Kessler, "Haggai, Book of," DOTP, p. 303; Baldwin, *Haggai, Zechariah, Malachi*, p. 29. Based on the evidence of over 100 Babylonian texts and new moon data from astronomical calculations it is possible to synchronize the old lunar calendar with the Julian calendar accurate to within one day.

> "These people say, 'The time has not yet come for the LORD's house to be built.'"
> (Haggai 1:2b)

Excuses, excuses. So easily we justify what we're doing, even if it's far from God's will for us. God questions their excuse.

> "Is it a time for you yourselves to be living in your paneled houses, while this house remains a ruin?" (Haggai 1:4)

The temple had been burned in 587 BC, with some walls remaining, but lots of rubble on the ground. In 537 BC the altar had been set up again for the regular sacrifices, and rebuilding had begun.

> "They gave money … and food, drink, and oil to the Sidonians and the Tyrians to bring cedar trees from Lebanon to the sea, to Joppa, according to the grant that they had from Cyrus king of Persia." (Ezra 3:7)

They had begun getting the timber needed for the project, but then stopped due to opposition. Now it was a roofless, ruined hulk, with priests working at the altar in front of the partially repaired structure.

"Paneled" (NIV, NRSV, ESV), "ceiled" (KJV) comes from the verb *sāpan*, "to cover, roof, panel," and so could refer to the fact that (1) the partially completed temple has no roof, or (2) that the leaders of the people lived in nice houses with paneling on the walls (walls covered).[29] Whichever it is, the Lord's house is a ruin,[30] and the leaders' homes are nice and snug.

The Result of God Withholding Blessing (Haggai 1:5-11)

The problem is clear. God's house still lies in ruins, but there is a cost to disobeying God. God is withholding his blessing.

> "5 Now this is what the LORD Almighty says: 'Give careful thought to your ways.[31] 6 You have planted much, but have harvested little. You eat, but never have enough. You drink, but never have your fill. You put on clothes, but are not warm. You earn wages, only to put them in a purse with holes in it.'" (Haggai 1:5-6)

---

[29] *Sāpan*, Holladay, *Hebrew Lexicon*, p. 259; TWOT #1537. See the word also in 1 Kings 6:9; 7:3.

[30] "Remains a ruin" (NIV) "lies in ruins" (ESV, NRSV), "lie waste" (KJV) is the adjective *ḥārēb*, "waste, desolate" from the verb *ḥārēb*, "dry up, lie in ruins (Holladay, *Hebrew Lexicon*, p. 115). The word is also found in verse 9.

[31] "Give careful thought to your ways" (NIV), "consider" (ESV, NRSV, KJV) here and verse, constitutes four words in the Hebrew text, literally, "set your heart/mind on your ways," or "on your paths." A similar expression in 2:15, 18 might be translated, "take careful note of."

Think about your situation, says God. You're just barely getting by. You are by no means flourishing. Now it's time to obey.

> "7 This is what the LORD Almighty says: 'Give careful thought to your ways. 8 Go up into the mountains and bring down timber and build the house, so that I may take pleasure[32] in it and be honored,'[33] says the LORD." (Haggai 1:7-8)

The people are centered in themselves. They give no thought to what pleases God, or what God desires.

Has it ever occurred to you that God can be pleased? That he can enjoy something like a temple built to honor him? Do you know that God smiles when you, his child, begin to obey and serve him deliberately and joyfully? Paul challenges us, "try to discern what is pleasing to the Lord" (Ephesians 5:10, ESV).

Q1. (Haggai 1:8) God wishes to "take pleasure" in the temple, but the people have stopped working on the project. When is God displeased with you? When does he "take pleasure" in you? What is keeping you from serving him deliberately and joyfully? http://www.joyfulheart.com/forums/topic/1724-q1-taking-pleasure/

The next verses are scary when you think of what they are saying. Because of the people's disobedience, God begins to withhold material blessings from them.

> "9 You expected much, but see, it turned out to be little. What you brought home, I blew away. Why?' declares the LORD Almighty. 'Because of my house, which remains a ruin, while each of you is busy with[34] his own house. 10 Therefore, because of you the heavens have withheld[35] their dew and the earth its crops. 11 I called for a drought[36] on the fields and the mountains, on the grain, the new wine, the oil and

---

[32] "Take pleasure" is *rāṣâ*, "be pleased with, be favorable to" (TWOT #2207).

[33] "Be honored" (NIV, NRSV), "be glorified" (ESV, KJV) is *kābēd*, "be heavy, grievous, hard, rich, honorable, glorious" (TWOT #943).

[34] "Busy with" (NIV), "hurry off to" (NRSV), "busies himself with" (ESV), "run" (KJV) is *rûs*, "run, make haste by running." (TWOT #2137). Here it has the sense of "be busy" (Holladay, *Hebrew Lexicon*, p. 336).

[35] "Withheld" is *kālā'*, "keep back, keep in detention," then "withhold" something from someone (Holladay, *Hebrew Lexicon*, p. 157). "The basic meaning of this root is to restrict the flow or movement of a thing or person" (John N. Oswalt, TWOT #980).

[36] "Drought" is *ḥōreb*, "Dryness, drought, heat, desolation," from the verb *ḥārab*, "to be dry." Mt. Horeb, an alternative name for Mt. Sinai, is derived from this word, signifying a desolate region (Edwin Yamauchi, TWOT #731b).

whatever the ground produces, on men and cattle, and on the labor of your hands.'"
(Haggai 1:9-11)

I have a three-year-old granddaughter. When she disobeys by playing with her food
and throwing it on the floor, her parents take it away. This has a way of getting her
attention. Crude, perhaps, but effective. God sometimes does the same thing to get our
attention.

When we get to Lesson 10, we see a similar situation in Malachi's day. People have
neglected to tithe to support the now-built temple. As a result, God is withholding his
blessings from them. If they resume tithing, God promises to abundantly bless them
(Malachi 3:10-11). The implication is that until they obey, God's protection has been
lifted. The floodgates of heaven have been closed. Obedience opens them.

Some people have taken turned these truths into a Prosperity Doctrine. Poverty is
bad; God desires you to be rich. This teaching has some truth in it. God blesses those
who obey and partially withholds from his children who disobey. But it becomes
unbiblical when it declares material wealth to be God's standard to be desired and
expected. Jesus certainly doesn't teach materialism to his disciples,[37] nor did Paul[38] or
James.[39]

> **Q2. (Haggai 1:6, 9-11) God sometimes disciplines us through hardships and cir-
> cumstances (Hebrews 12:7-11). Sometimes through us not having all that we need.
> What is such discipline intended to do in our lives? Are you experiencing hard-
> ship? What is God trying to say to you in the midst of it?**
> **http://www.joyfulheart.com/forums/topic/1725-q2-discipline/**

Prophecy 2. Belief and Obedience (Haggai 1:12-15)

The people believe Haggai's prophecy. They connect their struggle with disobeying
God regarding completing the temple.

---

[37] Jesus: Matthew 6:19-34; 8:20; 19:23-24; Mark 4:19; Luke 6:24; 8:14; 12:21.
[38] Paul: 1 Timothy 6:9, 17-18.
[39] James: James 1:10-11; 2:6; 5:1-2.

"Then Zerubbabel son of Shealtiel, Joshua son of Jehozadak, the high priest, and the whole remnant[40] of the people obeyed the voice of the LORD their God and the message of the prophet Haggai, because the LORD their God had sent him. And the people feared the LORD." (Haggai 1:12)

The people are afraid of continued disobedience. They are ready to obey. Now another prophecy comes, perhaps the same day. If the first word brings fear, the second prophecy brings assurance.

"[13] Then Haggai, the LORD's messenger, gave this message of the LORD to the people: 'I am with you,' declares the LORD. [14] So the LORD stirred up the spirit of Zerubbabel son of Shealtiel, governor of Judah, and the spirit of Joshua son of Jehozadak, the high priest, and the spirit of the whole remnant of the people. They came and began to work on the house of the LORD Almighty, their God, [15] on the twenty-fourth day of the sixth month in the second year of King Darius." (Haggai 1:13-15)

Yahweh's declaration, "I am with you," brings encouragement to Moses and the people of Israel (Exodus 33:14), and to Joshua when he prepares to cross the Jordan (Joshua 1:5). The Lord promises to be with the people when Jehoshaphat faces the combined armies of Edom and Moab (2 Chronicles 20:17). These words are our confidence also:

"God has said, 'Never will I leave you; never will I forsake you.'" (Hebrews 13:5)

Jesus told his disciples:

"Surely I am with you always, to the very end of the age." (Matthew 28:20)

The same promise comes in the second prophecy in Haggai 2:4, given a few weeks later.

Through this prophecy, the Lord "stirred up the spirit" of both the leaders and the people (Haggai 1:14). "Stirred up" is *ûr*, "rouse oneself, awake, incite." The word is also used of Cyrus being stirred to allow the Jewish exiles to return (2 Chronicles 36:22; Ezra 1:1).[41] Prophecy can have a profound effect upon a whole people.

And so, twenty-three days after Haggai first begins to prophesy, they begin to work.

---

[40] "Remnant" is *she'ērit*, "Remainder, remnant, posterity, residue, survivors." This noun, in every usage, carries forward the basic root idea of *shā'ar* and speaks of that which has survived after a previous elimination process or catastrophe (Gary G. Cohen, TWOT #2307b).

[41] "Stirred up" is the Hiphil (causative) stem of *ûr*, "rouse oneself, awake, incite." The word is also used of Cyrus being stirred to allow the Jewish exiles to return (2 Chronicles 36:22; Ezra 1:1; TWOT #1587).

" [14b] They came and began to work on the house of the LORD Almighty, their God,
[15] on the twenty-fourth day of the sixth month in the second year of King Darius."
(Haggai 1:14b-15).

Haggai's first prophecy is on August 29, 520 BC. The project resumes on September 21st the same year, probably after the people have finished the harvest and returned to Jerusalem to build. We read in Ezra how there had been a big celebration on the day when work began in 537 BC.

"[11] With praise and thanksgiving they sang to the LORD: 'He is good; his love to Israel endures forever.' And all the people gave a great shout of praise to the LORD, because the foundation of the house of the LORD was laid."[42] (Ezra 3:11-13)

Now, they begin the work again with joyful hearts.

Prophecy 3. The Promised Glory of the New House (Haggai 2:1-9)

"On the twenty-first day of the seventh month, the word of the LORD came through the prophet Haggai...." (Haggai 2:1)

It is now October 17th. The work has started again and has been going on for a full month. The encouragement of the prophets is helpful in getting them restarted. But now there is a need to overcome discouragement that can easily derail the progress already made.

The Danger of Discouragement

We saw this discouragement when we studied Ezra 3. Solomon's temple has been a world-class building, gilded inside with extravagant decoration and impressive tapestries, built when Israel is united, wealthy, and at the apex of its power. But now Judah doesn't even have a king. Judah (Yehud) is merely a sub-province of the Persian Empire, just hanging on to survival, surrounded by enemies who don't want them there. Funds are limited. By comparison with their memory of Solomon's Temple, the beginnings of the Second Temple seem a huge let-down.

Sometimes the way to deal with a problem is to acknowledge what people are feeling and deal with it directly. By this time,[43] the prophet Zechariah has begun prophesying,

---

[42] As mentioned in footnote 18 above, and as we will see in Haggai 2:18, the phrase "the foundation of the Lord's temple was laid," and similar verses in Ezra using the verb *yasad* could have been adequately translated by the simple verb 'build,'" rather than being restricted to laying the foundation only (Baldwin, *Haggai, Zechariah, Malachi,* pp. 52-53).

as we'll see in Lesson 3. He deals with the same problem – a sense of hopelessness and dejection.

> "**Who despises the day of small things?** Men will rejoice when they see the plumb line in the hand of Zerubbabel." (Zechariah 4:10)

In a similar way, Haggai acknowledges the leaders' discouragement and speaks God's words of encouragement.

> "2 Speak to Zerubbabel son of Shealtiel, governor of Judah, to Joshua son of Jehoza-dak, the high priest, and to the remnant of the people. Ask them, 3 'Who of you is left who saw this house in its **former glory**? How does it look to you now? Does it not **seem to you like nothing**?'" (Haggai 2:2-3)

Be Strong and Work (Haggai 2:4-5)

The Lord acknowledges their discouragement. Now he calls them to action.

> "But now be strong, O Zerubbabel,' declares the LORD. 'Be strong, O Joshua son of Jehozadak, the high priest. Be strong, all you people of the land,' declares the LORD, 'and work. For I am with you,' declares the LORD Almighty." (Haggai 2:4)

Be strong[44] and work.[45] Be strong means to take courage. We see a similar command to Joshua as he prepares to cross the Jordan and take Jericho:

> "Have I not commanded you? Be strong and courageous. Do not be terrified; do not be discouraged, for the LORD your God will be with you wherever you go." (Joshua 1:9)

So often we're faced with challenges and shrink from them. We're afraid, lack self-confidence, and run away, often to denial or avoidance. God's word is "be strong, be courageous" and then "work." Set out to do the task that God has put before us, trusting him to give us strength to do it. Whatever God gives us to do, is possible when he is with us.

God being with them is not a new idea, but part of God's ancient covenant promise.

> "This is what I **covenanted**[46] **with you** when you came out of Egypt. And my Spirit remains among you. Do not fear.'" (Haggai 2:5)

---

[43] Zechariah's first prophecy is dated more generally to approximately the month of November 520 BC. Haggai's word comes on October 21, 520 BC

[44] "Be strong" (NIV, ESV, KJV), "take courage" (NRSV) is the Qal stem of *ḥāzaq*, "be(come) strong" (TWOT #636).

[45] "Work" is *'āśâ*, "do, fashion, accomplish" (TWOT #1708).

God has made covenants with Abraham, Isaac, and Jacob. Then in the Wilderness he renews that covenant with the people of Israel with the "book of the covenant" and the "blood of the covenant" (Exodus 24:7-8). The Presence of the Lord with them is key. The tabernacle in the very center of the camp of Israel, and the pillar of cloud by day and fire by night symbolize Yahweh's presence with them. After the people sin, Moses pleads with the Lord:

> "If your Presence does not go with us, do not send us up from here.... What else will distinguish me and your people from all the other people on the face of the earth?" (Exodus 33:15-16)

Through Haggai the prophet, God recalls the covenant and the Spirit of his Presence, and affirms to the exiles that Yahweh is still with them to protect and help them.

> "My Spirit remains among you. Do not fear." (Haggai 2:5b)

Q3. (Haggai 2:1-5) Discouragement is a common experience. What command does God give Joshua the high priest? What assurance does he give? To deal with your own times of discouragement, what would God's command and assurance be for you? How would you implement them?
http://www.joyfulheart.com/forums/topic/1726-q3-discouragement/

Shaking and Glory (Haggai 2:6-9)

Now the Lord speaks further to their concern that the new temple is little compared to Solomon's grand temple that had been destroyed.

> "⁶ This is what the LORD Almighty says: 'In a little while I will once more shake the heavens and the earth, the sea and the dry land. ⁷ I will shake all nations, and the desired of all nations will come, and I will fill this house with glory,' says the LORD Almighty. ⁸ 'The silver is mine and the gold is mine,' declares the LORD Almighty. ⁹ 'The glory of this present house will be greater than the glory of the former house,'

---

[46] "Covenanted" (NIV, ESV, KJV), "the promise that I made to you" (NRSV) is two words: *dābār*, "word, matter" and the Qal stem of *karat*, "to cut off" The most important use of the root is "to cut" a covenant *berît*. The word here is pregnant with theological meaning. A covenant must be cut because the slaughter of animals was a part of the covenant ritual (Elmer B. Smick, TWOT, #1048). In verse 5, however, the word *dābār* ("word") is used instead of *berît* ("covenant"), which is implied.

says the LORD Almighty. 'And in this place I will grant peace,' declares the LORD Almighty." (Haggai 2:6-9)

God promises that this Second Temple will see more glory than Solomon's Temple. Let's look at this amazing statement.

"Yet once more, in a little while..." (Haggai 2:6a). The fulfillment of this promise of glory is not for now, but "in a little while."[47] The time is not specified. But I believe Haggai is looking forward to Christ's presence in this temple some 550 years later.

"I will ... shake the heavens and the earth, the sea and the dry land. I will shake all nations" (Haggai 2:6b-7a). Between the time of the prophecy and its fulfillment in Christ, God will shake[48] the nations. This period sees the fall of the Persian Empire, the rise and fall of the Greek Empires and the rise of the Roman Empire. In this period the temple is desecrated by Antiochus Epiphanes and restored by the Maccabees, celebrated by Hanukkah. Then this Second Temple is added onto and beautified by Herod the Great to become the glorious building that Jesus and the Apostles saw.

"The treasures of all nations shall come in, and I will fill this house with glory" (Haggai 2:7b, ESV). The NIV follows the KJV tradition using the word "desired" to translate the Hebrew ḥemdâ, "desire." Translated this way it would refer to Jesus as the "Desire of All Nations."[49] But the context is clearly treasure, silver and gold (verse 8). The noun often refers to treasure, yielding the translation "the desirable, precious things of all nations" (such as in Hosea 13:15; 2 Chronicles 32:27; 36:10; Daniel 11:8).[50] Thus, Haggai's prophecy probably underscores Isaiah's prophecies that the wealth of the nations will come to Jerusalem (Isaiah 60:5-7, 10-11; 66:12).

"The silver is mine and the gold is mine" (Haggai 2:8). The people were concerned that the Second Temple of their day was unadorned with silver and gold compared to

---

[47] "In a little while" (NIV), "once again, in a little while" (NRSV), "yet once more, in a little while" (ESV, cf. KJV), involves several words: the adverb 'ôd, "continuance, besides, still, again" + a number 'eḥād, "one, first, once" + an adjective me'aṭ, "little, few, small."

[48] "Shake" is rā'ash, "quake, shake" in verses 6, 7, and 21 (TWOT #2195).

[49] This usage follows a passage where Saul is referred to as the one "to whom is all the desire of Israel turned" (1 Samuel 9:20).

[50] Hemdâ, BDB, p. 326. "The desired of the nations" (NIV), "the treasure of all nations" (NRSV), "the treasures of all nations" (ESV), "the desire of all nations" (KJV) involves two words: (1) gôy, "gentile, heathen, nation, people" (TWOT #326e), and (2) ḥemdâ, "desire," also an adjective, "pleasant, precious," from ḥāmad, "to desire, delight in" (TWOT #673b). Baldwin observes that while the Latin Vulgate that underlies the KJV has a singular subject, "the Hebrew verb is plural and requires a plural subject," that is "treasures" (Baldwin, *Haggai, Zechariah, Malachi*, p. 48).

Solomon's temple. God assures them that this isn't due to God's poverty. It all belongs to him.

"The glory of this present house will be greater than the glory of the former house" (Haggai 2:9a). Several hundred years later, Herod the Great adds on to and beautifies the Second Temple to the point that it is indeed glorious and far exceeds Solomon's temple. Of course, Christ's presence in the temple is the ultimate fulfillment of the greater glory of this temple.

"And in this place I will grant peace" (2:9b). "Peace" is *shalom*. Of course, the name Jerusalem, carries the word "peace" in it. Ultimately, the peace of the Messiah will be proclaimed from this temple.

Our work may seem small and unimpressive, but God can make it great. It may be that God is calling you to lay foundations in a child or in a work that only much later will bear great fruit. We obey what God calls us to do, and then leave the results in his hands. We may not even see those results in our lifetimes. We walk by faith, not by sight (2 Corinthians 5:7).

Prophecy 4. You Are Defiled. Repent. (Haggai 2:10-19)

A Defiled People (Haggai 2:10-14)

"[10] On the twenty-fourth day of the ninth month, in the second year of Darius, the word of the LORD came to the prophet Haggai: [11] 'This is what the LORD Almighty says: "Ask the priests what the law says: [12] If a person carries consecrated meat in the fold of his garment, and that fold touches some bread or stew, some wine, oil or other food, does it become consecrated?"'

The priests answered, 'No.'

[13] Then Haggai said, 'If a person defiled by contact with a dead body touches one of these things, does it become defiled?'

'Yes,' the priests replied, 'it becomes defiled.'

[14] Then Haggai said, '"So it is with this people and this nation in my sight," declares the LORD. "Whatever they do and whatever they offer there is defiled."'" (Haggai 2:9-14)

It is hard for twenty-first century Christians to understand this. I'll explain it, but you'll need to follow closely. Haggai is appealing to the Levitical rules of ceremonial uncleanness, of how holiness and uncleanness are conveyed. Haggai asks the priests for a ruling on this question.

Conveying Holiness and Defilement (Haggai 2:12-13)

In the time of the tabernacle and temple, the priests had a right to take portions of the sacrifices on the altar as food for their families (Leviticus 6:17-18, 24-29). Haggai raises a hypothetical situation where a priest might carry meat from the altar, that is, "holy, consecrated"[51] meat. Haggai asks a technical question: If the holy meat comes in contact with the priest's clothing, does the meat convey ceremonial holiness to the garment? The priests answer, "No."

Now Haggai asks a second technical question. "If a person defiled[52] by contact with a dead body touches one of these things, does it become defiled?" (2:13). The answer is, "Yes."

You Are Defiled (Haggai 2:14)

Haggai gets the people's attention by his technical questions of holiness and defilement. Now he makes his point – our whole nation is defiled! Working on the temple (or doing church work) doesn't make a person holy. Rather, defiled people defile whatever they touch.

To interpret this passage correctly, it is important to observe the context. Haggai gives this prophecy on December 18, 520 BC The prophet Zechariah, who began prophesying in November 520 BC, has just called the people to repent.[53]

> "'**Return to me**,' declares the LORD Almighty, 'and I will return to you....' **Then they repented** and said, 'The LORD Almighty has done to us what our ways and practices deserve, just as he determined to do.'" (Zechariah 1:3b, 6)

Thus Haggai's message about a defiled people reminds them of the importance of repenting and consecrating themselves.

---

[51] "Consecrated" (NIV, NRSV), "holy" (ESV, KJV) in verse 12a is *qōdesh*, which "connotes the concept of 'holiness,' i.e., the essential nature of that which belongs to the sphere of the sacred and which is thus distinct from the common or profane (Thomas E. McComiskey, TWOT #1990a).

[52] "Defiled" (NIV), "unclean" (NRSV, ESV, KJV) in verse 13a and 13b is the adjective *ṭāmē*. "Animals and foods were considered clean or unclean by their nature. Persons and objects could become ritually unclean. Personal uncleanness could be incurred through birth, menstruation, bodily emissions, 'leprosy,' sexual relations and misdeeds and contact with death. Priests and Levites were especially concerned with the issues of cleanness and uncleanness. The greatest uncleanness was idolatry which defiled the temple and the land" (Edwin Yamauchi, TWOT #809a).

[53] D. J. Wiseman, "Haggai," *The New Bible Commentary Revised* (Eerdmans, 1970), p. 784.

Q4. (Haggai 2:10-14) What kinds of things defile a disciple today? What is the danger of acting as if doing church work somehow makes us holy by association? How does a believer deal with spiritual defilement and sin? http://www.joyfulheart.com/forums/topic/1727-q4-defilement/

With Repentance Comes God's Blessing (Haggai 2:15-19)

Haggai is saying: You have sinned, and your sin has resulted in meager crops and blighted blessing. But now that you have repented and begun again the work on the temple, God will bless you abundantly.[54]

> "15 'Now give careful thought to this from this day on – consider how things were before one stone was laid on another in the LORD's temple. 16 When anyone came to a heap of twenty measures, there were only ten. When anyone went to a wine vat to draw fifty measures, there were only twenty. 17 I struck[55] all the work of your hands with blight,[56] mildew[57] and hail, yet you did not turn to me,' declares the LORD. 18 'From this day on, from this twenty-fourth day of the ninth month, give careful thought to the day when the foundation of the LORD's temple was laid. Give careful thought: 19 Is there yet any seed left in the barn? Until now, the vine and the fig tree, the pomegranate and the olive tree have not borne fruit. 'From this day on I will bless you.'" (Haggai 2:15-19)

Most translations of verse 18 suggest the foundation of the temple has just been laid in 520 BC. However, Ezra 3:10 indicates that the people celebrated laying the foundations back in 537 BC. Is this a discrepancy? No. As indicated in footnotes above, the Hebrew word translated "lay the foundation" is the verb *yasad*, "to found." However, sometimes *yasad* is used more generally, as in 2 Chronicles 24:27; 31:7. The verses in Ezra

---

[54] Other commentators credit the refoundation ceremony of 520 BC itself as clearing away ceremonial defilement and assuring the people of God's blessing (John Kessler, "Haggai, Book of," DOTP p. 305).

[55] "Struck" (NIV, NRSV, ESV), "smote" (KJV) is the Hiphil stem of *nākâ*, "smite, strike, hit, beat," then, the result, "to slay, kill." Here it is used metaphorically in the sense of to bring judgment upon man for his sins (Marvin R. Wilson, TWOT #1364).

[56] "Blight" (NIV, NRSV, ESV), "blasting" (KJV) is *shiddāpôn*, "scorching" (Holladay, *Hebrew Lexicon*, p. 361), "blight," a natural catastrophe. "Blight" is the effect produced by the dry, hot wind that blows into Palestine from the Arabian desert, sometimes blowing for two or three days at a time. Its destructiveness is such that it is capable of withering grass, flowers, and standing grain in a day (Victor P. Hamilton, #TWOT 908a).

[57] "Mildew" is *yērāqôn*, disease of grain, "rust" or "mildew" (Holladay, *Hebrew Lexicon*, p. 145).

and Haggai where *yasad* is used are best translated by the simple verb "build." Thus the people celebrate *beginning the building* in 537 BC and the *resumption of building* in 520 BC.[58]

Prophecy 5. Zerubbabel: the Lord's Signet Ring (Haggai 2:20-23)

A second prophecy comes to Haggai on that same day, December 17, 520 BC, an encouragement to Zerubbabel.

> "[20] The word of the LORD came to Haggai a second time on the twenty-fourth day of the month: [21] 'Tell Zerubbabel governor of Judah that I will shake the heavens and the earth. [22] I will overturn[59] royal thrones and shatter[60] the power of the foreign kingdoms. I will overthrow chariots and their drivers; horses and their riders will fall, each by the sword of his brother.
>
> [23] On that day,' declares the LORD Almighty, 'I will take you, my servant Zerubbabel son of Shealtiel,' declares the LORD, 'and I will make you like my signet ring, for I have chosen you,' declares the LORD Almighty." (Haggai 2:20-23)

One of the reasons that the rebuilding of the temple has faltered is because the leaders are discouraged, disheartened by opposition and constant pressure from provincial officials who are trying to frustrate and derail the project.

Now, God speaks directly to Zerubbabel, governor of the Persian province of Judah (Yehud). As Haggai had prophesied in Haggai 2:6-7, so God's shaking of governments will overthrow the status quo. Those officials who have prevented rebuilding the temple will no longer be able to do so.

Moreover, God tells Zerubbabel that he is specially appointed by God himself to carry out the work. "I will make you like my signet ring" (Haggai 2:23). A signet ring (compare English "*signa*ture") is a seal made of engraved stone that is impressed in clay

---

[58] Baldwin, *Haggai, Zechariah, Malachi*, pp. 52-53; Fensham, *Ezra and Nehemiah*, pp. 61-62, fn. 49. Other commentators note that more than one foundation ritual was commonly employed for temples. J.S. Wright, *Building of the Second Temple*, 1958, p. 17; D. J. Wiseman, "Haggai," *The New Bible Commentary Revised* (Eerdmans, 1970), p. 784.

[59] "Overturn" and "overthrow" (NIV), "overthrow" (NRSV, ESV, KJV) is *hāpak*, "turn," then, as used here, "overturn" (upside down) a throne,, "overthrow, destroy" a city (Holladay, *Hebrew Lexicon*, p. 82). It is used twice in verse 22, first of thrones, then of chariots.

[60] "Shatter" (NIV), "destroy" (NRSV, ESV, KJV) *shāmad* in the Hiphil stem, "destroy, exterminate." The destruction depicted by *shāmad* usually involves a rather sudden catastrophe such as warfare or a mass killing (Hermann J. Austel, TWOT #935).

or wax to authenticate a document or an order.[61] The person who carries the signet carries the authority of the person who has given the order. Zerubbabel is like Yahweh's own signet ring, one who will execute Yahweh's orders with Yahweh's own authority.

What an encouragement this prophecy would have been to Zerubbabel. Not only does this public prophecy bolster his authority among the people to complete the temple project, it is also a humbling and deeply personal assurance from God himself that the Lord is with him to enable him.

God desires to encourage you as a worker and a leader in His kingdom. He knows you personally and loves you. You are important to God, as you help execute his kingdom here on earth.

We, too, have been authorized to serve Jesus, to speak and act on his behalf (Matthew 10:40; Luke 10:16; John 13:20-21; 2 Corinthians 5:20). And he has promised never to leave us or forsake us – to the very end of the age (Matthew 28:18-20). When that kind of realization breaks over us, we become bold in the Lord to do his will, despite the obstacles we face. My dear friends, you are God's man, God's woman, to the people around you! Jesus said that as people listen to you, in a very real sense, it is like listening to Jesus

Just as Zerubbabel is encouraged by the assurance that he is God's signet ring, executing God's orders with God's own authority, as we listen to his Spirit, we today can act and speak with God's own authority, with Jesus' own words of love and power. May it be so in our lives!

> **Q5. (Haggai 2:20-23) In what way is Haggai's image of Zerubbabel being God's signet intended to encourage Zerubbabel? What is the power of a leader's signet? How does listening to God's Spirit make you effective as his agent? In what ways are you authorized to speak and act for Jesus?**
> http://www.joyfulheart.com/forums/topic/1728-q5-gods-agents/

---

[61] "Signet ring" (NIV, NRSV, ESV), "signet" (KJV) is *ḥôtām*, from *ḥātam*, "affix a seal, seal up." A seal was made of engraved stone impressed in clay or wax to authenticate a document. If it were a cylinder seal like those used in Mesopotamia it would be suspended around the neck on a string (Genesis 38:18). A stamp seal, such as was more common in Palestine, would be carried or worn on a finger. "The signet on the right hand" is a figure for that which is particularly precious to one (Jeremiah 22:24; Haggai 2:23; Jack P. Lewis, *ḥôtām*, TWOT #780a).

Lessons for Disciples

Haggai's prophecy offers a number of principles for disciples.

1. We may justify to ourselves and one another our neglect to do what God has called us to do. But our rationalization does not impress God (Haggai 1:2-4).
2. Our disobedience can result in God's discipline, or in God withholding his blessing (Haggai 1:5-6, 9-11).
3. God takes pleasure in us – and in his House – when we obey him. We should seek his pleasure, not our own (Haggai 1:8).
4. God "stirs up the spirit" of people (that is, brings additional motivation) to obey God, sometimes through prophecy, and sometimes through other means (Haggai 1:14; 2 Chronicles 36:22; Ezra 1:1).
5. Discouragement is commonplace. God commands us to "be strong and work," to take courage and not to fear. And to realize that God is with us. Courage and obedience are the earmarks of a disciple (Haggai 2:1-5).
6. We can be defiled by participating in the unclean practices of the world. Contact with holy things (such as church work) does not make us holy. We are cleansed only through repentance, confession, and faith that God forgives us (Haggai 2:10-14)
7. We do what God calls us to do, but the results are in his hands. Our work may seem small and unimpressive, but God can make it great (Haggai 2:1-9; Ezra 3:11-13; Zechariah 4:10).
8. Repentance and obedience change things. As we follow Jesus we can expect to see his blessings, both spiritually and materially (Haggai 2:15-19).
9. Just as Zerubbabel is encouraged by the assurance that he is God's signet ring, executing God's orders with God's own authority, so we today can act and speak with God's own authority, with Jesus' own words of love and power, as we listen to him (Haggai 2:20-23).

Your participation in God's work is important – and expected. However, we can be thankful that ultimately it depends upon his grace, his words of encouragement, his stirring, his shaking, and his raising up of people. And the wonderful thing is that we get to participate in both his kingdom as well as in his blessings. Hallelujah!

Prayer

Father, thank you for the privilege we have of laboring together with you. We pray that you would lift us up when we are discouraged. Stir our spirits, bring us to a place of repentance and reconsecration, that we might please You. In Jesus' name, we pray. Amen.

Key Verses

"'You expected much, but see, it turned out to be little. What you brought home, I blew away. Why?' declares the LORD Almighty. 'Because of my house, which remains a ruin, while each of you is busy with his own house.'" (Haggai 1:9, NIV)

"'But now be strong, O Zerubbabel,' declares the LORD. 'Be strong, O Joshua son of Jehozadak, the high priest. Be strong, all you people of the land,' declares the LORD, 'and work. For I am with you,' declares the LORD Almighty." (Haggai 2:4, NIV)

"'I will shake all nations, and the desired of all nations will come, and I will fill this house with glory,' says the LORD Almighty." (Haggai 2:7, NIV)

"'On that day,' declares the LORD Almighty, 'I will take you, my servant Zerubbabel son of Shealtiel,' declares the LORD, 'and I will make you like my signet ring, for I have chosen you,' declares the LORD Almighty." (Haggai 2:23, NIV)

3. Encouragement for the Builders (Zechariah 1-6)

Haggai's prophecy concluded with a highly personal encouragement to Zerubbabel, governor of the Persian province of Judah (Yehud). The first six chapters of Zechariah's prophecy concern themselves with continued encouragements to Judah's two prime leaders, Zerubbabel, who governed civil affairs of the community, and Jeshua (Joshua) the high priest, who governed religious affairs.

James J. Tissot, detail of 'Zechariah the Prophet' (1898-1902) The Jewish Museum, New York.

Zechariah the Prophet (Zechariah 1:1)

"In the eighth month of the second year of Darius, the word of the LORD came to the prophet Zechariah son of Berekiah, the son of Iddo." (Zechariah 1:1)

Zechariah was a common name in the Bible, meaning in Hebrew, "Yahweh remembers." We don't know a great deal about Zechariah, but we do know that he is:

- A **prophet**, one who receives the word of the Lord to share with the people.
- A **contemporary of Haggai.** Haggai begins prophesying on August 29, 520 BC. Zechariah begins to prophecy in November 520, and while Haggai's ministry seems to end in 520 BC, Zechariah's ministry extends to about 515 BC and perhaps beyond.
- Grandson of Iddo, who is probably the head of a priestly family, mentioned in Nehemiah 12:4. If it is the same Iddo, then Zechariah is **a priest-prophet.**

A Call to Return to the Lord (Zechariah 1:2-6)

Now let's consider the word that God gave him for the people.

"2 The LORD was very angry with your forefathers. 3 Therefore tell the people: This is what the LORD Almighty says: 'Return to me,' declares the LORD Almighty, 'and I will return to you,' says the LORD Almighty." (Zechariah 1:2-3)

"Return," "turn" is used here in the sense of "to repent,"[62] to come back to following the Lord. Notice the exalted title that Yahweh assumes – "LORD of hosts," "LORD Almighty," which means, "Yahweh of heaven's armies." The title is used 46 times in this book.

The returned exiles have only been in Judah for 17 years or so, but they have already lapsed into a kind of lethargy concerning obeying God. So the Lord reminds them about their former sin and its disastrous consequences.

> "⁴'Do not be like your forefathers, to whom the earlier prophets proclaimed: This is what the LORD Almighty says: 'Turn from your evil ways and your evil practices.' But they would not listen or pay attention to me, declares the LORD." (Zechariah 1:4)

Human life is short.

> "Where are your forefathers now? And the prophets, do they live forever?" (Zechariah 1:5)

Consider the consequence of disobedience. Zechariah has no need to spell it out. The pain of exile is still fresh.

> "But did not my words and my decrees, which I commanded my servants the prophets, overtake your forefathers?" (1:6a)

"Overtake," "take hold" is a hunting term, "overtake, catch up with."[63] The same word is used in a warning in Deuteronomy:

> "All these curses will come upon you. **They will pursue you and overtake you** until you are destroyed, because you did not obey the LORD your God and observe the commands and decrees he gave you." (Deuteronomy 28:45, cf. 28:15)

We humans rationalize our behaviors, and having done that, we imagine that God won't mind so much. But God's commands and words do not die. They will catch up with us. There is no escaping truth or judgment. As the Law says:

> "You may be sure that your sin will find you out." (Numbers 32:23)

Our only hope is to repent. Fortunately, these returned exiles listen and obey.

---

[62] The Qal stem of the very common verb *shûb*, "turn, return" physically, used theologically in a two-fold sense here to describe God's people returning to God (repentance), and, turning away from evil (renouncing and disowning sin) (Victor P. Hamilton, *shûb*, TWOT #2340). The word is also used in the sense of return from exile.

[63] *Nāśag*, Holladay, *Hebrew Lexicon*, p. 247, 1.

"Then they repented and said, 'The LORD Almighty has done to us what our ways and practices deserve, just as he determined to do.'" (Zechariah 1:6b)

Dear friend, are there "ways and practices" in your life that you know to be contrary to God's word? Don't expect God to give you a "pass," or a "Get Out of Jail Free Card" (a reference to the game of Monopoly). Continual patterns of sin both (1) keep you from closeness to God, and (2) subject you to severe discipline from God if you continue in them. Will you turn? Will you repent? Repentance can be difficult and sometimes embarrassing, but the fruits of repentance are joy, peace, and intimacy with God. His Spirit is speaking to you. Now is the time of repentance.

> **Q1. (Zechariah 1:3) Why is a message of repentance from sin such an important part of the Gospel? What happens when we remove repentance from the core message of Jesus? Why do you think God wants you to repent of all known sin?**
> **http://www.joyfulheart.com/forums/topic/1729-q1-repentance/**

The Night Visions (Zechariah 1:7-6:15)

Zechariah's first word is dated in November 520. Over the first six chapters is a whole series of Night Visions that Zechariah receives in one momentous night a couple of months later, on Feb 15, 519 BC. These Night Visions consist of eight symbolic words from God, designed to encourage the people and their leaders to rebuild the temple.

1. A Man Among the Myrtle Trees (Zechariah 1:8-17)
2. Four Horns and Four Craftsmen (Zechariah 1:18-21)
3. A Man with a Measuring Line (Zechariah 2)
4. Clean Garments for the High Priest (Zechariah 3)
5. The Gold Lampstand and the Two Olive Trees (Zechariah 4)
6. The Flying Scroll (Zechariah 5:1-4)
7. The Woman in the Basket (Zechariah 5:5-11)
8. Four Chariots (Zechariah 6)

Apocalyptic

Many of Israel's prophets had used objects or word pictures as a starting point for a prophetic word. But the book of Zechariah is different. It belongs to the genre of prophecy termed "apocalyptic." The word comes from the Greek *apokalypsis*, "revelation, making fully known," literally, "take the cover off." In the Greek Bible, the title of the Book of Revelation is *Apokalypsis*.

Daniel seems to be the earliest apocalypse (about 600 to 520 BC), followed directly by parts of Ezekiel (597-573 BC) and Zechariah (520-515 BC or a bit later). Then a whole body of Jewish literature sprang up between 200 BC and 100 AD in imitation of Daniel.[64]

Apocalyptic literature is full of symbols that are seen in dreams and visions, such as rich symbolism in the Book of Revelation. Another characteristic of apocalyptic prophecy is a deterministic view – that history must run its course, but the end is predetermined by God. The end of history will be a violent in-breaking by God to establish his kingdom.[65] Longman writes:

> "Apocalyptic is a metaphor-rich genre. In this regard it is like poetry. Metaphors and similes teach by analogy. They throw light on difficult concepts and things by relating them to something we know from common experience. As such, images speak truly and accurately, but not precisely. We often do not know where the analogy stops."[66]

The symbols are designed to communicate not just facts, but also emotional feelings. It is important not to over-interpret these apocalyptic images. The course of history is littered with hundreds of dogmatic interpretations of Daniel, Revelation, and Zechariah, that, in hindsight, appear to be overworked and bizarre.

The book of Zechariah is one of the most difficult books of the Bible to interpret. St. Jerome referred to it as "that most obscure book." So don't be disappointed if we can't unravel all the figures and symbols completely. However, we'll do our best.

Vision 1. Man Among the Myrtle Trees (Zechariah 1:8-17)

We begin with the first of the seven "Night Visions." Zechariah sees people astride red, brown, and white horses in a myrtle grove, which have returned from surveying the whole earth.

---

[64] Some of the Jewish apocalyptic writings include: First and Second Enoch, Book of Jubilees, Testaments of the Twelve Patriarchs, Psalms of Solomon, Assumption of Moses, Fourth Ezra, and the Apocalypse of Baruch.

[65] George Eldon Ladd, "Apocalyptic Literature," ISBE 1:151-160; also George Eldon Ladd, *Jesus and the Kingdom* (Harper & Row, 1964), chapter 3, later published under the title, *The Presence of the Future*.

[66] Tremper Longman III, *The NIV Application Commentary: Daniel* (Zondervan, 1999), p. 178.

'Vision of Zechariah,' detached leaf, Sicily (c. 1300), tempera with gold on parchment, 2-7/8 x 6-7/8 inches, J. Paul Getty Museum, Los Angeles.

"¹² Then the angel of the LORD said, 'LORD Almighty, how long will you withhold mercy from Jerusalem and from the towns of Judah, which you have been angry with these seventy years?' ¹³ So the LORD spoke kind and comforting words to the angel who talked with me.

¹⁴ Then the angel who was speaking to me said, 'Proclaim this word: This is what the LORD Almighty says: "I am very jealous for Jerusalem and Zion, ¹⁵ but I am very angry with the nations that feel secure. I was only a little angry, but they added to the calamity."

¹⁶ Therefore, this is what the LORD says: "I will return to Jerusalem with mercy, and there my house will be rebuilt. And the measuring line will be stretched out over Jerusalem," declares the LORD Almighty.

¹⁷ 'Proclaim further: This is what the LORD Almighty says: "My towns will again overflow with prosperity, and the LORD will again comfort Zion and choose Jerusalem.'" (Zechariah 1:8-17)

The color and number of the horses in the vision have no sure meaning. But they seem to represent horsemen who have been sent on a reconnaissance mission to evaluate what is going on in the earth, perhaps to the four corners of the earth. They report: "We have gone throughout the earth and found the whole world at rest and in peace."

Some Jews had been saying, "The time has not yet come for the LORD's house to be built" (Haggai 1:2). Perhaps they felt they needed revenue from the Persian government to continue building, but the government's attention had been elsewhere putting down rebellions.[67] But now by February 519, the horsemen's report is "rest and peace." Now was the time. There are encouraging words:

- The Lord speaks "kind and comforting words" (verse 13).
- God is "very jealous for Jerusalem and Zion," and will defend them against "the nations that feel secure" (verse 14), perhaps referring to the surrounding provinces that are trying to stop work on the temple.
- God will "return to Jerusalem with mercy" to rebuild the temple, indicated by "the measuring line" used by surveyors and builders (verse 16).
- He promises that the towns and cities of Judah "will again overflow[68] with prosperity"[69] (verse 17a).
- That Yahweh will again "comfort" Zion[70] and "choose" Jerusalem (verse 17b).

Yahweh offers two actions: (1) to comfort, and (2) to choose. "Comfort"[71] recalls the great passage from Isaiah:

"Comfort, comfort my people…
Speak tenderly to Jerusalem,
and proclaim to her that her hard service
has been completed." (Isaiah 40:1-2)

While comfort is God's response to Israel's discipline, "to choose" (verse 17) indicates that he now has a positive intention to further his plans through them. He "chooses" and "decides for"[72] Jerusalem. He removes his people from the sideline of history in

---

[67] The historical background may illuminate the horsemen's report of "rest and peace." Cyrus's son and successor, Cambyses, died in July 522 BC, at reports of unrest in the eastern part of the Persian Empire. Darius, an officer in Cambyses entourage, siezed the throne, dealt with the rebels, and then proceeded to put down rebellions in other parts of the Empire. It seems that by 520 BC, when Haggai and Zechariah had begun to prophesy, Darius had secured his throne.

[68] "Overflow" (NIV, NRSV, ESV), "spread abroad" (KJV) is the Qal stem of *pûs*, "scatter, disperse," here in the sense of "overflow," as in Proverbs 15:7 (Holladay, *Hebrew Lexicon*, p. 290, 3).

[69] "Prosperity" is the common noun *tôb*, "good, goodness," here referring to economic or material good (TWOT #793a).

[70] Here Zion is a synonym of Jerusalem. Originally, Zion was the part of the city that David conquered from the Jebusites.

[71] "Comfort" is the Piel stem of *nāham*, "comfort (with words)" (Holladay, *Hebrew Lexicon*, p. 234). The root seems to reflect the idea of breathing deeply, hence the physical display of one's feelings, usually "sorrow, compassion, or comfort" (Marvin R. Wilson, TWOT #1344).

[72] "Choose" is the Qal stem of *bāhar*, "to choose, elect, decide for" TWOT #231), "select" (Holladay, *Hebrew Lexicon*, p. 37, I, 2).

Babylon where they languished for 70 years, back into the center of history, rebuilding his house in Jerusalem. We see this theme elsewhere:

"The LORD, who has **chosen Jerusalem**, rebuke you!" (Zechariah 3:2)

"The LORD has **chosen Zion**." (Psalm 132:13)

"Once again he will **choose Israel**." (Isaiah 14:1a)

God had spoken through Isaiah concerning this time:

"The Lord … says of Jerusalem, 'It shall be inhabited,' of the towns of Judah, 'They shall be built,' and of their ruins, 'I will restore them.'" (Isaiah 44:26)

For a people who had started rebuilding the temple, then faltered, God's words of encouragement through Zechariah must have been energizing.

Vision 2. Four Horns and Four Craftsmen (Zechariah 1:18-21)

The next vision Zechariah sees that night is not of horses, but of the curious symbols of horns and craftsmen.

"[18] Then I looked up – and there before me were four horns! [19] I asked the angel who was speaking to me, 'What are these?' He answered me, 'These are the horns that scattered Judah, Israel and Jerusalem.'

[20] Then the LORD showed me four craftsmen. [21] I asked, 'What are these coming to do?' He answered, 'These are the horns that scattered Judah so that no one could raise his head, but the craftsmen have come to terrify them and throw down these horns of the nations who lifted up their horns against the land of Judah to scatter its people.'" (Zechariah 1:18-21)

"Horn" refers to military power. Hebrew *qeren* primarily denotes the horn(s) of various animals (ram, wild oxen) that they would use to fight for dominance. But the meaning extends to physical and military might, as well as arrogance and pride.[73] Powerful foreign invaders have scattered[74] God's people and dispersed them in exile to Assyria and Babylon.[75]

The other important figures in this prophecy are four "craftsmen" (NIV, ESV), "blacksmiths" (NRSV), "carpenters" (KJV) is the verb *ḥārāsh*. The basic idea is cutting

---

[73] *Qeren*, TWOT #2072a.

[74] "Scattered" is *zārâ*, "to scatter, spread, cast away, disperse" (TWOT #579).

[75] Some have attempted to define the four horns as Assyrians, Babylonians, Medes, and Persians, but it's harder to identify the four craftsmen. Perhaps it's better to see four as representing the totality of opposition from every direction, the four winds (Baldwin, *Haggai, Zechariah, Malachi*, p. 104).

into some material, such as engraving metal or plowing. The noun can mean "engraving, carpenter, smith, mason." Craftsman is a generic way of expressing these kinds of workers.[76] The craftsmen correspond to those who destroy Israel's enemies (think of a blacksmith's heavy hammer). That's the big picture.

There's a similar prophecy in Daniel 2, where a rock, representing the Kingdom of God, crushes all the previous world powers (Daniel 2:34-35, 45). Or, to switch analogies, Jeremiah speaks of God's word as a hammer that breaks in pieces those who oppose God (Jeremiah 23:29).

The returned exiles who began to build the temple have been frustrated by their enemies. God's people have enemies, but they don't have the last word. God is with us and will ultimately destroy our enemies – the theme of many of the Psalms (Psalm 18:3; 23:5; Psalm 59:10; etc.).

Vision 3. Man with a Measuring Line (Zechariah 2)

"Measuring line" is two words: *ḥ̣ebel*, "rope, cord," and *middâ*, "measure, measurement." Twenty-first century contractors use phased infrared light beams to determine distances. But until recently, builders have used rods, chains, and tapes to measure distances. The "measuring line" is a simple cord or rope of a definite length or with distances marked on it – used by both carpenters (Isaiah 44:13) and surveyors, as in our passage.

> "¹ Then I looked up – and there before me was a man with a measuring line in his hand! ² I asked, 'Where are you going?' He answered me, 'To measure Jerusalem, to find out how wide and how long it is.' ³ Then the angel who was speaking to me left, and another angel came to meet him ⁴ and said to him: 'Run, tell that young man, "Jerusalem will be a city without walls because of the great number of men and livestock in it. ⁵ And I myself will be a wall of fire around it," declares the LORD, "and I will be its glory within."'" (Zechariah 2:1-5)

Zechariah has a vision of someone who comes to measure the now-small city of Jerusalem, probably to build a wall to protect it. But then God says, that the city, which is now small with few people, will become so large that no wall will be able to contain all the people and livestock that will be in it.

---

[76] Leon J. Wood, *ḥ̣ārāsh*, TWOT #760a.

> "6 'Come! Come! Flee from the land of the north,' declares the LORD, 'for I have scattered you to the four winds of heaven,' declares the LORD. 7 'Come, O Zion! Escape, you who live in the Daughter of Babylon!'" (Zechariah 2:6-7)

"Daughter of Babylon" means "inhabitants of Babylon." God invites the remaining exiles in Babylon to return to Jerusalem, for God himself will protect and avenge them.

> "8 For this is what the LORD Almighty says: 'After he has honored me and has sent me against the nations that have plundered you – for whoever touches you touches the apple of his eye – 9 I will surely raise my hand against them so that their slaves will plunder them. Then you will know that the LORD Almighty has sent me." (Zechariah 2:8-9).

God says that to touch Israel, is to touch God's own pupil,[77] the sensitive part of one's eye. God will not let this go unpunished.

> "'Shout and be glad, O Daughter of Zion.
> For I am coming,
> and I will live among you,'
> declares the LORD." (Zechariah 2:10)

The idea of God being in the midst of his people goes back to the tabernacle residing in the very center of the camp of Israel in the Wilderness.

> "11 Many nations will be joined with the LORD in that day and will become my people. I will live among you and you will know that the LORD Almighty has sent me to you. 12 The LORD will inherit Judah as his portion in the holy land and will again choose Jerusalem." (Zechariah 2:11-12)

Here is a promise that the Gentiles will become one with God's people, with Jerusalem at its center. We see this theme in Psalms, Isaiah, and elsewhere (e.g., Zechariah 8:20-23; Psalm 22:27-30; 68:29-31; Isaiah 2:2-5; 60:3-7).

What is the modern-day equivalent of God in the midst of his people? God dwelling in the midst of his gathered people, the church. In congregations around the world, people experience God in their midst – as God in his temple (1 Corinthians 3:16; Ephesians 2:21-22; 1 Peter 2:5). It is sad that Christians feel free to separate themselves

---

[77] "The apple of one's eye," that is, the "pupil," is an English idiom, not a Hebrew one. The phrase goes back to King Alfred in the 9th century AD. The Hebrew idiom is different. In Zechariah 2:8, "apple" is bābâ, "pupil, eyeball," of uncertain derivation. (Holladay, *Hebrew Lexicon*, p. 33). Hebrew 'îshôn (literally, "little man" of the eye) is used elsewhere for "pupil" (Holladay, *Hebrew Lexicon*, p. 14; Deuteronomy 32:10; Psalm 17:8; Proverbs 7:2). In Lamentations 2:18, the phase is literally the "daughter" of the eye.

from a congregation and live their lives independent from church. Yes, this is sometimes necessary. But it is not normal, nor is it the place of God's desired blessing. We are part of a people, not "Lone Ranger" Christians.

"The Lord ... has roused himself from his holy dwelling." (Zechariah 2:13b)

God has "roused himself," he is active and ready to fight for his people.[78] There is a 13th century English proverb, "Let sleeping dogs lie," alluding to a time when dogs were trained to be fierce watchdogs, and to wake them would put a person in danger. God is ready to act on behalf of his people – certainly an encouraging word to the returned exiles who have struggled to build the temple against the opposition of their neighbors.

Be Still before the Lord (Zechariah 2:13a)

Because God is ready to act, it is a time to be still before him in awe and fear.

"Be still[79] before the LORD, all mankind,

because he has roused himself from his holy dwelling." (Zechariah 2:13)

So often we yammer and complain to God. We fault him for not acting on our behalf according to our own timetable. We act as if we know best and that God is asleep. How foolish. Faith doesn't need noise. Stillness before our awesome God is appropriate.

After escaping Egypt, God told Moses to pitch the Israelite camp next to the Red Sea. When Pharaoh's chariots were spotted pursuing them, and with nowhere they could escape, the people panicked and blamed Moses. But Moses had been with God, and spoke words of faith:

"The LORD will fight for you, and you have only to **be silent**."[80] (Exodus 14:14)

We see this theme elsewhere:

"The LORD is in his holy temple;   1

let all the earth **be silent** before him." (Habakkuk 2:20)

---

[78] "Roused" (NIV, NRSV, ESV), "raised up" (KJV) is the Niphal stem of 'ûr, "be stirred up, be set in motion" (Holladay, *Hebrew Lexicon*, p. 268).

[79] "Be still" (NIV), "be silent" (NRSV, ESV, KJV) is *hasâ*, "an interjection with imperative force meaning be silent, hush" (Carl Philip Weber, TWOT #511). Also in Habakkuk 2:20 and Zephaniah 1:7a.

[80] "Be still" (NIV), "keep still" (NRSV), "be silent" (ESV), "hold your peace" (KJV) is the Hiphil stem of *ḥārēsh*, "keep still, be silent, let someone do something without objection" (Holladay, *Hebrew Lexicon*, p. 118). The basic idea is of non-communication, expressed by either not speaking or not hearing (Leon J. Wood, TWOT #761).

"**Be silent** before the Sovereign LORD,
for the day of the LORD is near." (Zephaniah 1:7a)

"**Be still**,[81] and know that I am God." (Psalm 46:10a)

Silence before the Lord could be from frustration, having given up. Or from fear and awe. But it is best used by disciples as a silent trust in God to take care of us and our situation. We can trust him!

> **Q2. (Zechariah 2:13) Why, in this passage, do you think the prophet calls all mankind to be still before him? In the context of God aroused to protect his people from attack, why is silence appropriate? For the enemy of God, what does silence represent? For the believer, what does silence before God represent?**
> **http://www.joyfulheart.com/forums/topic/1730-q2-be-still/**

Vision 4. Clean Garments for the High Priest (Zechariah 3)

One of the things that causes us to lag in serving the Lord is sin. Guilt. The sense of being a hypocrite. I am guessing from this vision that Joshua the high priest (called Jeshua in Ezra and Nehemiah) has fallen into sin. We know that later, two of his sons had married foreign women. But Joshua is high priest, one of the two most important leaders in all Jerusalem. He has been compromised by sin; sin has destroyed his ability to lead effectively. So God gives Zechariah a vision of cleansing and redemption.

> "[1] Then he showed me Joshua the high priest standing before the angel of the LORD, and Satan standing at his right side to accuse him. [2] The LORD said to Satan, 'The LORD rebuke you, Satan! The LORD, who has chosen Jerusalem, rebuke you! Is not this man a burning stick snatched from the fire?'" (Zechariah 3:1-2)

The name Satan (śāṭān) means "adversary, one who withstands," from śaṭan, "be an adversary, resist, accuse."[82] Occasionally, it is used as a title of God's chief opponent, Satan. It appears in the Old Testament in Job 1:6-12; 2:1-8; and 1 Chronicles 21:1 (compare 2 Samuel 24:1). The intertestamental period sees increased interest in Satan. In the New Testament, the title Satan is transliterated from the Hebrew 34 times, though

---

[81] "Be still" is the Hiphil stem of rāpâ, "leave someone alone" (= not bother)" (Holladay, pp. 344-345; William White, TWOT #2198).

[82] J. Barton Payne, śaṭan, TWOT #2252.

more often he is referred to as "the devil."[83] In opposing God, Satan is a tempter, a corrupter, and then an accuser. Wonderful is the day when we read:

> "The accuser of our brothers,
> who accuses them before our God day and night,
> has been hurled down." (Revelation 12:10)

In our day, Satan no longer has access before the throne of God, as he seems to have had in Job's day. However, in Zechariah's vision, Satan is accusing Joshua before the Lord. God reproves him most sharply:

> "Yahweh rebuke[84] you, Satan!
> Yahweh, who has chosen[85] Jerusalem, rebuke you!" (Zechariah 3:2a)

A Brand Plucked from the Fire (Zechariah 3:2b)

> "Is not this man a burning stick[86] snatched[87] from the fire." (Zechariah 3:2b)

This is similar to Amos's admonition of Israel:

> "'I overthrew some of you,
> as when God overthrew Sodom and Gomorrah,
> and you were as **a brand plucked out of the burning**;
> yet you did not return to me,' declares the LORD." (Amos 4:11)

This figure is also used by Jude in the New Testament:

> "Be merciful to those who doubt;
> **snatch others from the fire** and save them…." (Jude 22-23a)

If you've observed a fireplace or campfire, then you know that sometimes a piece of wood begins burning when you don't want it to. So you quickly pull it out or rescue it from the fire so it won't burn any more. It had begun to burn, but it has now been rescued, saved. That is Joshua the high priest's situation. He is guilty, condemned, accused, washed up as a leader. But God saves him, silences Satan, and cleanses him for his service.

---

[83] Daniel P. Fuller, "Satan," ISBE 4:344.

[84] "Rebuke" is *gā'ar*, "rebuke, reprove." This root indicates a check applied to a person or peoples through strong admonitions or actions (Harold G. Stigers, TWOT #370).

[85] Also Zechariah 1:17; 2:12.

[86] "Burning stick" (NIV), "brand" (NRSV, ESV, KJV) is *ûd*, "log" (Holladay, *Hebrew Lexicon*, p. 6), "brand, firebrand" (BDB, 15).

[87] "Snatched" (NIV), "plucked" (NRSV, ESV, KJV) is the Hofal stem of *nāṣal*, "rescue, save," here, Hofal, "snatched away" (Holladay, *Hebrew Lexicon*, p. 244).

I think of Peter. Jesus' closest disciple betrays him three times. He's done! He feels unworthy until Jesus restores him and commissions him afresh, "Feed my lambs."

Perhaps you're a believer or a leader who has sinned. Who feels Satan's harsh condemnation. Who has been believing Satan's accusations. I have good news for you. Gospel news! Jesus is in the cleansing and restoration business.

Here's how the gospel of redemption plays out in Zechariah's vision.

> "³ Now Joshua was dressed in filthy clothes as he stood before the angel. ⁴ The angel said to those who were standing before him, 'Take off his filthy clothes.' Then he said to Joshua, 'See, I have taken away your sin, and I will put rich garments on you.' ⁵ Then I said, 'Put a clean turban on his head.' So **they put a clean turban on his head and clothed him**, while the angel of the LORD stood by.
>
> ⁶ The angel of the LORD gave this charge to Joshua: ⁷ 'This is what the LORD Almighty says: "If you will walk in my ways and keep my requirements, then you will govern my house and have charge of my courts, and I will give you a place among these standing here."'" (Zechariah 3:3-7)

The Lord promises him the privilege of governing the temple – all by grace!

The angel removes his "filthy clothes" (representing his sin) and clothes him with clean, rich garments (representing cleansing and forgiveness). We see this kind of imagery elsewhere in the Bible:

> "He has clothed me with **garments of salvation**
> and arrayed me in a **robe of righteousness**." (Isaiah 61:10)

> "You have taken off your old self with its practices
> and have put on the new self,
> which is being renewed in knowledge in the image of its Creator."
> (Colossians 3:9-10)

Q3. (Zechariah 3:1-7) What do Joshua's filthy clothes represent? How does God deal with this? What message is this prophecy intended to convey to Joshua the High Priest? How might this message apply to Christian leaders who have sinned? http://www.joyfulheart.com/forums/topic/1731-q3-clean-clothes/

My Servant, the Branch (Zechariah 3:8-10)

The next passage introduces a clearly messianic image.

"Listen, O high priest Joshua and your associates seated before you,
who are men symbolic of things to come:
I am going to bring **my servant, the Branch**." (Zechariah 3:8)

"Branch" is *ṣemaḥ*, "sprout, growth, branch," from *ṣāmaḥ*, "to sprout, spring up." A similar term appears in a Phoenician inscription as "the rightful shoot." A Ugaritic inscription refers to "shoot or progeny." Thus *ṣemaḥ* is a technical term signifying a scion or son.[88] Already by Zechariah's time, the concept of the Branch springing up from David's line is a recognized messianic figure, introduced by Isaiah, and reinforced by Jeremiah, Ezekiel, and the Psalmist.

"A **shoot**[89] will come up from the stump of Jesse;
from his roots a **Branch**[90] will bear fruit." (Isaiah 11:1)

"In that day **the Branch** (*ṣemaḥ*) of the LORD will be beautiful and glorious,
and the fruit of the land
will be the pride and glory of the survivors in Israel." (Isaiah 4:2)

"He grew up before him like a **tender shoot**,[91]
and like a root out of dry ground." (Isaiah 53:2a)

"'The days are coming,' declares the LORD,
'when I will raise up to David a **righteous Branch** (*ṣemaḥ*),
a King who will reign wisely
and do what is just and right in the land.'" (Jeremiah 23:5; compare 33:15)

"There I will make a horn to **sprout** (*ṣāmaḥ*) for David;
I have prepared a lamp for my anointed." (Psalm 132:17)

"On that day I will cause a horn to **spring up** (*ṣāmaḥ*) for the house of Israel,
and I will open your lips among them." (Ezekiel 29:21)

In our passage, the Branch is referred to as "my servant" and seems to be a different person than Joshua himself. (In Zechariah 6:12 the Branch seems to be the same person as Joshua. More on that shortly.) Here Yahweh promises that the Branch (the Messiah, the Son of David) will come in the future. This prophecy has two more figures.

---

[88] *Semah*, TWOT #1928.
[89] *Hōṭer*, "branch or twig" (TWOT #643a).
[90] *Nēṣer*, "branch, shoot, sprout" (TWOT #1408a).
[91] *Yônēq*, "suckling, sapling, young plant" (TWOT #874a).

The 7-Faceted Stone (Zechariah 3:9a)

Next, the prophet refers to a seven-faceted stone (ʾeben). Yahweh is often referred as the Rock (ṣûr), but this is different. Ṣûr is "rock, boulders or formations of stone and for the material which composes mountains."[92] But a "stone" (ʾeben) was smaller. Stone was used for building – houses, the temple, altars, markers, pillars. Stone is used several times in the Old Testament as a messianic title – and quoted in the New Testament.

> "He will be a **stone** (ʾeben) that causes men to stumble
> and a rock that makes them fall.
> And for the people of Jerusalem he will be a trap
> and a snare." (Isaiah 8:14)

> "See, I lay a **stone** (ʾeben) in Zion, a tested stone,
> a **precious cornerstone** for a sure foundation;
> the one who trusts will never be dismayed." (Isaiah 28:16)

Daniel sees a Stone that will crush all former kingdoms (Daniel 2:34). Now we come back to the stone before Joshua the high priest in Zechariah's vision.

> "'9 See, the **stone** I have set in front of Joshua!
> There are seven eyes on that one stone,
> and I will engrave an inscription on it,'
> says the LORD Almighty,
> 'and I will remove the sin of this land in a single day.
> 10 In that day each of you will invite his neighbor
> to sit under his vine and fig tree,'
> declares the LORD Almighty.'" (Zechariah 3:9-10)

The stone in Zechariah's vision seems to be one of these messianic symbols, particularly since Branch and Stone are in adjacent verses.

The seven "eyes" (NIV, ESV, KJV) or "facets" (NRSV)[93] represent the completeness and perfection of this stone. True, Vision 6 has a menorah with seven lights on it, which represent "the eyes of the LORD, which range throughout the earth" (Zechariah 4:10b), but I think here "facets" is the idea, rather than symbolic eyes. Apocalyptic prophecies often shift around symbols from one prophecy to another.

---

[92] John E. Hartley, ṣûr, TWOT #1901a. In only one case is Yahweh referred to as "the Stone (eben) of Israel" (Genesis 49:24).

[93] "Eyes" (ESV, KJV) or "facets" (NIV, NRSV) is ʾayin, "eye." Here they refer to "facets," used in the sense of "surface" as in Exodus 10:15 ("the eye [surface] of the whole land") (Carl Schultz, TWOT #1612a).

What the inscription signifies, we can't be sure and speculation doesn't help us much. The image of sitting "under his vine and fig tree" means to enjoy peace and prosperity in the messianic age (1 King 4:25; Isaiah 36:16; Hosea 2:18; Micah 4:4).

Removing Sin in a Single Day (Zechariah 3:9d)

The messianic promise of atonement is clear to us in light of Christ.

'And I will remove the sin of this land in a single day." (Zechariah 3:9d)

Messiah Jesus is rather clear about his role.

"For even the Son of Man did not come to be served, but to serve,
and to give his life as **a ransom for many**." (Mark 10:45)

Jesus' words "for many" are intended to echo Isaiah's great prophecy:

"He poured out his life unto death,
and was numbered with the transgressors.
For **he bore the sin of many**,
and made intercession for the transgressors." (Isaiah 53:12b)

On the day Jesus the Messiah dies on the cross, he takes upon himself not only the "sins of this land" (Judah), but also "the sins of the whole world" (John 1:29; 1 John 2:2). In a later prophecy, Zechariah declares:

"On that day a fountain will be opened to the house of David
and the inhabitants of Jerusalem,
to cleanse them from sin and impurity." (Zechariah 13:1)

Praise God!

Vision 5. The Gold Lampstand and the Two Olive Trees (Zechariah 4)

Now we come to the fifth of Zechariah's seven night visions. While Vision 4 was intended to encourage Joshua the high priest, Vision 5 is given primarily to encourage Zerubbabel the governor. Here's Zechariah's vision.

"2 I see a solid gold lampstand with a bowl at the top and seven lights on it, with seven channels to the lights. 3 Also there are two olive trees by it, one on the right of the bowl and the other on its left." (Zechariah 4:2-3)

When Zechariah asks an angel what they represent, the angel doesn't immediately solve the riddle, but replies:

" [6] This is the word of the LORD to Zerubbabel: 'Not by might nor by power, but by my Spirit,' says the LORD Almighty. [7] 'What are you, O mighty mountain? Before Zerubbabel you will become level ground.'" (Zechariah 4:6-7a)

Construction of the temple had been blocked, frustrated by Judah's enemies. For years the partly-constructed temple site lay silent from the sounds of workmen. The task has seemed like a "mighty mountain." But now the project shall become easy – "level ground."

What is the difference? This time they will build relying upon God's strength, not their own – God's Holy Spirit.

As I look back on my life, I can see many times when I relied on my own talents and hard work, than on the Spirit of God – and achieved little. I believe that one of the vital lessons of discipleship is to listen to discern what God is saying and doing, and then cooperate with that, rather than trying to force things to happen by our own will and efforts. This is Jesus' way (John 5:19).

Zerubbabel to Complete the Temple (Zechariah 4:7b-9)

" [7b] Then he will bring out the capstone to shouts of 'God bless it! God bless it!'

[8] Then the word of the LORD came to me: [9] "The hands of Zerubbabel have laid the foundation of this temple; his hands will also complete it. Then you will know that the LORD Almighty has sent me to you." (Zechariah 4:7b-9)

Verse 7 and 8 contrast two types of stones used in construction: foundation stones and capstones. The foundation stones are placed first, before any other construction takes place. The capstone or capstones go at the very top of the structure to finish it off.[94] Zechariah prophesies even the words that will be spoken when the top stone is placed: The NIV's translation, "God bless it!" is a stretch. More accurate is "Grace to it!" (NRSV, ESV, KJV). "Grace" is *hēn*, "favor, grace."[95] When Zerubbabel lays the final stone the people will shout and attribute the completion to God's favor, God's grace.

Despising the Day of Small Things (Zechariah 4:10a)

Remember how the people had wept when they saw the humble, plain beginnings of the Second Temple that was to replace Solomon's glorious temple? (Ezra 3:12). As the

---

[94] "Capstone" (NIV), "top stone" (NRSV, ESV), is literally "headstone" (KJV). The word modifying stone (*'eben*) is *rō'shâ*, "top, i.e. the topmost stone," from *rō'sh*, "head," then "top, summit" (TWOT #2097b).

[95] *Hēn*, "favor, grace," from the verb *hānan*, to be gracious, pity." The verb *hānan* depicts a heartfelt response by someone who has something to give to one who has a need (Edwin Yamauchi, TWOT #694a).

partly-finished temple lay in ruins. Haggai reminds them of their attitude: "Is it not in your sight as nothing?" (Haggai 2:3b).

Sometimes we castigate ourselves for our mistakes and false starts by telling ourselves that we never could have done it anyway. The returned exiles were thoroughly discouraged, from the people to the governor, Zerubbabel. Now Zechariah's prophecy shakes him.

> "Who despises the day of small things?
> Men will rejoice when they see the plumb line in the hand of Zerubbabel."
> (Zechariah 4:10a)

Zechariah had despised that early start. How weak, how insignificant, how naive he had been. Yet, in spite of all that, God had been in those beginnings.

How often our efforts for God are attacked by the enemy. We can get so discouraged we don't even want to try again. But God delights in taking the insignificant and making something out of it. Down through history we can see the pattern:

- Moses' rod that delivers a nation from Egypt (Exodus 4:1-9),
- The jawbone of an ass that in Samson's hand kills a thousand Philistines (Judges 15:14-16),
- Five smooth stones that fell the giant Goliath (1 Samuel 17),
- The handful of meal and a jar of oil that sustain a widow through years of famine (2 Kings 4:1-7),
- Five barley loaves and a couple of fish that feed a multitude (Matthew 14:13-21), and
- The mustard seed Jesus said will become a great tree for birds to find shelter (Matthew 13:31-32).

What little thing, what dream, what false start, have you despised? Your small church, your tiny Bible study, your hopes of ministry for Christ? Do you despise your failures? Don't. Surrender them to the God who delights in taking human weakness and showing his strength. Take another look at your discarded dreams, this time through God's eyes:

> "Not by might, not by power, but my Spirit says the Lord Almighty." (Zechariah 4:6)

Trust God, Zerubbabel. Try again, this time with his leading, his Spirit, and his power. And the people who have been thoroughly disheartened by the failure to build the temple will be encouraged by your example. They'll see Zerubbabel out on the ruins of the temple, plumb line in hand, beginning to direct the project again, and they'll rejoice.

Incidentally, a plumb line is still used in building to this day to make sure the wall of a building is straight up and down – plumb. Essentially, a plummet or plumb bob, is a stone or weight on a string.[96] Gravity pulls the line straight down. Simple, but effective.

Q4. (Zechariah 4:1-10) Why do we so easily fall into the trap of trying to do God's work with our own strength? What does it mean, "Not by might, not by power, but by my Spirit"? How might you apply this truth to your life?
http://www.joyfulheart.com/forums/topic/1732-q4-by-my-spirit/

Two Olive Trees and Golden Pipes (Zechariah 4:10b-13)

Now Zechariah returns to some of the more difficult symbols of this vision: olive trees, a pedestal lampstand holding seven lamps, and golden pipes that transmit olive oil from the olive trees to the lamps.

> "I see a solid gold lampstand with a bowl at the top and seven lights on it,
> with seven channels to the lights." (Zechariah 4:2)

The lamp described in Zechariah's vision is probably a pedestal lampstand. These are normally a cylindrical column made of pottery, tapering slightly towards the top, with a bowl on top. Here the seven lamps are wicks are set around the bowl, apparently with a channel to each of the lights to bring oil from a central supply in the middle. But this lampstand is gold!

> "(These seven are the eyes of the LORD,
> which range throughout the earth.)" (Zechariah 4:10b)

The seven lamps represent the seven all-seeing eyes of Yahweh (2 Chronicles 16:9; Proverbs 15:3; Revelation 5:6). Zechariah asks the angel what this means.

> "These are the two who are anointed to serve the Lord of all the earth." (Zechariah 4:13)

It seems to me that here's how it works, though the symbols are somewhat bizarre. The "two olive trees" represent Zerubbabel and Joshua, the two men whom Yahweh is

---

[96] "Plumb line" (NIV, ESV), "plummet" (NRSV, KJV) is *eben*, "stone," a word we've seen before in this passage.

encouraging through this vision. They are "anointed[97] to serve the Lord of all the earth." The golden pipes seem to run from the olive trees to pour out "gold oil" that lights the lamp, which probably represents Israel. We see an echo of this in Revelation in the Two Witnesses:

> "These are the two olive trees and the two lampstands
> that stand before the Lord of the earth." (Revelation 11:4)

Taken together, Vision 5 encourages Zerubbabel that God's Spirit will help build the temple and that, together, the anointed leaders of Judah, Zerubbabel and Joshua, will provide what is needed to accomplish God's plan. It will all be by God's grace, however, not man's effort. Yes, Zerubbabel and Joshua must lead well and the people will work, but it is God's grace that allows it to come to completion.

Visions 6 The Flying Scroll (Zechariah 5:1-4)

Just when are beginning to make sense out of Zechariah's night visions, along comes one that is full of mystery. Though the details may be unclear, the overall thrust of visions 7 and 8 is clear: condemnation of sin and its removal from the land.

Again, the figures are somewhat bizarre.

> "I looked again – and there before me was a flying scroll! [2] He asked me, 'What do you see?' I answered, 'I see a flying scroll, thirty feet long and fifteen feet wide.'" (Zechariah 5:1)

Highway billboards can be that large. When I lived in Los Angeles, I would often see small airplanes pulling long banners to advertise a product or promote a cause. Such aerial banners might be 15 to 30 feet tall and as long as 100 feet – or larger. So when I read of Zephaniah's flying scroll I can picture it. By

any standard, Zephaniah's banner was huge 15 by 30 feet (4.6 by 9 meters). The size of the banner is to indicate that its message is intended to be read by all God's people.

> "[3] And he said to me, 'This is the curse that is going out over the whole land; for according to what it says on one side, every thief will be banished, and according to what it says on the other, everyone who swears falsely will be banished. [4] The LORD

---

[97] The Hebrew text uses the phrase "sons of oil," or those full of oil. Anointing, of course, is accomplished by using olive oil. Olive oil also is also used in the lamps on the menorah.

Almighty declares, "I will send it out, and it will enter the house of the thief and the house of him who swears falsely by my name. It will remain in his house and destroy it, both its timbers and its stones."'" (Zechariah 5:3-4)

The message is a curse upon those who steal and those who lie under oath – thieves and perjurers. These are violations of the third, eighth, ninth, and tenth commandments of the Ten Commandments (Exodus 20). Here are the sins:

- **Stealing** is a double violation of both the eighth and tenth commandments. Stealing is taking something that belongs to someone else (Exodus 20:15). It comes from letting selfishness run rampant, from "coveting" what belongs to someone else (Exodus 20:17). This violates Jesus' second greatest commandment, to love one's neighbor as oneself (Mark 12:31). Paul even has to reinforce this command in the New Testament church (Ephesians 4:28; 1 Corinthians 6:10).

- **Swearing falsely**[98] **in Yahweh's name** is also a double violation. The ninth commandment is "You shall not give false testimony against your neighbor" (Exodus 20:16). This, of course, is lying, but in particular, lying in court with the intent of hurting another person. Perhaps even more serious, however, is breaking the second commandment: "You shall not misuse the name of the LORD your God, for the LORD will not hold anyone guiltless who misuses [99]his name" (Exodus 20:7). When we use our association with God or Christianity to deceive or perpetrate a wrong, we show utter disregard – not only for the people we are defrauding, but for God himself! This completely breaks Jesus' first command to love the Lord your God fully (Mark 12:30).

This vision of the flying banner focuses on the sins of stealing and lying under oath, but probably is intended to be understood as a curse[100] against all sin. A curse is a solemn

---

[98] "Swears falsely." In verse 3, most translations supply "false" from its use in verse 4. *Shāba ʿ* , "to swear, adjure," in the Niphal stem, means "to bind oneself by an oath" (TWOT #2319). "Falsely" is *sheqer*, "lie," from the verb *shāqar*, "to deal falsely, be false," used of words or activities which are false in the sense that they are groundless, without basis in fact or reality (Herman J. Austel, TWOT #2461a).

[99] To "misuse" (NIV), "make wrongful use of" (NRSV), "take ... in vain" (ESV, KJV) means to make a false statement followed by "so help me God."

[100] "Curse" in Zechariah 5:3 is *ʾālā,* "an oath, solemn statement, promise, curse" (for broken oath) (TWOT #94a). Hebrew uses a variety of words for "curse."

oath or promise against a person or people. A curse was considered to possess an inherent power of carrying itself into effect.[101]

God had promised a blessing for keeping the covenant commandments and a curse[102] for breaking them (Deuteronomy 11:26-29). Half a chapter of Deuteronomy is devoted to describing the curses that will rest upon those who break God's covenant by disobedience (Deuteronomy 29:15-68).

When God is for us, life is good. But when God himself turns his anger against us to bring us down, the results are devastating.

The penalty for sin that Zechariah pronounces is harsh – or so our world would judge it. The penalty is two-fold:

1. **Banishment.** The sinner is "banished" (NIV), "cut off" (NRSV, KJV), "cleaned out" (ESV).[103] The sinner is to be cut off from the community – banished, excommunicated.

2. **Destruction.** The sinner's own house is consumed, "both timber and stones." The curse is a kind of devouring thing, "destroy" (NIV), "consume" (NRSV, ESV, KJV). The word is often used of violent destruction, such as in war.[104] The curse continues until the man's house is completely gone. He has nothing to return to.

Terrible judgment is pronounced against sinners. We recoil from this. How can God be loving if he punishes sin so savagely? We can't be *that* bad! Our attitude comes from being immersed in a culture that both belittles sin and emasculates God. In both the Old and New Testaments, the punishment for sin is horrific. Jesus himself said:

"If your hand causes you to sin, cut it off.

It is better for you to enter life maimed

---

[101] T. Lewis and R.K. Harrison, "Curse," ISBE 1:83.

[102] "Curse" in Deuteronomy 11:26-29; 29:15-68 is *qelālâ*, "curse," from *qālal*, "be slight, trifling, of little account." The primary emphasis here is the absence (or reversal) of a blessed or rightful state and lowering to a lesser state (Leonard J. Coppes, TWOT #2028d).

[103] The word is the Niphal stem of *nāqâ*, a verb with the original sense of "pour out" and "be empty, clean." The word can be used with positive connotations, but here the use is obviously negative – a punishment. Probably the best sense here is "to be cut off" (Milton C. Fisher and Bruce K. Waltke, #1412). Baldwin says, "The verb means 'purged out' (RV), or 'exempted from obligation' imposed with the covenant, and so will be 'cut off' from the community" (*Haggai, Zechariah, Malachi*, p. 127). See also Holladay, *Hebrew Lexicon*, p. 245.

[104] This is the Piel stem of *kālâ*. The basic idea of this root is "to bring a process to completion." Here it is used negatively, "[Qal] used up, vanished, spent, [Piel] consumed" The idea of being consumed is most commonly applied to violent destruction, often by war (John N. Oswalt, TWOT #982).

than with two hands to go into hell,
where the fire never goes out." (Mark 9:43)

Jesus talked more about hell than any other person in the entire Bible. Sin is an offense against the holiness of God.

God is love. But he is also holy, righteous, and just. This is part of the Good News. And without it, the Good News of grace doesn't appear nearly as gracious.

While the punishment for sinners is terrible in its utter completeness, so the redemption of sinners is wonderful in contrast. Jesus' death on the cross on our behalf is the reason that God says in Vision 4 above:

"I will remove the sin of this land in a single day." (Zechariah 3:9)

Vision 7. The Woman in the Basket (Zechariah 5:5-11)

Vision 7 carries on a discussion of sin and its removal, and belongs closely to Vision 6.

"Then the angel who was speaking to me came forward and said to me, 'Look up and see what this is that is appearing.'" (Zechariah 5:5)

There has been a flying scroll or banner. Now there is a flying basket with a lead lid.

"[6] I asked, 'What is it?' He replied, 'It is a measuring basket.' And he added, 'This is the iniquity of the people throughout the land.' [7] Then the cover of lead was raised, and there in the basket sat a woman! [8] He said, 'This is wickedness,' and he pushed her back into the basket and pushed the lead cover down over its mouth." (Zechariah 5:6-8)

This measuring basket was the size of an ephah, about two-thirds the size of our bushel basket.[105] Sometimes you see large baskets of wicker or woven rushes that might have looked like this. But what makes it unique is what is inside.

A woman. If you take the size of the basket literally, this would be a small woman indeed. But we're dealing with symbols in a vision – concepts, not exact sizes. The women is identified by the angel as "wickedness." She tries to escape, but the angel pushes her back into the basket and covers it with a lid of lead. Near the end of the Bible,

---

[105] "Measuring basket" (NIV), "basket" (NRSV, ESV), "ephah" (KJV) is *'êpâ*, a dry measure, frequently mentioned in the OT, estimated to be equivalent to from three-eighths to two-thirds of a bushel. A "bath" was a liquid measure of the same size. An ephah would be the basket used to measure out this standard dry measure (Jack B. Scott, TWOT #82; E.M. Cook, "Weights and Measures," ISBE 4:10).

we see a another woman represent wickedness, "the great prostitute" (Revelation 17:1-6).

"Wickedness" is a concept far removed from Western culture in our day. Yes, we have "the wicked witch of the West" in "The Wizard of Oz," and "wicked" stepmothers in fairytales. But the word "wicked" is seldom used to describe people these days. Instead, we tend to use the word "evil" for really bad people – not ourselves, of course.

"Wickedness" is *rish 'â*, "guilt, wickedness,"[106] a comprehensive word, often used as the antithesis of righteousness, including civil, religious, and ethical evil.[107] In the Bible, the wicked are often contrasted with the righteous (Genesis 18:25; Proverbs 10:3; etc.). Psalm 1 describes the wicked as those who give evil counsel, take advantage of the poor, renounce the Lord, murder the innocent, curse, and lie.

Our problem comes with the realization that, "There is no one righteous, not even one" (Romans 3:10). We have all gone astray. We seek for our own interests. We are selfish. We rebel against God. We do what we know we shouldn't do. "And there is no health in us," as the prayer of confession in the *Book of Common Prayer* puts it.

Our pretended righteousness cannot save us.

> "All of us have become like one who is unclean,
> and all our righteous acts are like filthy rags." (Isaiah 64:6a)

In Zechariah's day, even the high priest is compromised, corrupted, and needs cleansing. You and I are wicked enough that Jesus had to die for us.

I've spent some time on this so that we can grasp the importance of God removing sin from us. In Zechariah's vision, the basket of wickedness is transported to Babylon, to a kind of shrine where people worship wicked gods (Zechariah 5:9-11). This brings to mind a wonderful verse about God's complete forgiveness.

> "He does not treat us as our sins deserve
> or repay us according to our iniquities.
> For as high as the heavens are above the earth,
> so great is his love for those who fear him;
> as far as the east is from the west,
> so far has he removed our transgressions from us." (Psalm 103:10-12)

---

[106] *Rish 'â*, TWOT #2222d.
[107] Baldwin, *Haggai, Zechariah, Malachi*, pp. 128-129.

This vision is intended to encourage the returned exiles that God had cleansed their sin. This gives them hope to complete the work on the temple. It also gives us courage to serve the God of Grace.

Vision 8. Four Chariots (Zechariah 6:1-8)

Now we consider the eighth night vision – of four chariots patrolling[108] the earth. These indicate the hosts or armies of heaven.

> "7 When the powerful horses went out, they were straining to go throughout the earth. And he said, 'Go throughout the earth!' So they went throughout the earth. 8 Then he called to me, 'Look, those going toward the north country have given my Spirit rest in the land of the north.'" (Zechariah 6:7-8)

The command to go patrol the earth is the same as in Vision 1 in Zechariah 1:10. It indicates God's sovereignty over the whole earth, with swift chariots ready to do his bidding.[109] In Revelation we see various colored horses that are the Four Horsemen of the Apocalypse (Revelation 6:1-8), executing God's judgment on earth.

The horsemen see the power of the nations, but God is sovereign. His chariots are stronger than any army. Remember the terror of Elisha's servant when he saw the mighty army of Aram surrounding the city of Dothan. God assurance is: "Those who are with us are more than those who are with them" (2 Kings 6:16-17). We need not be afraid of Satan and his minions, nor the nations of this world!

> "You, dear children, are from God and have overcome them, because the one who is in you is greater than the one who is in the world." (1 John 4:4)

The Coronation of Joshua (Zechariah 6:9-15)

The night visions conclude with a strange symbolic coronation of Joshua the high priest.

> "10 "Take [silver and gold] from the exiles Heldai, Tobijah and Jedaiah, who have arrived from Babylon. Go the same day to the house of Josiah son of Zephaniah. 11 Take the silver and gold and make a crown, and set it on the head of the high priest, Joshua son of Jehozadak." (Zechariah 6:10-11)

---

108 "Go throughout" (NIV), "go, patrol" (NRSV, ESV), "walk to and fro" (KJV) represent the verb *hālak*, "go, walk," a word denoting movement in general, usually of people (Leonard J. Coppes, TWOT #498). Here the word is doubled for emphasis, a Hebrew grammatical device known as an infinitive construct. Combined here, with the preposition *le*, it perhaps indicates obligation or permission (Gesenius, *Hebrew Grammar*, p. 350). Satan patrols the earth in Job 1:8.

109 Phillips, *Zechariah*, p. 135.

If I were Zechariah, I would be having a dispute with Yahweh about now. O God, kings wear crowns,[110] not priests! This just isn't proper. It goes against all custom and tradition.[111] But the command is clear. With the crowning comes an amazing word:

> "12 Tell him this is what the LORD Almighty says: 'Here is the man whose name is the Branch, and he will branch out from his place and build the temple of the LORD. 13 It is he who will build the temple of the LORD, and he will be clothed with majesty and will sit and rule on his throne. And he will be a priest on his throne. And there will be harmony between the two.'" (Zechariah 6:12-13)

"Branch" is *semah*, which we saw above in Zechariah 3:8, which refers to the family tree line of a legitimate royal son. The high priest is of the line of Moses and Aaron, not David's line. Nevertheless, the prophet is told to put this crown on the high priest's head, symbolically combining the roles of king and priest. This is fulfilled in Christ Jesus centuries later.

This symbolic crowning ceremony doesn't institute a permanent change in the government of the province, since we know that Nehemiah is appointed governor several decades later. Nor is Zerubbabel thrust aside; he is part of the rebuilding leadership (Zechariah 4:6-10; Haggai 1:1, 12, 14; 2:2, 4, 20-23). If you recall, the Lord declares Zerubbabel as his signet ring (Haggai 2:23). The crowning here seems to be primarily a prophetic symbolic act. Nevertheless, to remember the event, the crown is to be placed in the temple for preservation (Zechariah 6:14).

This whole section concludes with the promise that those from afar – perhaps Jews returning from exile as well as Gentiles – will come and help build the temple.

> "Those who are far away will come and help to build the temple of the LORD, and you will know that the LORD Almighty has sent me to you. This will happen if you diligently obey the LORD your God." (Zechariah 6:15)

---

[110] "Crown" (NIV, ESV, NRSV), "crowns" (KJV) is *'aṭārâ*, "crown, wreath." This is the general term for crown, should be distinguished from *nēzer*, the royal and priestly crown. The word in Hebrew is plural, perhaps to indicate the superlative, the ultimate crown (Carl Schultz, TWOT #1608a).

[111] High priests did wear a sort of crown, though different than a regal crown. It was a small golden plate fastened with blue cord to the front of the high priest's turban. Inscribed on the plate were the words: "Holy to the Lord" (Exodus 28:36-38; 39:30-31; Leviticus 8:9). This called by two words. The first is "plate" (NIV, ESV, KJV), "rosette"(NRSV), *ṣîs*, "flower," as an ornament on the forehead of the priest (Holladay, *Hebrew Lexicon*, p. 306). The second is *nēzer*, "consecration, ordination," then a kind of crown, "diadem, headband," of silver or gold with lacing-holes as a mark of being consecrated (Holladay, *Hebrew Lexicon*, p. 233). *Nēzer* is also used in Zechariah 9:16 to indicate a crown with jewels set in it.

The promise we saw in Zechariah 2:8-11 is repeated here, that people far away will help build the temple. One interpretation of this is that these are the Gentiles who come to the Lord in fulfillment of prophecy (Isaiah 56:6-8; 57:19; 60:10; Ephesians 2:13-22).

Finally, Zechariah calls for diligent obedience[112] – that is, repentance from their former neglect of the temple project, and continued work to bring the project to completion.

Lessons for Disciples

We've covered a lot of territory in the first six chapters of Zechariah. It's amazing how many lessons God has revealed to his people through the prophet. Rather than rehearse the prophetic images themselves, let's consider the discipleship lessons that we learn from these chapters.

1. The way to God begins with repentance – away from evil and toward God. Otherwise, the consequences of our sin will overtake us (Zechariah 1:3-6).
2. The rebuilding of Jerusalem and the temple – indeed all things – comes through God's choice and grace (Zechariah 1:7-17).
3. God is our protector. We can trust him to deal with our enemies (Zechariah 1:18-21).
4. God has chosen to live in the midst of his people – but has extended to all the invitation to be part his people. The modern expression of this is God living in the midst of his gathered people, the church (Zechariah 2:1-12).
5. Sometimes the only appropriate response to God is stillness and awe (Zechariah 2:13).
6. We are unworthy to stand before God and touch holy things. But he desires to cleanse us and clothe us with his righteousness. This is all by his grace, not because we deserve it (Zechariah 3:1-7).
7. In Zechariah's prophecy we see the Messiah represented by titles such as The Branch, and the Stone, and the One who removes sin from the land in a single day – the day he died for our sins on the cross (Zechariah 3:8-9).
8. God's work doesn't need man's power and might; rather it requires people of faith who will rely on the might and power of the Spirit (Zechariah 4:6-7a).

---

[112] "Diligently obey" is *shāma'*, "hear, listen to, obey" (TWOT #2212). However, here the word is repeated for emphasis, using a Hebrew construction known as the Infinitive Absolute.

9. We must not be discouraged by "the day of small things." Rather, we trust God to increase what he has begun (Zechariah 4:10a).

10. God chooses anointed men and women to build his Kingdom. Not perfect men and women, but those who will stand as channels of his anointing, his Spirit, and his power (Zechariah 4:1-14).

11. God expects us to keep His commandments. If people persist in disobedience, rather than turn in repentance, their destiny is terrible – banishment from the presence of God and destruction (Zechariah 5:1-4).

12. Temptation to wickedness is present; our only hope is God's cleansing and removing wickedness far from us (Zechariah 5:5-11).

13. God is sovereign over all the earth; nothing is hidden from him (Zechariah 6:1-8).

14. The crowning of Joshua the high priest symbolizes Jesus Christ, our Messiah, who holds in himself two roles: Priest and King.

Prayer

Father, thank you for your love that never gives up on us. Thank you for your gifts of repentance, cleansing, forgiveness, and restoration. Without you we fumble and bumble and are ultimately lost. But you stoop to dwell in our midst because you have chosen us. You love us. Thank you. In Jesus' name, we pray. Amen.

Key Verses

"'Return to me,' declares the LORD Almighty, 'and I will return to you,' says the LORD Almighty." (Zechariah 1:3, NIV)

"'I will return to Jerusalem with mercy, and there my house will be rebuilt. And the measuring line will be stretched out over Jerusalem,' declares the LORD Almighty." (Zechariah 1:16, NIV)

"'And I myself will be a wall of fire around it,' declares the LORD, 'and I will be its glory within.'" (Zechariah 2:5, NIV)

"… Whoever touches you touches the apple of his eye." (Zechariah 2:8b, NIV)

"The LORD said to Satan, 'The LORD rebuke you, Satan! The LORD, who has chosen Jerusalem, rebuke you! Is not this man a burning stick snatched from the fire?'" (Zechariah 3:2, NIV)

"This is the word of the LORD to Zerubbabel: 'Not by might nor by power, but by my Spirit,' says the LORD Almighty." (Zechariah 4:6, NIV)

"Who despises the day of small things? Men will rejoice when they see the plumb line in the hand of Zerubbabel." (Zechariah 4:10a)

4. Prophecies of the Messiah (Zechariah 7-14)

Though it seems to be somewhat obscure, the second half of Zechariah includes a number of messianic prophecies that you're familiar with in the New Testament. Zechariah turns our focus to justice, Yahweh's future deliverance.

As mentioned in Lesson 3, Zechariah's name means, "Yahweh remembers." He is a prophet who ministers about 520 to 515 BC, and perhaps beyond. He is also a contemporary of the Prophet Haggai, and is probably from a priestly family.

Chapters 1-6 of Zechariah, which we considered in Lesson 3, focus primarily on encouraging the returned exiles to complete the temple, and are dated about 520 AD. The prophecies we'll be looking at in this lesson have a broader focus of ethical justice, authentic worship, and the End Times. Of this group, the first prophecy is dated to 518 BC, but the rest are not.

As I have written about these prophecies, a rather long lesson has emerged. Please forgive me. But I'd rather not pass over these words without careful study.

Zechariah prophesies that the Jews will finally, "look on me, the one they have pierced, and they will mourn" (Zechariah 12:10). This painting of the crucifixion is by Matthias Grünewald, 'Die Kreuzigung Christi' (1523-1524), Tauberbischofsheimer Altar, 193 x 151 cm. Kunsthalle, Karlsruhe, Germany.

Prophecy 1. Justice and Mercy, Not Fasting (Zechariah 7)

This prophecy is dated December 7, 518 BC, nearly two years after Zechariah's earlier Night Vision prophecies.

"¹ In the fourth year of King Darius, the word of the LORD came to Zechariah on the fourth day of the ninth month, the month of Kislev. ² The people of Bethel had sent Sharezer and Regem-Melech, together with their men, to entreat the LORD ³ by asking the priests of the house of the LORD Almighty and the prophets, 'Should I mourn and fast[113] in the fifth month, as I have done for so many years?'" (Zechariah 7:1-2)

Most modern translations (NIV, NRSV, ESV) see the subject of verse 2 as "the people of Bethel."[114] Bethel, a town 12 miles north of Jerusalem, was once a center of pagan worship in the Northern Kingdom. Now it is one of the towns in which returned exiles have settled (Ezra 2:28). A delegation has come to seek God's favor[115] in Jerusalem and ask the priests there a technical question regarding ritual and worship.

Ever since Jerusalem had fallen in 587 BC, the Jewish exiles had remembered with fasting that tragic event that had taken place in the fifth month so many years before (2 Kings 25:8). The priests in Jerusalem would be the ones to make any changes in the ritual worship of the people. Their question is: Now that the temple is nearly finished, should we continue to fast and mourn? Or should this custom cease, since it is no longer relevant? Zechariah, a priest who is now recognized as a prophet of God, answers them – but doesn't really reply directly to their question until Zechariah 8:19 (where he declares that the fast should become joyful festivals).

Worship that Pleases Us – not God (Zechariah 7:4-7)

Instead of answering their question, he uses the occasion to ask them – and all the people – an important question that lays bare their motives in fasting.

> "⁴ Then the word of the LORD Almighty came to me: ⁵ 'Ask all the people of the land and the priests, "When you fasted and mourned in the fifth and seventh months for the past seventy years, was it really for me that you fasted? ⁶ And when you were eating and drinking, were you not just feasting for yourselves?"'" (Zechariah 7:4-6)

By these rhetorical questions, Yahweh indicts the people for self-serving worship, rather than worship that is really directed towards God.

---

[113] "Fast" (NIV), "practice abstinence" (NRSV), "abstain" (ESV), "separating myself" (KJV) is *nāzar*, "separate, consecrate (oneself)." The basic meaning of the verb is "to separate," hence the term Nazirite, "a consecrated person" (Thomas E. McComiskey, TWOT #1340). There is no object given in verse 3. It could have been separation from food or sexual relations. But from the context in verse 4 (the verb *ṣûm*, "to fast"), it seems to refer to fasting.

[114] The KJV translates the Hebrew word Bethel as a "house of God" rather than the place name of a town 12 miles north of Jerusalem, though this translation is unlikely. It is possible to see the subject as a person with the compound name "Bethel-Sharezer." Baldwin (*Haggai, Zechariah, Malachi*, pp. 142-143) thinks it likely that this is a delegation from the Jewish community in Babylon to inquire at Jerusalem. Whether or not this is the case, the general meaning and context of the passage remain the same.

[115] Entreat" (NIV), "entreat the favor of" (NIV), "to pray before" (KJV) is the Piel stem of *ḥālâ* with *penê* ("the face of") means to "entreat, seek the favor of" (Carl Philip Weber, TWOT #656).

- **Fast days turned to self-pity** as they remembered the terrible events of the fall of Jerusalem and subsequent exile. Repentance and humbling, true reasons to fast, had given way to whining.
- **Feast days had become an excuse to party**, rather than real celebration of Yahweh.

That's a pretty strong rebuke! Zechariah continues.

> "Are these not the words the LORD proclaimed through the earlier prophets when Jerusalem and its surrounding towns were at rest and prosperous, and the Negev and the western foothills were settled?" (Zechariah 7:4-7)

Zechariah is saying that this is not a new message. Previous prophets have said the same thing. Here are just a few of the many, many prophecies calling people to repentance in the way they worship.

> "You seek your own pleasure on your fastdays...." (Isaiah 58:3b)

> "These people come near to me with their mouth
> and honor me with their lips,
> but their hearts are far from me.
> Their worship of me is made up only of rules taught by men." (Isaiah 29:13)

Much less than our worship being empty and by rote, such self-serving worship actually annoys God.

> "Stop bringing meaningless offerings!
> Your incense is detestable to me.
> New Moons, Sabbaths and convocations –
> I cannot bear your evil assemblies." (Isaiah 1:13)

Rather than outward worship, God desires a repentant and humble heart that worships him in spirit and in truth (John 4:24).

How do we apply Zechariah's word to our situation? Dear friends, I think that Almighty God might rebuke our worship too. Too often...

- We neglect gathering to worship God so that we might be involved in recreation and sports – or sleep in. Yes, sometimes there are special circumstances, but often gathering to worship is an accurate gauge of our love for God.
- We seldom fast at all, though our hearts are often far from repentance.
- Worship at church is about *our* enjoyment – feeling good, receiving comfort, and being "fed" – rather than offering honor and fresh heart surrender to

God. In many congregations, our singing has become a rock concert (or classical exercise in choral music), rather than authentic heart worship.

Consider our family exercises on the great celebration days of the Christian church. Too often…

- Christmas has become all about presents and family, not about the Christ Child.
- Easter has turned to spring dresses and candy and family meals, rather than a celebration of Christ's resurrection.
- Pentecost (Whitsunday) is neglected by most traditions, and the coming of the Holy Spirit is poorly understood at best.

I don't mean to be some negative prophet of doom. But we need to apply what Yahweh is saying through the prophet Zechariah to ourselves and our own failings. "Repent, for the Kingdom of heaven is at hand!" (Matthew 4:17).

> **Q1. (Zechariah 7:4-6) In what ways have we Christians tended to make worship about us, rather than about God? How should we evaluate our churches and our worship patterns? What can we do to make our personal worship a matter of the heart, and not just rote readings and prayer?**
> http://www.joyfulheart.com/forums/topic/1733-q1-authentic-worship/

Ethical Righteousness (Zechariah 7:8-10)

Now God speaks another word, this time about ethical justice, a common theme of the prophets who had spoken God's word prior to the exile.

> "⁸ And the word of the LORD came again to Zechariah: ⁹ This is what the LORD Almighty says: 'Administer true justice; show mercy and compassion to one another. ¹⁰ Do not oppress the widow or the fatherless, the alien or the poor. In your hearts do not think evil of each other.'" (Zechariah 7:8-10)

Later in this lesson we'll consider an overlapping list of ethical commands in Zechariah 8:16-17.

Positive Attributes: Justice, Mercy, and Compassion (Zechariah 7:9)

Verse 9 deals with positive commands, while verse 10 deals with prohibitions, things not to do. I think we'll learn a lot be examining these commands one at a time.

"Administer true justice" (Zechariah 7:9a) is the first command. The verb *shāpaṭ* involves providing good, just government. The noun *mishpāṭ*, "justice," usually refers to litigation before a magistrate or judge who hears testimony and then renders a verdict or decision according to law.[116] But justice can be corrupted by the rich and powerful – both in Zechariah's day and ours. Justice can be corrupted when the judge is influenced either by obvious self-interest or by bribery. It is appropriate for a judge to recuse himself when his own self-interest might be construed to guide his decision. Bribery, of course, is a clear opponent to justice. The Pentateuch clearly forbids offers of money or advantage to influence a decision.

> "Do not accept a bribe,
> for a bribe blinds those who see
> and twists the words of the righteous." (Exodus 23:8)

Disclosure of one's business interests is therefore basic to those who desire the privilege of governing and dispensing justice in a just society. Our verse adds the word *'emet*, "truth, faithfulness, verity," to distinguish real justice from what passes for justice in many parts of our fallen world.

"Show mercy and compassion to one another" (Zechariah 7:9b) is the second command. Though it is difficult to achieve, we must combine justice with mercy. A society that relies on legal precision, but refuses to practice mercy and show compassion, is harsh and, by definition, unforgiving. James affirms: "Mercy triumphs over judgment" (James 2:13). Let's look at the words used here.

"Mercy" (NIV, KJV), "kindness" (NRSV, ESV) is *ḥesed*, often translated "steadfast love." *Hesed* is difficult to define precisely, since no one English word encompasses its full meaning. Essentially, *hesed* is unremitting love within a covenant relationship, even when one party fails or is unfaithful to the covenant. In his landmark study, Gordon Clark concludes:

> "*Hesed* is not merely an attitude or an emotion; it is an emotion that leads to an activity beneficial to the recipient. The relative status of the participants is never

---

[116] "Administer true justice" (NIV), "render true judgments" (NRSV, ESV), "execute true judgment" (KJV) is three words: the verb *shāpaṭ*, "judge, govern." The verb means basically to exercise the processes of government, not just judicial functions (Robert D. Culver, #TWOT 2443). So the NIV's "administer" is probably a pretty good translation of the idea. The noun is *mishpāṭ*, from the same stem. It means "justice." Though it can refer to any kind of religious or civil government, *mishpāṭ* most often refers to litigation before a civil magistrate who hears evidence and testimony and then renders a decision according to law (TWOT #2443c). The qualifying word is *'emet*, "truth, faithfulness, verity" (TWOT #116k).

a feature of the *hesed* act, which may be described as a beneficent action performed, in the context of a deep and enduring commitment between two persons or parties, by one who is able to render assistance to the needy party who in the circumstances is unable to help him or herself."[117]

When you consider *hesed*, you think of a word developed by Paul in the New Testament, grace, Greek *charis* – favor that is extended to a person unilaterally, not on the basis of how well one performs or behaves or reciprocates love.

Now we'll consider the word that Zechariah uses alongside *hesed*:

"Compassion" (NIV), "mercy" (NRSV, ESV), "compassions" (KJV) is *raḥamîm*, "tender mercy, compassion." It comes from the verb *rāḥam*, "deep love (usually of a 'superior' for an 'inferior') rooted in some 'natural' bond."[118]

These two words are often used together in the Old Testament. The story of Hosea and his unfaithful wife Gomer illustrates this kind of love and commitment to a fallen covenant partner that goes way beyond one's duty (Hosea 2:19).

"Love" and "compassion" are central to David's great Psalm of Confession (Psalm 51). They also appear in the great hymn, "Great Is Thy Faithfulness," based on Lamentations 21:23:

> "The steadfast love (*hesed*) of the LORD never ceases;
> his mercies (*raḥamîm*) never come to an end;
> they are new every morning;
> great is your faithfulness. (Lamentations 3:22-23, ESV)

Justness, steadfast love, and compassion are attributes of God's character. That is why the prophet Zechariah calls on us humans to emulate them.

Negative Commands: Don't Oppress the Powerless (Zechariah 7:10a)

The positive attributes to emulate are followed by negative actions for us to avoid.

> "Do not oppress the widow, the fatherless,
> the sojourner, or the poor,
> and let none of you devise evil against another in your heart." (Zechariah 7:10, ESV)

---

[117] Gordon R. Clark, *The Word* Hesed *in the Hebrew Bible* (Sheffield: Sheffield Academic Press, 1993), p. 267. See also Robin Routledge, "*Hesed* as Obligation: A Re-Examination," *Tyndale Bulletin*, Vol. 46, No. 1 (1995), pp. 179-196. See also R. Laird Harris, *hesed*, TWOT #698).

[118] Coppes notes that this word shows the link between *rāḥam*, 'to have compassion' (Piel) and *reḥem/raḥam*, 'womb,' for "*raḥămîm* can refer to the seat of one's emotions or the expression of one's deep emotion" (Leonard J. Coppes, TWOT #2146b).

Oppression in Biblical terms involves abuse of power and authority to take advantage of the powerless.[119] On a national scale, for example, Israel is oppressed in Egypt when their overlords make slaves of them (1 Samuel 12:8; etc.). The Babylonians oppress the Israelites in exile (Isaiah 14:4; Jeremiah 50:16). By definition, enslaving someone who has not wronged you is oppression. It's one thing for a person to work off his debt; it is entirely another to keep an individual, his family, and descendants in slavery in perpetuity.

But oppression can be more individual. It is common in Zechariah's time – and common in our own time – for the rich and powerful to oppress the weak and disadvantaged. Our passage lists four such groups.

Widows often have no male to protect them in a patriarchal society. Since few women are educated, widows are often tricked in court and deprived of whatever land or goods their family might possess. They are seen as easy prey for the unscrupulous (Job 22:8-9; 24:2-3, 21; Isaiah 10:1-2; Mark 12:40). Jesus tells a parable about a crooked judge who is hounded by a persistent widow until he gives her justice (Luke 18:1-5).

Fatherless children and orphans have no one to protect their interests. If they've inherited anything from their parents, it is at risk of being taken by fraud or theft, with little ability to find relief in the courts.

The poor also have no voice. They can't afford to go to court; they don't have a good enough education to defend themselves. Against the powerful, they are easy pickings.

The sojourner is the fourth group, one which we need to consider carefully. "Alien" (NIV, NRSV), "sojourner" (ESV), "stranger" (KJV) is *gêyr*, "alien, sojourner, stranger," from the verb *gûr*, "abide, be a stranger, sojourn." The root means to live among people who are not blood relatives.[120] In our day, with aliens flooding Europe from wars in Africa and the Mideast, residents feel overwhelmed and that their social services and traditional ways of life are threatened. This is also true in parts of America, especially in states adjoining Mexico. America is a country made up almost exclusively of sojourners, who moved to the New World, and then began oppressing Native Americans and slaves brought from Africa. There's plenty of blame to go around.

---

[119] "Oppress" is *āshaq*, "oppress, get deceitfully, defraud, do violence." (Ronald B. Allen, TWOT #1713). The verbal root *āshaq* is concerned with acts of abuse of power or authority, the burdening, trampling, and crushing of those lower in station.

[120] Harold G. Stigers, *gêyr*, TWOT #330a.

In our modern society we make a distinction between legal and illegal aliens. But in Bible days there were no such distinctions. No one had papers that were checked at the border. People moved around due to drought, famine, persecution, war, and forced exile to quell rebellion. Examples of aliens or sojourners in the Bible include most of the famous characters, including: Abraham, Isaac, and Jacob; Joseph; the Israelites in Egypt and the Wilderness; Ruth and Naomi; David; Ezra and Nehemiah; Jesus and his parents; Paul; Aquila and Priscilla; and many more.

The Old Testament law gives legal rights to aliens who live with Israel.

> "The alien had a legal right (along with the fatherless and the widow) to glean what was left after the harvesters had completed a field, vineyard, or orchard." (Deuteronomy 24:20-21)

Moreover, the Israelites are commanded not to mistreat[121] aliens, because they (as former aliens) remember how it feels to be aliens (Exodus 23:9; Deuteronomy 24:14; Ezekiel 22:29).

God himself defends aliens.

> "[Yahweh] defends the cause of the fatherless and the widow,
> and **loves the alien**,
> giving him food and clothing." (Deuteronomy 10:18)

God's backing of the poor and downtrodden has two consequences. First, he who oppresses them, opposes God himself (Proverbs 14:31). Second, since God loves the alien, we are commanded to follow his example:

> "When an alien lives with you in your land, do not mistreat him.
> The alien living with you must be treated as one of your native-born.
> **Love him as yourself**, for you were aliens in Egypt.
> I am the LORD your God." (Leviticus 19:33-34)

I say all this because Scripture clearly teaches it. This doesn't mean that countries should not control their borders. But clearly, we must not oppress, or take advantage of aliens in our midst – whether legal or illegal. Rather we must love them and assist them.

God commands us not to oppress the weak. He also commands us to watch our hearts, lest we try to devise ways to take advantage of anyone – whether helpless or not.

> "Let none of you devise[122] evil against another in your heart." (Zechariah 7:10, ESV)

---

[121] "Mistreat" (NIV), "oppress" (NRSV), "do wrong" (ESV), "vex" (KJV) is the Hiphil stem of *yānâ*, "oppress" (Holladay, *Hebrew Lexicon*, p. 136), "maltreat" (BDB, p. 413).

The Fruit of Rebellious Hearts (Zechariah 7:11-14)

God is saying through the prophet Zechariah to turn from evil. Their parents were sent into exile because of their rebellious hearts. Their descendants are only in "the pleasant land"[123] because of God's grace.

> [11] 'But they refused to pay attention; stubbornly they turned their backs and stopped up their ears. [12] They made their hearts as hard as flint and would not listen to the law or to the words that the LORD Almighty had sent by his Spirit through the earlier prophets. So the LORD Almighty was very angry.
>
> [13] 'When I called, they did not listen; so when they called, I would not listen,' says the LORD Almighty. [14] 'I scattered them with a whirlwind among all the nations, where they were strangers. The land was left so desolate behind them that no one could come or go. This is how they made the pleasant land desolate.'" (Zechariah 7:8-14)

Prophecy 2. The Lord Promises to Bless Jerusalem (Zechariah 8-11)

Chapters 8-11 primarily consist of memorable sayings, declarations of blessing over Jerusalem.

1. Yahweh is jealous for Zion (verse 2, see 1:14). Yahweh isn't passive about Jerusalem. Rather he has strong emotions toward it – his residence on earth.[124] Zion is used as a synonym for Jerusalem.
2. Yahweh will dwell in Jerusalem. It will have two titles: (1) "City of Truth" (NIV, KJV) or "faithful city" (NRSV, ESV), and (2) "the Holy Mountain (verse 3; cf. Isaiah 1:26).

---

[122] "Think evil of" (NIV), "devise evil against" (NRSV, ESV), "imagine evil against" (KJV) is two words: *ra'*, "evil, distress," and the Qal stem of *hāshab*, "think, plan, make a judgment, imagine, count." The basic idea of the word is the employment of the mind in thinking activity. The most frequent idea is one of "planning, devising" (Leonard J. Wood, TWOT #767). The NIV's translation, "think evil of" is based on taking *hāshab* to mean "make a judgment." While this is possible, I think it is unlikely, since the context of Zephaniah 7:10 seems to be condemning unjust actions, not heart attitudes, which are covered in verse 9. Also the NIV translates *hāshab* in a parallel passage as "plot evil" (Zechariah 8:17).

[123] The "pleasant land" uses the adjective *hemdâ*, "pleasant, precious," from *hāmad*, "desire, delight in." (TWOT #673). This has a similar idea to Beulah Land (Isaiah 62:4), from *beulah*, "married."

[124] "Jealous" is the Piel stem of *qānā'*, "be jealous, envious, zealous." This verb expresses a very strong emotion whereby some quality or possession of the object is desired by the subject. Coppes notes, "It may prove helpful to think of 'zeal' as the original sense from which derived the notions zeal for another's 'property'='envy' and zeal for one's own 'property'='jealousy'" (Leonard J. Coppes, TWOT 2038).

3. Jerusalem will have both old men and women and boys and girls (verses 4-5). This is a big contrast to the narrow age range of most of the returnees who undertook the arduous journey from Babylon back to Jerusalem. Children have a future in Jerusalem.
4. Jerusalem will seem marvelous[125] to the returned exiles, yet to God it is a small thing compared to his unlimited power. Nothing is impossible with God (verse 6).
5. God will save his people from the countries where they are scattered and bring them back to Jerusalem. They will again be God's people, and God will be to them "faithful and righteous" (verses 7-8).

Now we move from short sayings to a longer passage.

"This is what the LORD Almighty says: 'You who now hear these words spoken by the prophets who were there when the foundation was laid for the house of the LORD Almighty, let your hands be strong so that the temple may be built.'" (Zechariah 8:9)

Zechariah is probably referring to the prophecy of Haggai in 520 AD, who had contrasted the hardships they were experiencing before commencing work on the temple (Haggai 1:6-11), to Yahweh's promise of material blessings that would date from the time they restart building the temple (Haggai 2:15-19).

Zechariah reminds them of their former plight:

- No wages (verse 10a).
- No security (verse 10b).
- The Jews as an object of cursing (verse 13)
- God brought disaster without pity (verse 14)

But now they will experience blessing as their inheritance:

- Productive seeds (verse 12a).
- Productive vines (verse 12b).
- Productive ground (verse 12c).
- Plentiful dew and rain (verse 12d)
- Salvation and blessing (verse 13a)

---

[125] "Marvelous" (NIV, ESV, KJV), "impossible" (NRSV) is the Niphal stem of *pālā'*, "be marvelous, wonderful" (TWOT #1768).

- God determines to do good to Jerusalem (verse 15)

Twice he tells them not to be afraid (verses 13a, 15) and to let their hands be strong (verses 9, 13b), that is, to be willing to work to complete the temple.

Ethical Commands (Zechariah 8:16-17)

As we saw a call to righteousness in Zechariah 7:9-10, so it is repeated here.

"16 'These are the things you are to do: Speak the truth to each other, and render true and sound judgment in your courts; 17 do not plot evil against your neighbor, and do not love to swear falsely. I hate all this,' declares the LORD." (Zechariah 8:16-17)

Some of these we saw in the first ethical passage. Others are new.

Zechariah 7:9-10	Zechariah 8:16-17
	Speak the truth to each other (8:16a).
Administer true justice (7:9a).	Render true and sound judgment in your courts (8:16b).
Show mercy and compassion to one another (7:9b).	
Do not oppress the widow or the fatherless, the alien or the poor (7:10a).	
Let none of you devise evil against another in your heart (7:10b, ESV).	Do not plot evil against your neighbor (8:17a).
	Do not love to swear falsely (8:17b).

The commands *not* included in the list of Zechariah 7:9-10 relate to being truthful.

"Speak truth to each other" (verse 16a).

"Do not love to swear falsely" (verse 17b).

"Love truth and peace" (verse 19b).

Swearing falsely (Zechariah 8:17b) relates to court testimony. Zechariah spoke strongly against it in the prophecy of the flying scroll in Zechariah 5:4. It is prohibited by the Third and Ninth Commandments (Exodus 20:7, 16). Yahweh, through his prophet Zechariah, is determined that the courts be a place of justice.

However, the command to "**speak the truth to each other**" (Zechariah 8:16a) refers to everyday communication between the people of Israel. Though it's not part of the Ten

Commandments, truthful speech is commanded in both the Old and New Testaments (Psalm 15:1-2; Proverbs 12:22; and often).

"Do not lie. Do not deceive one another." (Leviticus 19:11)

"Simply let your 'Yes' be 'Yes,' and your 'No,' 'No';
anything beyond this comes from the evil one." (Matthew 5:37)

"Therefore each of you must put off falsehood
and speak truthfully to his neighbor,
for we are all members of one body." (Ephesians 4:25)

"Do not lie to each other,
since you have taken off your old self with its practices." (Colossians 3:9)

Why are we to tell the truth? Because our God is a God of truth. Notice the command is to speak truthfully to "one another" or to our "neighbor." There is no requirement to speak the truth to an enemy.

> **Q2. (Zechariah 7:9-10; 8:16-17) What does it look like to operate from a policy of mercy and compassion? God commands justice for the poor and oppressed in our culture. How can we be sure that the poor are treated justly in our courts? How do you treat aliens in your country, sojourners from another land? Why is speaking truthfully with others so important to God?**
> **http://www.joyfulheart.com/forums/topic/1734-q2-mercy-and-compassion/**

Happy Feasts (Zechariah 8:18-19)

Now the prophet picks up the question that began chapter 7:

"Should I mourn and fast in the fifth month, as I have done for so many years?" (Zechariah 7:3)

The people have been in mourning since the fall of Jerusalem. The prophet declares the answer to this question:

"The fasts of the fourth, fifth, seventh and tenth months[126] will become joyful and glad occasions and happy festivals for Judah. Therefore love truth and peace." (Zechariah 8:19)

---

[126] Baldwin (*Haggai, Zechariah, Malachi*, p. 143) notes that the fourth month commemorated the breach of the city wall (Jeremiah 39:2); The fifth, the destruction of the temple (2 Kings 25:8). The seventh month

The Gentiles Come to Jerusalem (Zechariah 8:20-23)

This prophecy concludes with a future vision of the Gentiles flowing to Jerusalem to seek the Lord in the day of the Messiah.

> "[20b] Many peoples and the inhabitants of many cities will yet come, [21] and the inhabitants of one city will go to another and say, 'Let us go at once to entreat the LORD and seek the LORD Almighty. I myself am going.' [22] And many peoples and powerful nations will come to Jerusalem to seek the LORD Almighty and to entreat him…. [23b] In those days ten men from all languages and nations will take firm hold of one Jew by the hem of his robe and say, 'Let us go with you, because we have heard that God is with you.'" (Zechariah 8:21-23)

In the future, the Jew who has been a byword among the nations is now sought out, as Yahweh's name begins to draw people from all nations. The gathering of the Gentiles to Jerusalem is a theme of Zechariah's (Zechariah 2:11; 14:16-17). It is also a theme found throughout the Old and New Testaments, which both promise that the gospel will go to the Gentiles.[127] Here is a sampling:

> "It shall come to pass in the latter days
>   that the mountain of the house of the LORD shall be established
>   as the highest of the mountains,
>   and it shall be lifted up above the hills;
>   and peoples shall flow to it,
>   and many nations shall come, and say:
> 'Come, let us go up to the mountain of the LORD,
>   to the house of the God of Jacob,
>   that he may teach us his ways
>   and that we may walk in his paths.'
> For out of Zion shall go forth the law,
>   and the word of the LORD from Jerusalem." (Micah 4:1-2)

God loves his chosen people, the Jews. Paul foresees that at the end – after "the fullness of the Gentiles has come in" (the event of which Zechariah is speaking), that all Israel will be saved (Romans 11:25).

---

commemorated the death of Gedaliah (2 Kings 25:25); the tenth, the beginning of Nebuchadnezzar's siege of Jerusalem (2 Kings 25:1-2).

[127] Psalm 22:27; 72:17; 117:1-2; 138:4-5; Isaiah 2:2-3; 11:10; 49:6, 22-23; 66:18-20; Isaiah 60; Malachi 1:11; Matthew 8:41; Revelation 11:15.

Judgment on Israel's Enemies (Zechariah 9:1-8)

Judah has been tormented by the hostile provinces surrounding it. Now Yahweh assures them that God will deal with those who have been discouraging them from building the temple.

Now a textual note. Verse 1b is difficult, it could be translated as "for the LORD has an eye on mankind and on all the tribes of Israel" (ESV), which would accord with Yahweh "keeping watch" in verse 8. Or it could be "for the eyes of men and all the tribes of Israel are on the LORD" (NIV, cf. KJV).[128]

In some cases, the prophecies against these enemies are quite specific, though we don't know enough of the history from this period to track the fulfillments.[129] Some of the punishments may refer to conquests under Alexander the Great and the Greek Empire, or later by the Romans.

The final part of this prophecy is intriguing.

> "I will take the blood from their mouths, the forbidden food from between their teeth. Those who are left will belong to our God and become leaders in Judah, and Ekron will be like the Jebusites." (Zechariah 9:7)

Zechariah prophesies that some who are enemies will be converted to Judaism, even become leaders. The "blood" and "forbidden food" refer to non-Kosher food eaten by pagans. The Jebusites under David's rule co-existed with the Israelites and were absorbed into Judah; so it will be with the residents of Ekron.

---

[128] Literally, verse 1a reads "the oracle of the word of the LORD" (NIV), or "the burden of the word of the LORD" (KJV). The word is *maśśā'*, "burden, oracle," from *nāśā'*, "to lift, carry, take." The phrase occurs often in prophecies. P.A.H. de Boer (*An Inquiry into the Meaning of the Term* Maśśā', Brill: Leiden, 1948) found that *maśśā'* is a burden, "imposed by a master, a despot, or a deity on subjects, beasts, men, or things." So *maśśā'* is a technical term, "a burden imposed on…." introducing the theme of a prophecy. If translated "oracle," it still contains the ideas of compulsion, urgency, dread (Baldwin, *Haggai, Zechariah, Malachi*, pp. 162-163).

[129] Hadrach, was a city-state in northern Syria, probably Hatarikka, present day Tell Afis, about 28 miles southwest of Aleppo (William Sanford LaSor, "Hadrach," ISBE 2:592). Damascus, was a leading city-state that often dominated cities around it. It remains as the capital of modern Syria. Hamath, was a royal city-state of the Hittites, present-day Hama, on the main road from Damascus to Aleppo. Tyre and Sidon are ancient Phoenician cities on the coast north of Israel in present-day Lebanon. Tyre (modern Ṣur) was heavily fortified and rich from extensive trade. Ashkelon, Gaza, and Ekron are three of the five ancient Philistine city-states that were Israel's ancient enemy.. Ashkelon and Gaza are port cities the coastal plain of the eastern Mediterranean, and are important today – Ashkelon within the State of Israel, Gaza controlled by the Palestinians. Incidentally, "Palestine" comes from the root of the word "Philistine." Only the ruins of Ekron are visible today as Tel Miqne (Hebrew) or Khirbet el-Muqanna (Arabic), on the eastern side of the coastal plain within the State of Israel.

Zechariah looks forward to the universal reign of the Messiah, as we'll see in the following passage. In that day, Judah will be free from enemies, for Yahweh is watching over his "house," the temple.

> "But I will defend my house against marauding forces.[130]
> Never again will an oppressor overrun my people,
> for now I am keeping watch." (Zechariah 9:8)

The Coming of Zion's King (Zechariah 9:9-10)

Now we come to a familiar passage, quoted in Matthew 21:5 and John 12:15 as fulfilled in Jesus' triumphal entry into Jerusalem on Palm Sunday at the beginning of Holy Week.

> "Rejoice greatly, O Daughter of Zion!
> Shout, Daughter of Jerusalem!
> See, your king comes to you,
> righteous and having salvation,
> gentle and riding on a donkey,
> on a colt, the foal of a donkey." (Zechariah 9:9)

The donkey was domesticated in Mesopotamia by the Third Millennium BC and was used as a beast of burden from the patriarchal period. It was renowned for its strength and was the animal normally ridden by nonmilitary personnel (Numbers 22:21; Judges 10:4; 1 Samuel 25:20).[131]

Scripture indicates that riding a donkey is not at all beneath the dignity of Israel's noblemen and kings (2 Samuel 18:9; 19:26). Indeed, David indicates his choice of Solomon to be king by decreeing that the young man should ride on the king's own mule (1 Kings 1:32-40).

James J. Tissot, 'Procession in the Streets of Jerusalem' (1898-1902), gouache on board, Brooklyn Museum, New York.

Jesus' instructions are clear that the donkey must be one that has never been ridden.[132] It is set apart, consecrat-

---

[130] The phrase is literally, "I will encamp at my house as a guard" (NRSV, ESV), better than "I will encamp about mine house because of the army" (KJV).

[131] R.K. Harrison, "Ass," ISBE 1:330.

[132] See Numbers 19:2; Deuteronomy 21:3; 1 Samuel 6:7; 2 Samuel 6:3.

ed for a specific use – for the Master's use. There is a rabbinical tradition that no one should use the animal on which a king rides.[133]

It is fascinating to me that in Zechariah's prophecy the gentle king that comes into Jerusalem riding a young donkey is the same one who will defeat chariots and war-horses and bring peace to the nations (Zechariah 9:10). One of the final scenes of Revelation is a picture of the conquering Christ riding a white war-horse (Revelation 19:11-16), but in this instance he rides a donkey in hope of peace.

When Jesus indicates to his disciples that he should ride on a donkey that no one had ever ridden before, he is initiating a public, kingly act. He is revealing openly that he is the Messiah spoken of by the prophets.

This Messianic King will bring peace.

> "I will take away the chariots from Ephraim
> and the war-horses from Jerusalem,
> and the battle bow will be broken.
> He will proclaim peace to the nations.
> His rule will extend from sea to sea
> and from the River to the ends of the earth." (Zechariah 9:10)

The mention of Ephraim (the largest of the tribes of the Northern Kingdom) indicates that the Messiah will reunite the divided kingdoms and restore the ten tribes from exile. All kinds of military weapons will be banished by this King who brings peace, not only to Israel, but to the whole earth!

Jubilation and Prosperity for God's Flock (Zechariah 9:11-17)

These words are given to encourage the returned exiles, who have come back to build their temple within Jerusalem with broken-down walls.

> "11 As for you, because of the blood of my covenant with you, I will free your pris-
> oners from the waterless pit. 12 Return to your fortress, O prisoners of hope; even
> now I announce that I will restore twice as much to you." (Zechariah 9:11-12)

God reminds the people of the blood covenant he has made with them (Genesis 15:9-11; Exodus 24:5-8), which guarantees that he will fight on their behalf when they are

---

[133] Joel B. Green (*The Gospel of Luke* (The New International Commentary on the New Testament; Eerdmans, 1997), p. 685, fn. 9) mentions Catchpole, "Triumphal Entry," in *Jesus and the Politics of His Day*, edited by Ernst Bammel and C.F.D. Moule (Cambridge University, 1984), p. 324, who cites *Sanh* 2.5.

attacked, as a Suzerain for his vassal. They are to return to their fortress[134] city, Jerusalem. God promises to restore to them double for what they have suffered, as Isaiah promised (Isaiah 40:2; 61:7).

The next passage describes the final war. "Greece" in verse 13 is *yāwān*, "Ionia, Greece,"[135] but also could refer to distant unknown peoples on the edge of civilization.[136] We're not sure if this prophecy refers to the Greek kings that followed Alexander the Great, or a future eschatological reference. The passage concludes with indications of the prosperity God will bring to his people. Notice that God is the Shepherd, who saves and takes delight in his sheep, who circle the hills like jewels on a crown.[137]

> "[16] The LORD their God will save them on that day
> as the flock of his people.
> They will sparkle in his land like jewels in a crown.
> [17] How attractive and beautiful they will be!
> Grain will make the young men thrive,
> and new wine the young women." (Zechariah 9:16-17)

The Lord Will Care for Judah (Zechariah 10-11)

The prophecy in chapter 10 derides the people's lack of godly leadership. Yahweh declares that he will be a shepherd to Judah.

> "[2b] Therefore the people wander like sheep
> oppressed for lack of a shepherd.
> [3] My anger burns against the shepherds,
> and I will punish the leaders;
> for the LORD Almighty will care for his flock,
> the house of Judah,
> and make them like a proud horse in battle." (Zechariah 10:2-3)

Zechariah affirms that the leader will come from the tribe of Judah.

> "From Judah will come the cornerstone,
> from him the tent peg,

---

[134] "Fortress" (NIV), "stronghold" (NRSV, ESV, KJV) is *biṣṣārôn*, "stronghold, fortified (or fenced) city" (John N. Oswalt, TWOT #270c).

[135] *Yāwān*, TWOT #855.

[136] Baldwin, *Haggai, Zechariah, Malachi*, p. 169.

[137] Baldwin, *Haggai, Zechariah, Malachi*, p. 170.

> from him the battle bow,
> from him every ruler." (Zechariah 10:4)

This is fulfilled in Jesus the Messiah, born in Bethlehem, the city of David, of the tribe of Judah, also prophesied in Micah 5:2.

> "See, the Lion of the tribe of Judah,
> the Root of David, has triumphed." (Revelation 5:5b)

When the Messiah returns, God will save the exiles from the Northern Kingdom, "the house of Joseph" (verse 6), the Ephraimites (verse 7), will gather them from exile (verses 9-10), and become their leader (verse 12). Zechariah 11:1-3 laments the ruin of Lebanon and Bashan, to the north of Judah.

Prophecy 3. The Two Shepherds (Zechariah 11:4-17)

This passage is confusing, to say the least. And it contains a verse that Baldwin calls "probably the most enigmatic in the whole Old Testament."[138] There are many, many interpretations, so I don't expect that we'll be able to decipher the whole prophecy. However, some things can be interpreted with some degree of certainty. Clearly the prophecy is about leadership and the consequences of bad leadership over God's people. Let's see what we can learn.

In the Bible, "shepherd" is used for:

1. A person who literally cares for animals, specifically sheep or goats.
2. Then, by extension, for a king, high priest, or leader – one who rules over a group of people. You see this metaphor used throughout the Ancient Near East for kings and leaders. In this sense, Shepherd is used of God, "The Lord is my shepherd...." (Psalm 23).

In verse 4a, the Lord tells Zechariah to act as shepherd over[139] "the flock marked for slaughter." It's quite possible Zechariah did not literally fulfill this, but rather that this shepherd role of his is some kind of prophetic symbol to make a point about the fate of rebellious Israel.

Now let's look at a few verses and make identifications.

> "4b 'Pasture the flock marked for slaughter. 5 Their buyers slaughter them and go unpunished. Those who sell them say, "Praise the LORD, I am rich!" Their own shepherds do not spare them. 6 For I will no longer have pity on the people of the

---

[138] Baldwin, *Haggai, Zechariah, Malachi*, p. 181.
[139] *Rā'â*, "pasture, tend, graze" (TWOT #2185).

land,' declares the LORD. 'I will hand everyone over to his neighbor and his king. They will oppress the land, and I will not rescue them from their hands.'" (Zechariah 11:4b-6)

- "The flock marked for slaughter" seems to be Israel, God's people. Some sheep are raised for their wool, shorn year after year. Others are raised for meat. The prophecy is saying that God's people are destined to be killed.
- "Their buyers" refer to their oppressors – the Assyrians, the Babylonians, the Persians (in Zechariah's time), and later, perhaps, the Greeks and the Romans.
- "Those who sell them" are their own leaders, "who ingratiated themselves with the authorities to their own material advantage,"[140] not caring for the welfare people in their charge. They are also referred to as "their own shepherds" (11:5b) and perhaps in verse 11 as "the sheep merchants" (NRSV), "sheep traders" (ESV).

The Detested Shepherd (Zechariah 11:7-9)

Zechariah takes on the task of leading this flock, with special care for those who are hurting – "the oppressed of the flock."

"7 So I pastured the flock marked for slaughter, particularly the oppressed of the flock. Then I took two staffs and called one Favor and the other Union, and I pastured the flock. 8 In one month I got rid of the three shepherds. The flock detested me, and I grew weary of them 9 and said, 'I will not be your shepherd. Let the dying die, and the perishing perish. Let those who are left eat one another's flesh.'" (Zechariah 11:7-9)

Zechariah, in this allegory, does his best. He gets rid of three shepherds or leaders who have been exploiting the sheep.[141] But the people don't appreciate what he is doing for them. "The flock detested me" (verse 8b). Finally, Zechariah tires of caring for people who have no appreciation for his work on their behalf, and leaves them to their fate.

People often don't appreciate their leaders, even the best leaders. Jesus, the Good Shepherd, "came to that which was his own, but his own did not receive him" (John 1:11). Jesus looks at the city of Jerusalem through his tears, and says:

---

[140] Baldwin, *Haggai, Zechariah, Malachi*, p. 180.

[141] Verse 8a is difficult to understand: "In one month I got rid of the three shepherds." There have been many attempts to identify the three shepherds historically, as kings, or high priests, or heads of successive empires. But there is absolutely no unanimity at all about an interpretation. It's best to understand it generally. For various views consult the commentaries.

"O Jerusalem, Jerusalem, you who kill the prophets and stone those sent to you, how often I have longed to gather your children together, as a hen gathers her chicks under her wings, but you were not willing. Look, your house is left to you desolate." (Matthew 23:37-38)

Jesus tells the Parable of the Tenants (Matthew 21:33-44), in which an owner builds a vineyard, but the tenants rebel, won't pay the rent, and finally kill the owner's son who comes to collect what is due. Of course, the rebellious tenants are the Jewish leaders who kill God's Son – and they finally get their due. They had a chance, but they rejected the Shepherd who could save them.

We know that Zechariah himself was detested, "murdered between the temple and the altar" (Matthew 23:35).

Breaking the Staff Called Favor and 30 Pieces of Silver (Zechariah 11:10-14)

Zechariah, the stand-in shepherd, has been given two shepherd's staffs. He breaks these staffs in symbolic acts.

"[10] Then I took my staff called Favor and broke it, revoking the covenant I had made with all the nations. [11] It was revoked on that day, and so the afflicted of the flock[142] who were watching me knew it was the word of the LORD." (Zechariah 11:10-11)

The first staff is named "Favor" (NIV, ESV, NRSV, NASB), "Goodwill" (NJB), "Beauty" (KJV). The Hebrew noun is nō'am, "pleasantness, beauty, kindness, favor," from the verb nā'ēm, "be pleasant, sweet, delightful, beautiful."[143] God's covenant protects Israel, as a suzerain has an obligation to protect vassal states that are attacked. But when God's gracious covenant is revoked because of his people's rebellion, their protection is lifted, and they are subject to the full onslaught of their enemies.

Zechariah is quitting his role as shepherd – as the Jewish leaders desire – but he brings up the matter of compensation for his service:

"[12] I told them, 'If you think it best, give me my pay; but if not, keep it.' So they paid me thirty pieces of silver.'

[13] And the LORD said to me, 'Throw it to the potter' – the handsome price at which they priced me! So I took the thirty pieces of silver and threw them into the house of the LORD to the potter." (Zechariah 11:12-13)

---

[142] The translation "afflicted of the flock" (NIV), "poor of the flock" (KJV) follows the Hebrew text. The translation "sheep traders" (ESV, cf. NRSV) follows the Greek Septuagint translation (Baldwin, *Haggai, Zechariah, Malachi*, p. 184).

[143] Nō'am, TWOT #1384a.

The Jewish leaders paid Zechariah 30 pieces of silver, the value of a slave (Exodus 21:32) – and the amount paid Judas to betray Jesus (Matthew 26:15). It shows how little they valued one who had been their leader! Zechariah rejects their insulting pay and throws it into the temple to the potter. "Potter" (NIV, ESV, KJV) translates the Hebrew text, while "treasury" (NRSV) translates the Syriac translation. The words have a similar sound in Hebrew – *yāṣar*, "potter" vs. *'ôṣār*, "treasury." There are various speculations about the relationship of potters and a treasury to the temple,[144] which are obscure to us today.

It is clear, however, that our Zechariah passage is referred to regarding the 30 pieces of silver paid to Judas for betraying Jesus (Matthew 26:15). Later, realizing what he has done, Judas throws the money into the temple (Matthew 27:5), and the money is used by the priests to purchase a potter's field in which to bury foreigners (Matthew 27:7). Matthew's reference is attributed to Jeremiah, a better known prophet, who he is also referencing (Jeremiah 18:2-3; 19:1-13; 32:6-15).[145] Lenzki notes,

> "In Zechariah the payment of thirty pieces of silver was made in order to get rid of Israel's shepherd. That same price was paid to get rid of Jesus who is Israel's Shepherd."[146]

Breaking the Staff of Union (Zechariah 11:14)

The second staff is named "Union" (NIV, ESV, NASB), "Unity" (NRSV), "Bands" (KJV), "Couplers" (NJB). The word is *ḥābal*, "to bind."

> "Then I broke my second staff called Union, breaking the brotherhood between Judah and Israel." (Zechariah 11:14)

The unity between the 12 tribes was broken. Though the leaders had been exiled under the Assyrians centuries before this, some members of the Ten Tribes remained in Samaria. This too was to be broken.

---

[144] See Baldwin, *Haggai, Zechariah, Malachi*, pp. 185-186.

[145] Leon Morris, *The Gospel According to Matthew* (Pillar Commentary; Eerdmans, 1992), pp. 696-698; R.T. France, *The Gospel of Matthew* (New International Commentary on the New Testament; Eerdmans, 2007), pp. 1041-1045.

[146] R.C.H. Lenzki, *The Interpretation of St. Matthew's Gospel* (Minneapolis, 1964), p. 1083.

The Foolish, Worthless Shepherd (Zechariah 11:15-17)

The Lord had called Zechariah to symbolically pastor the flock marked for slaughter. Now he calls him again to be a sign, a portent or warning of a future "foolish shepherd" who won't care for the people, but exploit them.

> "15 Then the LORD said to me, 'Take again the equipment of a foolish shepherd.
> 16 For I am going to raise up a shepherd over the land who will not care for the lost,
> or seek the young, or heal the injured, or feed the healthy, but will eat the meat of
> the choice sheep, tearing off their hoofs." (Zechariah 11:15-16)

This shepherd is called "foolish" in verse 15. The word, often used in Proverbs, denotes a person who is sinful rather than mentally stupid.[147] In verse 17 he is referred to as "worthless," that is, "weak, deficient."[148] The prophecy concludes with God's curse on the "worthless shepherd" in verses 15-17.

> **Q3. (Zechariah 11:4-17) Why is God so condemnatory towards shepherds or leaders who take advantage of their office and exploit the people? What is Jesus' standard for leaders (Mark 10:42-45). What would it look like in government if we followed Jesus' standard? What would it look like in your workplace? In your church? In your home? http://www.joyfulheart.com/forums/topic/1735-q3-servant-leaders/**

Prophecy 4. The Great Battle and New Jerusalem (Zechariah 12-14)

Zechariah 12-14 look forward to a future battle that has the nations of the earth gathering against Judah and Jerusalem. It sounds a lot like the final eschatological battle prophesied in Joel 3:8-16, Revelation 19-20, and elsewhere. The people will be attacked and conquered, but God will fight for them and will ultimately vanquish the enemy.

You'll probably find some Bible teachers who can tell you exactly how each of the elements of chapters 12-14 fit on some End Time chronological chart. I can't, though I recognize that this prophecy clearly belongs to the End Times.

Instead of a detailed exposition of future events that are vague at best, I'll conclude Zechariah by looking at some of the key prophecies here clearly fulfilled by Christ Jesus.

---

[147] "Foolish shepherd" (NIV, ESV, KJV), "worthless shepherd" (NASB) is *'ewîlî*, "foolish." This word, used often in Proverbs, denotes a person who is morally deficient (Louis Goldberg, TWOT #44b).

[148] "Worthless shepherd" (NIV, NASB, ESV) "idol shepherd" (KJV) – *'elîl*, "something worthless (particularly as an object of worship), from a root meaning "to be weak, deficient" (Jack B. Scott, TWOT #99a).

Mourning for the One they Have Pierced (Zechariah 12:10)

Here's a remarkable passage!

> "And I will pour out on the house of David and the inhabitants of Jerusalem a spirit of grace and supplication. **They will look on me, the one they have pierced**, and they will mourn for him as one mourns for an only child, and grieve bitterly for him as one grieves for a firstborn son." (Zechariah 12:10)

It prophesies that the Jews will look upon "the one they have pierced" and mourn for him. In the light of the New Testament, we see this as Messiah Jesus, who was crucified for our sins. This prophecy indicates that Jews will ultimately repent of crucifying Jesus! It is quoted in John's Gospel (John 19:36-37).

Paul indicates that in the End Times this repentance and cleansing will come:

> "A partial hardening has come upon Israel, until the fullness of the Gentiles has come in. And in this way all Israel will be saved"[149] (Romans 11:25b-26a)

A Fountain to Cleanse from Sin (Zechariah 13:1)

Along the same line is the wonderful promise of the End Time when washing and cleansing will come to the Jews.

> "On that day a fountain will be opened to the house of David and the inhabitants of Jerusalem, to cleanse them from sin and impurity." (Zechariah 13:1)

We see the phrase "fountain of life" a number of times in Scripture,[150] and the theme of washing from sins,[151] though the image of a fountain[152] is striking. The word "fountain" comes

William Adolphe Bouguereau, 'Compassion' (1897), oil on canvas, 130x280 cm, Musée d'Orsay, Paris

---

[149] Paul is referring to Isaiah 59:20-21, where Israel will repent and turn to the Lord, and God will restore his covenant with them.

[150] Proverbs 13:14; 16:22; 10:11; 14:27; Psalm 36:9; Jeremiah 2:13.

[151] Psalm 51:2, 7; Isaiah 1:16; Ezekiel 36:25; 1 Corinthians 16:11; Ephesians 5:25-27; Titus 3:5; Revelation 7:13-14.

[152] In Revelation 7:13-14 there is a vision of a great multitude wearing white robes. "They have washed their robes and made them white in the blood of the Lamb" (Revelation 7:14). In 1772, William Cowper wrote a vivid hymn based on this image and Zechariah 13:1. "There is a fountain filled with blood / drawn from Emmanuel's veins; / And sinners plunged beneath that flood / lose all their guilty stains."

from the idea of to dig a well.[153] At Jacob's well in Samaria, Jesus says,

> "Whoever drinks the water I give him will never thirst. Indeed, the water I give him
> will become in him a spring of water welling up to eternal life." (John 4:14)

Humans can't dig such a well or produce such a fountain by their own efforts. This is a
well only Jesus can draw from, offering cleansing from sin to those who will wash in its
waters.

Strike the Shepherd (Zechariah 13:7)

Now we consider a passage recalled by Jesus, when he looks forward to the disciples
fleeing at his capture and crucifixion (Matthew 26:31; Mark 14:27; cf. John 16:32).
Zechariah is speaking of striking another shepherd, the Great Shepherd, "the man who
is close to me."

> "'Awake, O sword, against my shepherd,
> against the man who is close to me!'
> declares the LORD Almighty.
> **'Strike the shepherd, and the sheep will be scattered,**
> and I will turn my hand against the little ones.'" (Zechariah 13:7)

This brings to mind another Messianic prophecy of this Shepherd, the Suffering Servant
who bears the sins of the sheep.

> "We considered him **stricken** by God,
> **smitten** by him, and afflicted.
> But he was pierced for our transgressions,
> he was crushed for our iniquities;
> the punishment that brought us peace was upon him,
> and by his wounds we are healed." (Isaiah 53:4b-5)

I'm skipping over the details of the final Battle, but note that the extreme testing of this
time brings a refining effect to the third of the people who are not killed.

> "This third I will bring into the fire;
> I will refine them like silver and test them like gold.
> They will call on my name and I will answer them;
> I will say, 'They are my people,'
> and they will say, 'The LORD is our God.'" (Zechariah 13:9)

---

[153] "Fountain" is *māqôr*, a from the root *qûr*, "to dig for water (TWOT #204a).

Q4. (Zechariah 12-13) Paul was broken-hearted for his countrymen the Jews, who had rejected the Messiah. We should be too. When do you think the prophecy will be fulfilled that says, "They will look on me, the one they have pierced, and they will mourn…?" (Zechariah 12:10). Concerning the fountain that cleanses from sin and impurity (Zechariah 13:1), has that been fulfilled, or will it be future? Why will it please God so much when all the Jews finally believe in Jesus?
http://www.joyfulheart.com/forums/topic/1736-q4-messiah/

The Lord Comes and Reigns (Zechariah 14)

Zechariah 14 recounts the coming terrible battle against Jerusalem. In spite of the heavy toll on the residents, we read that:

"Then the LORD will go out and fight against those nations,
as he fights in the day of battle." (Zechariah 14:3)

And at the victorious conclusion of the battle we read:

"Then the LORD my God will come,
and all the holy ones with him." (Zechariah 14:5b)

This coming of the "holy ones" sounds a lot like New Testament references to the event some call "The Rapture." Christ's coming will certainly include angels.

For the Son of Man is going to come in his Father's glory with his angels." (Matthew 16:27a; cf. 25:31; Jude 14)

But the "holy ones" will also include "the saints, the people of the Most High" (Daniel 7:27).

"And he will send his angels with a loud trumpet call,
and they will gather his elect from the four winds,
from one end of the heavens to the other." (Matthew 24:31)

"For the Lord himself will come down from heaven, with a loud command, with the voice of the archangel and with the trumpet call of God, and the dead in Christ will rise first. After that, we who are still alive and are left will be caught up together with them in the clouds to meet the Lord in the air. And so we will be with the Lord forever." (1 Thessalonians 4:16-17)

The concluding verses of Zechariah speak of the Day of the Lord in symbolic terms of the perfection when Christ returns to set the world aright – much like the imagery of Revelation 21 and 22 of the new heavens and new earth. We see symbolic language of:

- Light in the evening (verse 7).
- Living water flowing from Jerusalem (verse 8).
- Yahweh as king over the whole earth (verse 9).
- Jerusalem will be raised up and inhabited forever (verses 10-11).
- God's enemies will cease to be (verses 12-13, 15).
- The wealth of the nations will be collected (verse 14).
- The Gentiles will worship Yahweh in Jerusalem (verses 16-19).
- The inscription of the High Priest's plate, "Holy to the Lord" will be inscribed on the cooking pots of the common people – in effect, the common and unclean are made holy (verses 20-21a).
- No enemy of God (Canaanite) will pollute the temple, as they did in the days of Nehemiah (verse 21b, see Nehemiah 14:4-9).

Again, I apologize for the length of this chapter. I just hope it has helped you to understand these passages better.

Lessons for Disciples

A number of lessons for modern-day disciples emerge from Zechariah 7-14.

1. Rather than mere outward worship, God desires a repentant and humble heart that worships him in spirit and in truth. Too often, our worship is evaluated by what it does for us (makes us feel good, feeds us, etc.). Rather, worship needs to be towards God, and evaluated by how we come before him with humility and sincerity of heart. Our goal is to please God, not ourselves (Zechariah 7:4-7).

2. God calls us to ethical righteousness – true justice for the weakest in our society and an attitude of mercy and compassion rather than exploitation (Zechariah 7:8-10; 8:16-17).

3. Even when we are not under oath, we are also called to truthful speech with one another (Zechariah 8:16-17), rather than deceit.

4. We are to carry God's word to the Gentiles, those who don't know Jesus. As a result, they will begin to flow towards Jerusalem – an End Time prophecy and a theme of both Old and New Testaments (Zechariah 8:20-23).

5. As the King enters Jerusalem gently and humbly, riding on a donkey, so we are to exhibit a character of gentleness and humility (Zechariah 9:9-10).

6. God is concerned about leaders protecting his people from oppression, rather than oppressing them (Zechariah 10-11). We are not to be leaders who domineer over people, but who serve them.

7. Zechariah contains a number of prophecies of the Messiah, which are fulfilled in Jesus, encouraging us that God keeps his word, even if it doesn't find fulfillment in our lifetimes (Zechariah 12:10; 13:1, 7).

8. Zechariah reminds us of the New Testament prophecies of the Last Day – of battles, of judgments, and of the final place of peace in the New Heavens and the New Earth, themes that are echoed in the final chapters of Revelation.

> "On that day living water will flow out from Jerusalem, half to the eastern sea and half to the western sea, in summer and in winter. The LORD will be king over the whole earth. On that day there will be one LORD, and his name the only name." (Zechariah 14:8-9)

Come soon, Lord Jesus!

Prayer

Father, Zechariah speaks of many things I don't understand, but what I do understand frightens me. Keep me and other believers safe during the final Battle that will take place before you come. Help me to have courage to reach out to "the nations," so that they will hear the Good News and be drawn to you. Help me to represent your love and your justice to the weakest in my region, and love them as you love them. In Jesus' name, I pray. Amen.

Key Verses

Though much of Zechariah has some obscure images and prophecies, there are a number of verses that stand out – some of which are quoted in the New Testament.

> "When you fasted and mourned ... was it really for me that you fasted? And when you were eating and drinking, were you not just feasting for yourselves?" (Zechariah 7:5b-6, NIV)

> "Administer true justice; show mercy and compassion to one another. Do not oppress the widow or the fatherless, the alien or the poor. In your hearts do not think evil of each other." (Zechariah 7:9-10, NIV)

"'Speak the truth to each other, and render true and sound judgment in your courts; do not plot evil against your neighbor, and do not love to swear falsely. I hate all this,' declares the LORD." (Zechariah 8:16-17, NIV)

"In those days ten men from all languages and nations will take firm hold of one Jew by the hem of his robe and say, 'Let us go with you, because we have heard that God is with you.'" (Zechariah 8:23, NIV)

"Rejoice greatly, O Daughter of Zion!
Shout, Daughter of Jerusalem!
See, your king comes to you,
righteous and having salvation,
gentle and riding on a donkey,
on a colt, the foal of a donkey." (Zechariah 9:9, NIV)

"The LORD their God will save them on that day as the flock of his people. They will sparkle in his land like jewels in a crown. How attractive and beautiful they will be!" (Zechariah 9:16-17a, NIV)

"So I pastured the flock marked for slaughter, particularly the oppressed of the flock. Then I took two staffs and called one Favor and the other Union, and I pastured the flock." (Zechariah 11:7, NIV)

"They paid me thirty pieces of silver. And the LORD said to me, 'Throw it to the potter' – the handsome price at which they priced me! So I took the thirty pieces of silver and threw them into the house of the LORD to the potter. (Zechariah 11:12a-13)

"And I will pour out on the house of David and the inhabitants of Jerusalem a spirit of grace and supplication. They will look on me, the one they have pierced, and they will mourn for him as one mourns for an only child, and grieve bitterly for him as one grieves for a firstborn son." (Zechariah 12:10)

"On that day a fountain will be opened to the house of David and the inhabitants of Jerusalem, to cleanse them from sin and impurity." (Zechariah 13:1)

"Strike the shepherd, and the sheep will be scattered, and I will turn my hand against the little ones." (Zechariah 13:7b)

"On that day living water will flow out from Jerusalem, half to the eastern sea and half to the western sea, in summer and in winter. The LORD will be king over the whole earth. On that day there will be one LORD, and his name the only name." (Zechariah 14:8-9)

5. Confession and Repentance (Ezra 7-10)

Until now we've been looking at the period of rebuilding the temple – from the time the first exiles returned to Jerusalem about 537 BC, including the prophecies of Haggai and Zechariah, beginning in 520 BC, and the completion of the temple in 515 BC.

Now we fast-forward nearly 57 years to 458 BC. Most of a century has passed since the temple has been finished. The returned exiles in Jerusalem have fallen into both complacency about their situation, and have adopted a policy of compromise with their neighbors, in order to keep the peace.

Under Ezra's leadership, the priesthood is purified. James J. Tissot, detail of 'The Priests' (1898-1902), Gouache on board, The Jewish Museum.

Turbulence in the Persian Empire and Artaxerxes I

As you recall, the temple was finished in 515 BC by decree of Darius I, King of Persia (521-486 BC). After Darius the Great, the Persian Empire was ruled by Xerxes I (486-465 BC), known in the Book of Esther as King Ahasuerus, and also mentioned in Ezra 4:6.

But all is not well in the Persian Empire. In 465 BC, Xerxes is murdered by the commander of his royal bodyguard, and Xerxes' son and heir, Artaxerxes I Longimanus (464-424 BC), avenges his father's murder, and then takes firm steps to consolidate his throne. In the west, Egypt has revolted against Persia with the help of the Athenians. It's time for Artaxerxes to make sure that the buffer provinces near the border of Egypt are firmly committed to Persia. This seems to be the outward reason that Artaxerxes is particularly generous to Ezra's mission. The real reason, of course, is God's hand.

The text dates Ezra's journey to Jerusalem in "the seventh year of Artaxerxes" (Ezra 7:7) which is 458 BC. Artaxerxes commissions Ezra to take charge of the ecclesiastical and civil affairs of the province of Judah, and pays for sacrifices to be offered and prayers made for himself and his reign.

Ezra the Priest, Scribe, and Administrator (Ezra 7:1-10)

Though we've studied the first six chapters of Ezra already (Lesson 1), only now do we meet Ezra the Priest, after whom the book is named. We're introduced to Ezra in several ways.

Priest. Ezra is described as "the priest and scribe" (Ezra 7:11-12, 21; 10:16; Nehemiah 8:9; 12:26). A 16-generation genealogy is given in verses 1-5 to prove that his priestly lineage is of the highest order. He comes from a proud heritage of priests.[154] Ezra doesn't seem to serve as a high priest in the temple during his day. Rather, Ezra exercises his ministry by being a religious reformer.

Babylon. Ezra comes out of the large Jewish community centered near Babylon. In addition, Babylon is the main capital of the Persian kings at this period,[155] which helps explain his access to Artaxerxes.

Scribe. Ezra is also described as a "teacher" (NIV) or "scribe" (NRSV, ESV, KJV). The noun is *sōpēr*, from the verb *sāpar*, "to count" (mathematical), and "to recount," that is, "to declare, tell, show forth." Related words refer to "book" and "writing." Certainly, scribes were important in the Ancient Near East for keeping records. But gradually scribes evolved from mere copiers and recorders to influential members of the government and representatives of the king. During the Exile a professional class of scribes helps explain to the Jewish community how the Law should be obeyed in a foreign context. Thus the initial elaborations of the Torah, later known as "the scribal tradition," come into existence.[156] This is where Ezra excelled.

> "He was a teacher well versed in the Law of Moses, which the LORD, the God of Israel, had given." (Ezra 7:6a)

> "Ezra had devoted himself to the study and observance of the Law of the LORD, and to teaching its decrees and laws in Israel." (Ezra 7:10)

Courageous Leader. It is clear that Ezra takes the initiative while in Babylon to seek help from the Persian King in his plans to help Israel. "The king had granted him

---

[154] Several luminaries are found among his ancestors: **Hilkiah** is high priest during the reign of Josiah, who found the lost book of the law while repairing the temple. He was a leader in the ensuing reformation and purification of the temple in 621 BC (2 Kings 22:8ff; 23:4). **Zadok** is high priest under David (2 Samuel 8:17; 1 Chronicles 12:38-40), loyal to David's son Solomon (1 Kings 1). **Phinehas** is zealous against immorality and religious apostasy of Israel (Numbers 25). **Eleazar** succeeds his father Aaron as high priest after his death, and assisted both Moses and Joshua in their missions. **Aaron** is Moses' brother and the first high priest.

[155] The Kings of Persia also used other capital cities including Pasargadae, Ecbatana, Susa, and Persepolis.

[156] D. A. Hagner, "Scribes," ISBE 4:359-361.

everything he asked, for the hand of the LORD his God was on him" (Ezra 7:6b). Then he organizes a caravan of Jews to emigrate from Babylon to Judah.

Person of Faith. In Ezra 8, his role as a person of faith is seen. His caravan will be carrying the equivalent of millions of dollars in gold and silver without a military guard. So he organizes a fast to seek God for a safe journey before embarking.

Civil Administrator. Finally, Ezra is a civil administrator, one whom King Artaxerxes commissions to reform the government and justice system in the province of Judah (Ezra 7:25), though I don't think he is the actual governor of the Province of Judah (Yehud).

Artaxerxes sees in Ezra a religious man, but one who will reestablish Persian rule in this area so close to Persia's enemy Egypt. From a divine perspective, Ezra is the one God has chosen to bring religious reform. Perhaps by his largess, Artaxerxes thinks he is buying loyalty. But God is behind it all as a way to finance his own Kingdom work.

Ezra Comes to Jerusalem (Ezra 7:7)

Ezra's caravan includes not only Babylonian Jews wanting to emigrate to their ancestral home, but also a contingent of religious workers who can help Ezra bring reform when he gets there. Verse 8 gives us the date of the journey – 458 BC – and its duration – five months. Verses 9 and 10 attribute the success of the journey to God's grace and goodness[157] upon a man who has devoted himself to God's service.

King Artaxerxes' Letter to Ezra (Ezra 7:11-28)

Verses 11-28 include the text of a letter of authorization that Ezra brings with him. Artaxerxes authorizes:

1. **Emigration.** To emigrate with a band of Jews (verse 13)
2. **Official inquiry.** To inquire about the province of Judah and its capital, Jerusalem on behalf of "the king and his seven advisors." In other words, Ezra's inquiry and the measures he will take to correct problems have the king's authority. The Jews' enemies don't have much recourse (verse 14).
3. **Transmit money.** To transfer out of Babylon money from both the king himself and the Jewish community to offer sacrifices in Jerusalem, and whatever else is needed there (verses 15-19)

---

[157] "Gracious hand" (NIV, NRSV), "good hand" (ESV, KJV) uses the adjective *ṭôb*, "good" in a broad sense of the term.

4. **Royal treasury.** To draw on the royal treasury of the Satrapy of Trans-Euphrates (of which Judah is a sub-province) for other needs – essentially a blank check signed by the king (verses 19-21). Limits are set, but they seem generous indeed (verse 22).

5. **Prayer.** To pray and offer sacrifices for the king and the Persian government (verse 23). Artaxerxes isn't a believer but a polytheist. However, he believes that favor from the Jews' God – any god for that matter – is worth paying for.

6. **Waiver of taxation.** The priests and temple workers are free from taxation (verse 24).

7. **Governance.** To appoint magistrates and judges to administer justice (verses 25-26). Those who don't obey may be punished by death and other means, by the king's authority.

The chapter closes with a word of praise for God prompting such great favor from the government (verses 27-28a).

Recruiting Emigrants for the Journey (Ezra 7:28b-8:20)

Now that Ezra has official authorization for his journey, it is time to recruit people from the most distinguished families in Babylon to join him.

> "Because the hand of the LORD my God was on me, I took courage and gathered leading men from Israel to go up with me." (Ezra 7:28b)

The first part of chapter 8 details the names of the heads of families that join on the journey, as well as the numbers from each family.

When he finally gathers the group at the Ahava Canal to begin the journey, he finds that they have priests, but not Levites, the temple

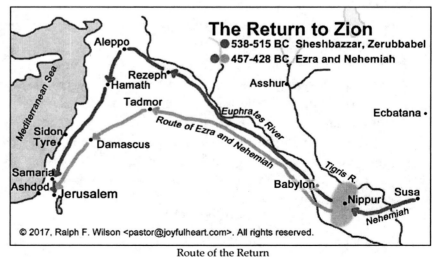

Route of the Return

workers who are required to run the temple enterprise. And so he sends a delegation to "Iddo, the leader in Casiphia" (Ezra 8:17), who heads a clan of temple servants. With his help, they assemble 258 men, enough to meet the need.

When you total the whole group, you come up with approximately 1,750 men. I am sure that these men additionally bring their wives, children, and servants, to emigrate with them. So the whole company may have numbered 10,000 or so.

Fasting and Prayer at the Ahava Canal (Ezra 8:21-23)

The company has assembled and are camping together, waiting for the order to embark. But first, there is business to do before God.

> "21 There, by the Ahava Canal, I proclaimed a fast, so that we might humble ourselves before our God and ask him for a safe journey for us and our children, with all our possessions. 22 I was ashamed to ask the king for soldiers and horsemen to protect us from enemies on the road, because we had told the king, 'The gracious hand of our God is on everyone who looks to him, but his great anger is against all who forsake him.' 23 So we fasted and petitioned our God about this, and he answered our prayer." (Ezra 8:21-23)

Ezra has been boasting to King Artaxerxes how mighty the Jewish God is, so he can't very well ask for an armed escort. That would display unbelief in God's power to protect him. But the danger is real. They are carrying a great deal of money. So Ezra calls a fast to humble them and to petition God for protection. We don't know the length of the fast, but when Ezra senses that God had answered them, they are ready to go.

Fasting isn't some form of spiritual blackmail or earning favor to manipulate God to do things for us. Rather it is a way of humbling ourselves before God. Fasting helps us to be aware of our need for him, rather than continue to be self-deceived by a sense of self-sufficiency. Our prayers become humble, earnest, faith-filled.

Q1. (Ezra 8:21-23) Why does Ezra call the people to fast? Does fasting compel God to answer our prayers? What does fasting accomplish in us?
http://www.joyfulheart.com/forums/topic/1737-q1-fasting/

Measures to Protect from Embezzlement (Ezra 8:24-30, 33-34)

Access to a money has a way of tempting people to steal it – or embezzle it from the organization they work for. So Ezra publicly weighs out the gold and silver articles and puts them in the care of twelve trusted men. He tells them that the treasure is "consecrated to the LORD," to put the fear of God in them. And then he explains that when they get to Jerusalem, the articles will be weighed again – and the weights compared with the original weights to make sure people haven't been shaving off bits of gold and silver during the journey (8:34).

It's both wise and biblical to set up measures to ensure that trusted people don't embezzle God's funds. Paul did this when conveying gifts for the poor of Jerusalem (1 Corinthians 16:3; 2 Corinthians 8:19-21). For example, most churches in our day have found it wise to have different people make bank deposits than those who pay the bills. It's not that we don't trust one another, but we know from sad experience that even the best people can be tempted by greed. Taking precautions is wise.

> **Q2. (Ezra 8:24-30, 33-34) Why does Ezra weigh out the gold and silver vessels when he entrusts them to individuals, and weigh them again when they are delivered to the temple? Is this an act of distrust? If not, why are steps to prevent embezzlement good for Christian organizations?**
> **http://www.joyfulheart.com/forums/topic/1738-q2-care-with-money/**

Safe Journey (Ezra 8:15-36)

> "[31] On the twelfth day of the first month we set out from the Ahava Canal to go to Jerusalem. The hand of our God was on us, and he protected us from enemies and bandits along the way. [32] So we arrived in Jerusalem, where we rested three days." (Ezra 8:31-32)

God protects his people during the five-month, 900 mile trek. Yes, a caravan of 10,000 people might be intimidating, but unarmed civilians are no match for mounted bandits, who are skilled at lying in wait where they can't be seen, and then attacking, spreading confusion, and stealing the goods they seek. The enemies and bandits[158] either didn't see them, or did but kept their distance through the sovereign protection of God.

---

[158] "Enemies" (NIV) or "the hand of the enemy" (NRSV, ESV, KJV) uses the noun *'ōyēb*, "a participle of the verb *'āyab*, "to be an enemy, be hostile to" (TWOT #78). "Bandits" (NIV), "ambushes" (NRSV, ESV), "of

On the other hand, a few years later, Nehemiah has no problem being accompanied by the king's "army officers and cavalry" on his journey from Susa (Nehemiah 2:9). There are no hard and fast rules here, rather we rely on the Spirit's guidance.

Intermarriage between Faiths (Ezra 9)

Ezra and his band of 10,000 pilgrims have delivered their treasure to the temple and are now encamped in Judah in tents while they go about the immense task of finding their ancestral villages and building houses in their homeland.

As for Ezra, he begins his campaign of teaching the Word of God. Within four months (Ezra 7:8; 10:9), his teaching mission bears fruit with agonizing intensity, as some of his students come to him with a devastating report.

> "[1] The people of Israel, including the priests and the Levites, have not kept themselves separate from the neighboring peoples with their detestable practices, like those of the Canaanites, Hittites, Perizzites, Jebusites, Ammonites, Moabites, Egyptians and Amorites. [2] They have taken some of their daughters as wives for themselves and their sons, and have mingled the holy race with the peoples around them. And the leaders and officials have led the way in this unfaithfulness.'" (Ezra 9:1b-2)

The leaders' report to Ezra echoes the very words of the Law that he had been teaching them, including a list of the pagan nations from whom Israel was to keep itself separate: "Canaanites, Hittites, Perizzites, Jebusites, Ammonites, Moabites, Egyptians and Amorites" (Exodus 23:23; Deuteronomy 20:17-18).

Spiritual Purity

To people in the West, the idea of prohibiting interracial marriage might seem petty, motivated by racial prejudice, the very prejudice that pluralistic societies like the United States and Western Europe have had to fight to keep peace and promote justice. But if we try to understand what is happening in the Judah of Ezra's day using that paradigm, we'll miss the point entirely.

The issue isn't about race. I would guess that most of the various peoples living in Palestine looked pretty much the same outwardly. And it isn't really about difference of

---

such as lay in wait" (KJV) is the noun *ōreb* , "ambuscade," from the verb *ārab*, "to lie in wait, ambush." David used the word to describe how his enemies waited for a time they could find him vulnerable and attack (Psalm 10:9; 59:3).

language itself.[159] People probably knew enough Aramaic to makes themselves understood to each other.

The real issue is spiritual. When people intermarry with those of another religion, there is usually a mixing of belief-systems in the family, known as syncretism. If this just happened here or there rarely, it isn't as much of a problem. But if intermarriage with people of other religions is widespread, then the purity of the Jewish faith is compromised.

The worship of Yahweh gets intermixed and confused with the worship of Baal and Ashtoreth, and other pagan gods of the region. Immoral sexual practices of the pagans gradually become acceptable to God's holy people. There is no longer a sense of "clean" and "unclean," and therefore no concept of holiness and righteousness before Yahweh, the holy God. Any kind of religious practice is now tolerated as acceptable. There is no single Truth as revealed by God. Relativism and tolerance now accept all religions and gods as equally valid. As a result, the nation of Israel loses its distinctive character as a people devoted to Yahweh, the one God who created heaven and earth.

This may sound overblown until you look at the history of Israel and Judah. In the Northern Kingdom, the national worship centers came to feature golden calves as objects of worship, intermixed with Yahweh worship (1 Kings 12:28-33). In Judah before the Exile, pagan worship is widespread (Jeremiah 32:26-35) – even in Solomon's Temple itself (Ezekiel 8; 2 Kings 16).

Before Israel ever entered the Promised Land, God's command is clear:

> "Do not intermarry with them. Do not give your daughters to their sons or take their daughters for your sons, for they will turn your sons away from following me to serve other gods, and the LORD's anger will burn against you and will quickly destroy you." (Deuteronomy 7:3-4)

Indeed, this command has been repeated time after time by godly leaders and prophets down through the years (Joshua 23:12-13). When this command is neglected, disaster follows (Judges 3:6-7; 1 Kings 11:2; Psalm 106:35).

Ezra's Reaction (Ezra 9:3-4)

Ezra, as a student of the Bible and the history of God's people, is well aware of the disastrous consequences of intermarriage and syncretism. So when he receives this report, he is appalled!

---

[159] Of course, a distinct language is part of the root of a unique culture; so is religion.

"³ When I heard this, I tore my tunic and cloak, pulled hair from my head and beard

and sat down appalled. ⁴ Then everyone who trembled at the words of the God of Israel gathered around me because of this unfaithfulness of the exiles. And I sat there appalled until the evening sacrifice." (Ezra 9:2-4)

The word "appalled" describes the horror and shock[160] that Ezra feel, when he realizes the terrible punishment that will come upon the nation – again – for this terrible sin. And those who believe the word of God had the same reaction. They are described as those "who trembled at the words of the God of Israel."

Gustav Doré, detail from 'Ezra in Prayer' (1866), engraving, from *La Grande Bible de Tours*.

Many of us live in cultures that have no concept of "sin" – only of bad behavior and mistakes. The average man or woman in Western cultures doesn't "tremble at the words of the God of Israel." Rather they don't really believe them or imagine any eternal punishment for disobedience. That's what the culture of Judah is becoming in Ezra's day – except for a few who still believe strongly that God's words must be taken seriously. They join Ezra in mourning.

The way the people from the Near East mourn is often different from Western cultures. Grief there is expressed publicly and loudly.

"When I heard this, I tore my tunic and cloak, pulled hair from my head and beard and sat down appalled." (Ezra 9:3)

Tearing his clothes and pulling out hair are ways of expressing grief, as well as shock at blasphemy, in that culture (Joshua 7:6; 2 Kings 19:1; Job 1:20; Micah 1:16; Mark 14:63; Acts 14:14). In verse 5 we see that "self-abasement" (NIV), "fasting" (ESV, NRSV), "heaviness" (KJV) accompanies this mourning.[161]

---

[160] "Appalled" (NIV, NRSV, ESV), "astonied" (KJV) is the Poel participle *shāmēm*, "be desolate, appalled." Basic to the idea of the root is the desolation caused by some great disaster, usually as a result of divine judgment. Here the word is used in the sense of 'horror' and 'shock' brought about by the vision of desolation. It is the inner response to the outward scene (Hermann J. Austel, TWOT #2409).

[161] The Hebrew noun is *ta'anît*, "humiliation (by fasting)", from *'ānâ*, "afflict, oppress, humble" (TWOT #1652f).

The Prophet Ezekiel had a vision of judgment on the city and the temple, of a man clothed in linen with a writing case at his waist, with the command:

> "Pass through the city, through Jerusalem, and put a mark on the foreheads of the men who sigh and groan over all the abominations that are committed in it." (Ezekiel 9:4)

How much do we grieve over the backsliding of our family, friends, and neighbors? How deeply do we grieve over the shallowness of our churches? Or do we revert to a quick judgmentalism that is the earmark of the church in the eyes of the world?

Q3. (Ezra 9:3-4) How does Ezra react when he hears of the sin of intermarriage? Does he react for show? Does he over-react? Why does he grieve over the sins of the people? What is wrong with us if we don't grieve over the sins of God's people? http://www.joyfulheart.com/forums/topic/1739-q3-heart-sick/

Ezra's Prayer Posture (Ezra 9:5-6a)

Ezra's mourning isn't some kind of show. The sins of the leaders of the nation rip at his heart. He is beside himself with anguish for Judah because he knows history. He knows the Word. He knows how punishment for these very sins have been visited upon the nation in the past, and he can see that happening in the future. But he can also see God's mercy. And that brings him to prayer.

> "5 Then, at the evening sacrifice, I rose from my self-abasement, with my tunic and cloak torn, and fell on my knees with my hands spread out to the LORD my God 6 and prayed." (Ezra 9:5-6a)

Observe Ezra's posture of humility and supplication. For the most part, Hebrews pray standing (Luke 18:10-13). But kneeling indicates a special kind of humbling oneself before someone who is greater. We see it especially in earnest prayers (Daniel 6:10; Acts 9:40; Psalm 96:6; Matthew 18:26; Luke 22:41-42) – in Solomon, for example.

> "When Solomon had finished all these prayers and supplications to the LORD, he rose from before the altar of the LORD, where he had been kneeling with his hands spread out toward heaven." (1 Kings 8:54)

Spreading of the hands is also a characteristic Hebrew prayer posture, seen throughout the Old Testament. It is also common in the early church (1 Timothy 2:8). One of the characteristic symbols found in the catacombs of Rome is the *orante*, a figure standing with hands lifted in prayer (though Ezra is kneeling in our passage).

We see in Ezra 9:6b, that Ezra he is praying with bowed head as an indication of his shame and disgrace. Often, the Jews prayed and praised with face uplifted (Job 22:26; Psalm 24:7; John 11:41; 17:1-2), but praying with bowed head is a sign not only of humility, but of shame (Job 10:15; 11:15).

Ezra is not quiet about his mourning and his prayer. He was quite demonstrative – not for show, but because of his deep shame, grief, and genuine fear that the people's sins will bring God's judgment upon them once again. Skipping down to chapter 10:1 we read:

> "Ezra was praying and confessing, weeping and throwing himself down before the house of God." (Ezra 10:1)

Four verbs describe Ezra's actions. Three out of the four verses use the Hithpael stem of the Hebrew verb to express an intensive type of action with a reflexive voice, that is, when the person performs the action upon himself.

- **"Praying"** is *pālal*, "intervene, interpose, pray," used especially of intercessory prayer, where one person pleads before God on behalf of others.[162]
- **"Confessing"** is *yādâ*, "to confess," to convey the acknowledgment or confession of sin, individually or nationally.[163]
- **"Weeping"** is *bākâ*, ""to weep by reason of joy or sorrow, the latter including lament, complaint, remorse or repentance." It is the natural and spontaneous expression of strong emotion.[164] This is the weeping of repentance at having offended God. In the Near East culture it is probably accompanied by loud wailing.
- **"Throwing himself down"** is *nāpal*, "fall, lie, be cast down." I picture this as Ezra's initial reaction to the news. He falls immediately to the ground before the temple and kneeling, begins to pray, confess, and wail for Israel's sins.

Ezra's Corporate Confession (Ezra 9:6b-7)

Ezra begins his prayer with a humble and contrite confession of sins.

---

[162] Victor P. Hamilton, *pālal*, TWOT #1776, Hithpael stem.

[163] The Hithpael form is normally employed when this verb is used to convey the confession of national sins (Daniel 9:4, 20; Nehemiah 1:6; 9:2-3). Ralph H. Alexander, *yādâ*, TWOT #847.

[164] John N. Oswalt, *bākâ*, TWOT #243, Qal stem.

"[6b] O my God, I am too ashamed and disgraced to lift up my face to you, my God, because our sins are higher than our heads and our guilt has reached to the heavens. [7] From the days of our forefathers until now, our guilt has been great. Because of our sins, we and our kings and our priests have been subjected to the sword and captivity, to pillage and humiliation at the hand of foreign kings, as it is today." (Ezra 9:6b-7)

Notice that Ezra is not confessing his own personal sins. As a priest, he is confessing the sins of the nation – "our sins." This is no shallow confession. Ezra is overcome with shame and a sense of how the nation has disgraced itself and God by its actions.[165] They have no one to blame but themselves. We'll see some of the same elements in Lesson 6, as we study Nehemiah's prayer of confession (Nehemiah 1:6-7).

Next, Ezra acknowledges God's great grace to Judah, allowing them to return to their land and rebuild the temple.

"[8] But now, for a brief moment, the LORD our God has been gracious in leaving us a remnant and giving us a firm place in his sanctuary, and so our God gives light to our eyes and a little relief in our bondage. [9] Though we are slaves, our God has not deserted us in our bondage. He has shown us kindness in the sight of the kings of Persia: He has granted us new life to rebuild the house of our God and repair its ruins, and he has given us a wall of protection in Judah and Jerusalem." (Ezra 9:8-9)

The "wall"[166] probably refers to spiritual protection by God, rather than a physical wall around Jerusalem, which will be restored under Nehemiah a few years later.

God's grace to them makes their subsequent sin even more inexcusable. Ezra doesn't seem to be quoting a particular verse, but summarizing the message of Moses in verses 10-12.[167] Now Ezra reiterates that God has been very gracious, and his punishment has been restrained.

"What has happened to us is a result of our evil deeds and our great guilt, and yet, our God, you have punished us less than our sins have deserved and have given us a remnant like this." (Ezra 9:13)

---

[165] "Ashamed" is *bôsh*, "to fall into disgrace, normally through failure, either of self or of an object of trust." John Oswalt notes, "The force of *bôsh* is somewhat in contrast to the primary meaning of the English 'to be ashamed,' in that the English stresses the inner attitude, the state of mind, while the Hebrew means 'to come to shame' and stresses the sense of public disgrace, a physical state" (John N. Oswalt, TWOT #222). "Disgraced" (NIV), "blush" (NRSV, ESV, KJV) is *kālam*, "be ashamed ... the sense of disgrace which attends public humiliation" (John N. Oswalt, TWOT #987).

[166] "Wall of protection" (NIV), "protection" (ESV), "wall" (NRSV, KJV) is *gādēr*, "wall, fence, hedge."

[167] Leviticus 18:24-30; Deuteronomy 7:1-3; 12:31; 18:12; Malachi 2:11.

Ezra concludes his prayer with utter reliance on God's grace.

> "O LORD, God of Israel, you are righteous! We are left this day as a remnant. Here we are before you in our guilt, though because of it not one of us can stand in your presence." (Ezra 9:15)

Ezra completely throws himself and his nation upon God's mercy. He doesn't even beg forgiveness, because they don't deserve the grace God has already extended to them. It is an amazing prayer of corporate forgiveness that ranks among the great prayers of the Bible.

Notice that though Ezra his lived a righteous life personally, he includes himself in his confession of the sins of the nation. It isn't, "They have sinned." Rather, "We have sinned."

The People's Response (Ezra 10:1-6)

Ezra's demonstrative prayer draws a crowd.

> "While Ezra was praying and confessing, weeping and throwing himself down before the house of God, a large crowd of Israelites – men, women and children – gathered around him. They too wept bitterly." (Ezra 10:1)

In times of revival, the Holy Spirit can use one person's obedience and prayer as a catalyst to a mighty revival breaking out. And that's what seems to have happened here. The leader, Ezra the priest, is wailing on his knees before God for the sins of the people. Then someone else understands Judah's great peril because of its sin, and begins to weep also. Then another and another. Before Ezra is finished, hundreds of people have gathered – men, women, and children – gathering about him weeping bitterly,[168] so that a great wailing before God is going up in the temple precincts.

After Ezra's prayer is completed and the people have quieted down, a man named Shecaniah[169] stands to speak of a way that there can be "hope for Israel."

> "2 Then Shecaniah son of Jehiel, one of the descendants of Elam, said to Ezra, 'We have been unfaithful to our God by marrying foreign women from the peoples around us. But in spite of this, there is still hope for Israel. 3 Now let us make a

---

[168] "Weep bitterly" translates what is literally "weep with very great weeping," using a common Hebraic repetition of the verbal root to indicate intensity. Here the intensity is increased even more by the addition of the participle *rābâ*, "become, great, many, much, numerous." The KJV translation, "The people wept very sore," is difficult to understand.

[169] Shecaniah's name means "Yahweh has taken (His) dwelling." This is the same word as the Shekinah glory of God.

covenant before our God to send away all these women and their children, in accordance with the counsel of my lord and of those who fear the commands of our God. Let it be done according to the Law. [4] Rise up; this matter is in your hands. We will support you, so take courage and do it.'" (Ezra 10:2-4)

It is remarkable that such a radical suggestion comes spontaneously from one of the people. Shecaniah is probably some kind of leading voice, though we know nothing more about him.[170] He clearly speaks for the people gathered. This isn't Ezra imposing his will, but God's Spirit leading his repentant people forward.

Shecaniah agrees with the Law, that marrying non-Jewish wives is a serious violation of God's will. His proposal is to "send away" or "put away"[171] these non-Jewish wives and the children they have borne. We'll consider the morality of this decision – and how we apply the principles today – in a moment. But first let's see how Ezra carries out this decision.

Ezra takes this radical counsel as from the Lord, and puts the leaders under oath to carry out this decision lest they change their minds later (as we also see in Nehemiah 5:12).

> "So Ezra rose up and put the leading priests and Levites and all Israel under oath to do what had been suggested. And they took the oath." (Ezra 10:5)

Ezra's mourning over the people's sins isn't just for public show. He continues to mourn and fast in a room provided by Jehohanan, probably the reigning high priest (Ezra 10:6).

Q4. (Ezra 10:2-4) Do you think Shecaniah's solution to the people's sin of intermarriage was from God? Can you think of any other examples in the Bible of prophetic "words of wisdom" directing God's people at crisis points? How do the people respond to Schecaniah's radical solution? How does Ezra implement it?
http://www.joyfulheart.com/forums/topic/1740-q4-shecaniahs-solution/

---

[170] In the apocryphal book 1 Esdras 8:92-96 relating this incident, he is stated to be Jechonias.

[171] "Send away" (NIV, NRSV), "put away" (ESV, KJV) is the Hiphil stem of *yāṣā'*. The basic idea of the verb is "go out, come out, go forth," used literally of going out from a particular locality or from the presence of a person. But the Hiphil adds the causative idea, "to cause to go out, send away" (Paul R. Gilchrist, *yāṣā'*, TWOT #893).

Implementing the Oath (Ezra 10:7-44)

Next, a proclamation is made for all the male exiles to assemble in Jerusalem three days hence; failure to appear will result in being expelled from the community. It is December by this time, with nasty weather, but at the appointed time they come. They are distressed by the situation facing Israel – and from sitting in the temple square in the rain! But they are present. Ezra addresses them:

> "10b You have been unfaithful; you have married foreign women, adding to Israel's guilt. 11 Now make confession to the LORD, the God of your fathers, and do his will. Separate yourselves from the peoples around you and from your foreign wives." (Ezra 10:10b-11)

The men agree loudly: "You are right! We must do as you say." But due to the rain, and the time necessary to study each individual situation carefully, they suggest a three-month period to complete the investigation.

Only four from among the whole company voice dissent.

> "Only Jonathan son of Asahel and Jahzeiah son of Tikvah, supported by Meshullam and Shabbethai the Levite, opposed this." (Ezra 10:15)

These are probably leading men – though, because the names are common it's not possible to identify them with others in the Book of Ezra who have the same name. They may have disagreed because of the drastic effect this would have on their own families. Or their disagreement may have been that no law required this, and it is not a good idea.

Nevertheless, the dissenters' view doesn't win the day. "So the exiles did as was proposed" (Ezra 10:16a). For the next three months Ezra and his team investigate each case. Perhaps Ezra had no idea how widespread the problem was – but they take the time needed (Ezra 10:16b-17).

Verses 18-44 list the names of the men. It begins with the priestly families, the descendants of Jeshua, the high priest who rebuilt the temple along with Zerubbabel. Each man offers a pledge to put away his foreign wife, something like our shaking hands on an agreement. Then each man offers a ram, a male sheep, as a guilt offering before the Lord to deal with his sin.

The book of Ezra concludes with these sad words:

> "All these had married foreign women, and some of them had children by these wives" (Ezra 10:44).

After this, we don't see Ezra for another thirteen years, when he reappears to read the law during Nehemiah's governorship of Judah – resulting in a revival (Nehemiah 8). Later he leads a procession to celebrate the completion of the wall around Jerusalem (Nehemiah 12:36).

The Morality of Putting Away Non-Jewish Wives and Children

We can't help but feel bad for the wives and children, who are suddenly sent away. The wives probably return to their parents' homes, for the most part. Hopefully, they are sent away with some money, as Abraham did when he sent away his children born after Isaac (Genesis 25:6). It must have caused great grief, for there is affection as well as economic bonds that are torn asunder. As we'll see in Lesson 9, God hates divorce (Malachi 2:14-16).

But even greater than love for one's wife and children is one's love for God. Jesus told his disciples:

> "Anyone who loves his father or mother more than me is not worthy of me; anyone who loves his son or daughter more than me is not worthy of me." (Matthew 10:37)

The real issue here is not whether breaking up homes is wrong, but whether Israel will continue to be faithful to Yahweh only, or be drawn away to worship other gods through intermarriage. Jesus said there are two great commandments (Matthew 22:36-40):

1. Love the Lord your God with all your heart, soul, mind, and strength; and
2. Love your neighbor as yourself.

Our humanistic culture, which has no love for God, exalts the second commandment over the first, man over God, rather than the other way around.

Application Today

So how do we apply this principle today? Should Christians divorce their non-Christian spouses? No. One of the differences is that Ezra's situation affects the future of the entire Jewish nation. This is a national decision that will profoundly influence the nation's faithfulness to Yahweh for centuries to come. In our cases, we live in a pluralistic world, not in what was essentially a theocracy in Ezra's day.

The Apostle Paul, who wrote in a pluralistic culture where Christians were a small minority, speaks to Christians about this issue with two basic principles:

1. The Christian should stay with his non-believing spouse and their children if that is possible (1 Corinthians 7:12-16).

2. If the Christian's unbelieving spouse divorces him or her, the believer is free to remarry (1 Corinthians 7:15), but only another believer, "only in the Lord" (1 Corinthians 7:39). Christians are *not* to marry unbelievers!

I know that there is disagreement in the Christian community about whether, or under what conditions, a divorced person is free to remarry.[172] But we all agree that the Scripture is clear: Christians must *not* marry non-Christians.

Any association that impedes our full-out participation in the Kingdom of God should be examined, and if appropriate, ended. Business and social contacts shouldn't compromise our witness. As Paul put it, we need to keep from being "unequally yoked" (2 Corinthians 6:14).

Lessons for Disciples

Ezra 7-10 deals with very difficult issues that face many believers today. They know first-hand how a mixed marriage hinders their ability to set a Christian tone in the family, to raise their children in a clearly Christian environment, and to minister freely with one's free time. Nevertheless, we must not skirt hard issues when it comes to being disciples. Here are some things we can learn from this passage.

1. Ezra exercises gifts as a priest, as a teacher and scribe, as a recruiter, as a leader, as a man of faith, and as a civil administrator. Multi-gifted people like him can be used powerfully in the Kingdom of God. Are you one of these? Perhaps you can encourage someone you know like this to use his or her gifts to serve God.

2. Ezra calls people to fast, especially when they face a crisis. Fasting helps us humble ourselves before God, so we are more able to hear him when he speaks, and obey him when the path is clear. It helps us understand our complete reliance upon God (Ezra 8:21).

3. Ezra lives out his testimony about his faith. Since he has boasted about God's greatness to Artaxerxes, he doesn't feel he can ask for an armed escort, so he seeks God earnestly for help, and God hears. People have to see us practice what we preach (Ezra 8:21-23).

---

[172] You can see my careful exposition of 1 Corinthians 7 in my book *1 Corinthians: Discipleship Lessons from a Troubled Church* (JesusWalk Publications, 2014), chapter 7, or on my website at http://www.jesuswalk.com/1corinthians/07_marriage_divorce.htm

4. It is wise for churches and Christian groups to take steps to avoid the temptation to embezzle money (Ezra 8:24-30, 33-34).

5. We must take sin seriously. Sin in the body of Christ (or in our own lives) should cause deep grief within us (Ezra 9:3-4).

6. We are free to pray with a posture that is appropriate to the prayer. Ezra prayed on his knees with hands spread out to God, head bowed (Ezra 9:5-6).

7. When we pray for a people of whom we are part, we shouldn't confess *their* sins, but confess *our* sins. Ezra intercedes as a mediator, a priest, between his people and God (Ezra 9:6-7). While in the New Testament all are priests (1 Peter 2:5), there is still a need for some to lead the group in prayer and confession before God.

8. Ezra's sincere and earnest prayer sparks a spontaneous revival among his hearers (Ezra 10:1). Revival and renewal often begin with the example of others. People imitate us as we imitate Christ (1 Corinthians 11:1).

9. The Holy Spirit moves one of the assembly to offer a solution to the community's problem of intermarriage (Ezra 10:2-4). When we seek God together, he can bring his answer through any who are open to his voice – and we must be humble enough to receive it.

10. Ezra used oaths to hold people to their commitments. In our day, leaders can use formal promises to serve the same function (Ezra 10:5).

11. Life is complicated. Instead of implementing an across-the-board rule, Ezra and his team met with each head-of-household individually to talk about his situation and help him figure out how best to implement separation from his wife and children. It is a good leadership example to follow in working with individuals personally (Ezra 10:16-17).

12. Intermarriage with unbelievers weakens our own lives and witness – and weakens the Christian community of which we are part. We Christians are forbidden to marry non-believers. But if we are now married to a non-believer, we must not divorce them if they want to live with us (Ezra 9-10; 1 Corinthians 7:12-16, 39).

Prayer

Lord, you take sin much more seriously than we do. Please help us to grieve over our sins – enough that we will repent and turn from them. And help us as we seek to order our lives so that you are truly King! In Jesus' name, we pray. Amen.

Key Verses

"Ezra had devoted himself to the study and observance of the Law of the LORD, and to teaching its decrees and laws in Israel." (Ezra 7:10, NIV)

"I was ashamed to ask the king for soldiers and horsemen to protect us from enemies on the road, because we had told the king, 'The gracious hand of our God is on everyone who looks to him, but his great anger is against all who forsake him.' So we fasted and petitioned our God about this, and he answered our prayer." (Ezra 8:22-23)

"They have taken some of their daughters as wives for themselves and their sons, and have mingled the holy race with the peoples around them. And the leaders and officials have led the way in this unfaithfulness." (Ezra 9:2)

6. Nehemiah's Prayer (Nehemiah 1:1-2:8)

As the Book of Nehemiah opens, Jerusalem is in trouble. Judah's enemies, the Samaritans, have prevented the Jews from repairing Jerusalem's broken-down defenses. All seems to be lost. But God has a plan.

It just so happens that Nehemiah, a Jew, is a high official in the Persian government. He lives in "the citadel[173] of Susa," the royal palace, the winter capital of the kings of Persia, home previously to Esther[174] – 700 miles and five or six months journey from Jerusalem. Susa is one of the oldest cities in the world, going back to 5000 BC.

Nehemiah's name means "Yahweh comforts." We know nothing about his background other than that he is said to be "son of Hacaliah." In Hebrew Bibles, Ezra and Nehemiah are combined. They are divided into two books in the third century in Christian Bibles.

William Brassey Hole (1846-1917), 'Nehemiah Makes His Petition to Artaxerxes,' oil on canvas, in *The Holy Bible. Containing The Old And New Testaments* (Eyre & Spottiswoode, 1925).

As Nehemiah opens, we find Nehemiah as a trusted official in the king's court, "cupbearer[175] to the king" (Nehemiah 1:11b). The cupbearer was in charge of the king's wine, and would sometimes be called upon to drink some of it before the king, to make sure it didn't contain poison. This was a position of high confidence, since kings would be the focus of various assassination

---

[173] Citadel" (NIV, ESV), "capital" (NRSV), "palace" (KJV) is *bîrâ*, "palace," an Akkadian loan word (TWOT #240).

[174] Daniel may also have lived there for a time, for it is mentioned in one of his visions (Daniel 8:2).

[175] "Cupbearer" is *mashqeh*, from *shāqâ*, "give to drink" (TWOT #2452c).

plots that might include poisoning. (The previous king had been assassinated by his chief bodyguard). It is quite possible that Nehemiah is a eunuch, since a cupbearer would probably have had contact with the king's harem.[176] Since the cupbearer is constantly with the king, he is in a position of great influence, since he has the king's ear. The cupbearer is also well-paid, if Nehemiah's wealth is any indication (Nehemiah 5:8, 10, 14, 17).

Nehemiah is cupbearer to Artaxerxes Longimanus, the most powerful man in the world of his day, who reigns over the vast Persian Empire from 464 to 424 BC. He is the son of Xerxes I (486-465 BC, called Ahasuerus in the book of Esther). Xerxes is famous to people today as the Persian king during the 2006 movie "300," which features 300 Spartans against the massive Persian army. His son, Artaxerxes, reigns in contentious times as well. He wars on and off with Greek kings, and has put down a revolt in Egypt (460-454 BC). But Artaxerxes is sympathetic towards his cupbearer Nehemiah.

Nehemiah, the King's Cupbearer (Nehemiah 1:1)

Nehemiah's brother,[177] just back from Judah, gives him a distressing report. Nehemiah gives us the date – November-December 446 BC. The temple had been completed in 515 BC, but the walls of Jerusalem, which had been severely damaged when the city was destroyed by the Babylonians in 587 BC, have many sections that are still in disrepair.

As we'll see in a moment, Judah's enemies have obtained an injunction from Artaxerxes stopping repair of the walls of Jerusalem. The Samaritans have been zealous in following the king's command. Perhaps they have not only halted construction of Jerusalem's defenses, but have burned newly-built gates and demolished new attempts to repair breaches in the wall – we're not sure. Whatever has happened, it's clear that Jerusalem has no defenses, no functional gates, and a broken down wall. The news his brother brings is deeply troubling to Nehemiah.

> "Those who survived the exile and are back in the province are in great trouble[178] and disgrace.[179] The wall of Jerusalem is broken down, and its gates have been burned with fire." (Nehemiah 1:3)

---

[176] Fensham, *Ezra and Nehemiah*, p. 157.

[177] The word *āh* can mean, "brother, relative, fellow countryman, friend," so it is difficult to be certain of the relationship (Herbert Wolf, *'hh*, TWOT #62a).

[178] "Trouble" (NIV, NRSV, ESV), "affliction" is *ra'*, a very common noun with a range of meanings, from "bad, evil," to "times of distress" and "physical injury" (TWOT #2191a).

Petitions to Xerxes and Artaxerxes (Ezra 4:7-23)

Nehemiah has long known of the condition of Jerusalem's walls resulting from the Babylonians destruction of the city in 587 BC. That is not new.

But now he hears firsthand from his brother and other eyewitnesses of the implications of how Jerusalem's enemies have successfully petitioned Artaxerxes to strip away royal patronage and backing (Ezra 4:7-23).

In Lesson 1, we skipped Ezra 4:7-23 because it had been inserted out of chronological order among passages discussing the return and rebuilding of the temple (538 to 515 BC). These verses include letters sent by the enemies of the Jews to two successive Persian Kings – first to Xerxes (486-465 BC) and then to Artaxerxes (465-424 BC).

Here's my reconstruction of the chronology:

538 BC	The rebuilding begins
520 BC	The rebuilding resumes after an 18-year hiatus
486-465 BC	Letter to Xerxes, the Persian emperor who reigned 486-465 BC. He is the King Ahasuerus known from the story of Esther.
460-454 BC	Artaxerxes I (reigned 465-424 BC) at war in Egypt against Pharaoh Inaros II and Greek allies to put down serious revolt against Persian domination.
458 BC	Ezra receives authorization from Artaxerxes I authorizing him to take money and people to Jerusalem (Ezra 7).
457-445 BC	Enemies' letter to Artaxerxes, presumably after Ezra's initial mission, in which Artaxerxes countermands his support of the Jews under Ezra.
449 BC	Peace of Callias between Persia and the Greek city-states (Athens, etc.) that have been their opponents in the Mediterranean.
445 BC	Nehemiah serves as cupbearer to Artaxerxes I, and in Nov/Dec 445 BC goes to Jerusalem to repair its walls (Nehemiah 1:1) with renewed authorization from Artaxerxes.

The senders of the letter in Ezra 4:7-10 are primarily the Samaritans. Notice the complaint doesn't involve the rebuilding of the *temple*, but the rebuilding of the *city* and

---

[179] "Disgrace" (NIV), "shame" (NRSV, ESV), "reproach" (KJV) is *ḥerpâ*, "to reproach," with the specific connotation of casting blame or scorn on someone. An adversary might reproach with scorn, insults, or taunts (TWOT #749a).

its *walls,* which took place perhaps 75 years after the temple was rebuilt. The enemies write to Artaxerxes:

> "Be it known to the king that the Jews who came up from you to us have gone to Jerusalem. They are rebuilding that rebellious and wicked city. They are finishing the walls and repairing the foundations." (Ezra 4:12)

Ezra, who had been sent to Jerusalem with the king's commission in 458 BC, has been working to restore Jerusalem's walls. The Samaritans and other powers in the area are afraid that if Jerusalem's defenses are repaired, they can no longer threaten and dominate the Jews. So they write a deceptive and poisonous letter to Artaxerxes:

> "Now be it known to the king that if this city is rebuilt and the walls finished, they will not pay tribute, custom, or toll, and the royal revenue will be impaired.... We make known to the king that if this city is rebuilt and its walls finished, you will then have no possession in the province Beyond the River." (Ezra 4:13, 16)

This is a time when the Persian position in the southeastern Mediterranean is unsettled, with Egypt first threatening to rebel and then actual rebellion breaking out in 460 BC. Artaxerxes had sent Ezra to shore up Persian control of the area, but now he believes Judah's enemies, that Jerusalem is threatening to rebel. Fearful of more rebellion, and as a result of the enemies' deceitful petition, Artaxerxes issues an order to the Satrapy or Province Beyond the River:

> "Therefore make a decree that these men be made to cease, and that this city be not rebuilt, until a decree is made by me. And take care not to be slack in this matter. Why should damage grow to the hurt of the king?" (Ezra 4:21-22)

Jerusalem's enemies, now with royal backing, "went immediately to the Jews in Jerusalem and compelled them by force to stop" (Ezra 4:23). As Kidner puts it:

> "It was an ominous development, for the ring of hostile neighbors round Jerusalem could now claim royal backing. The patronage which Ezra had enjoyed (cf. Ezra 7:21–26) was suddenly in ruins, as completely as the city walls and gates. Jerusalem was not only disarmed but on its own."[180]

Deeply Moved (Nehemiah 1:4)

The expedition under Ezra that had begun with such hope and promise has been thwarted and Nehemiah's countrymen are "in great trouble and disgrace." It is the

---

[180] Kidner, *Ezra and Nehemiah*, p. 85.

report of this recent decree and its results that troubles Nehemiah so greatly. The Jews are utterly defenseless.

> "When I heard these things, I sat down and wept. For some days I mourned and fasted and prayed before the God of heaven." (Nehemiah 1:4)

Immortal Persian guard, glazed brick Frieze of Archers found in Darius the Great's palace in Susa, now in the Louvre, Paris.

He is deeply affected. Standing when he hears his brother's report, he sinks to the ground and sits. Then he begins to weep[181] and mourn,[182] probably with loud laments. Weeping and mourning were accompanied by fasting.[183] The suffering of his countrymen in Jerusalem is Nehemiah's suffering. Their shame is his shame.

We'll take this lesson to examine Nehemiah's prayer, one of the great prayers of the Bible.[184] In the next lesson we'll consider how Nehemiah goes about rebuilding the walls.

Great and Awesome God (Nehemiah 1:5-6a)

During his days of mourning, "day and night," Nehemiah has been praying essentially the same prayer, over and over again. Here, Nehemiah shares with us the basic elements of his prayer.

---

[181] *Bākā*, "to weep, cry, shed tears." Weeping is associated with the voice. Semites do not weep quietly, but aloud (John N. Oswalt, TWOT #243).

[182] *'Ābal*, "mourn, lament." Biblical mourning for the dead involved emotion, usually expressed audibly (Jeremiah 22:18; Jeremiah 48:36) and visibly (Genesis 37:34; Psalm 35:14; Micah 1:8; J. Barton Payne, *'ābal*, TWOT #6).

[183] *Sûm*, "fast." Fasting is depriving the body of nourishment as a sign that one is experiencing great sorrow. Mourning is further expressed in weeping and lamentation and in putting on sackcloth and ashes (Esther 4:3). He who fasts claims to afflict himself or his soul, i.e., his inner person" (John E. Hartley, TWOT #1890).

[184] A portion of this lesson is adapted from my book *Great Prayers of the Bible* (JesusWalk Publications, 2005, 2011).

Nehemiah's terminology seems to have some similarities with Daniel's prayer of confession (Daniel 9:4b-5), which isn't surprising since they were part of the same Jewish community in exile.

Nehemiah begins to pray[185] to the LORD (that is, God's revealed name, "Yahweh"), whom he describes as "the God of heaven," a phrase commonly used in the Persian empire. Like the Lord's Prayer, Nehemiah's salutation lifts his eyes to view the expansiveness of the Maker of the heavens.

The phrase, "great and awesome God" is striking. "Awesome" (NIV, NRSV, ESV) or "terrible" (KJV) is *yārē*, "be afraid, revere," which can refer to the emotion of fear as well as to "reverence or awe."[186] We don't like the idea of a terrible or dreadful God. We would rather think of God as our buddy or "home boy." No! God is awesome. He has immense power under his sole control.

I can remember holding my firstborn son on my shoulders as I walked along the beach at Fort Bragg, California. The Pacific breakers crashed upon the shore and rocks with great noise and power. I could feel my son was almost shuddering in fear. "God made the ocean, David," I told him. Yes, God is awesome in his power. He cannot be domesticated or tamed.

He is God in all his might and power! The refrain to Rick Mullins' praise chorus has brought this phrase into our worship vocabulary:

> "Our God is an awesome God
> He reigns from heaven above
> With wisdom, power, and love
> Our God is an awesome God."[187]

Like Daniel, Nehemiah recalls God's "covenant and steadfast love" (NRSV), which the people of Israel have broken by their disobedience. Then he asks God to give him a hearing. He is about ready to go in before the most powerful monarch of his day, Artaxerxes. But first he begs a hearing from the God of heaven upon whom he depends.

Notice that this is not a single prayer, but "the prayer your servant is praying before you day and night" (1:6a). This prayer is only the latest in a series of supplications that, as we will see, has lasted four months.

---

[185] *Pālal*, "intervene, interpose, pray," the most common OT word for prayer, which we've seen in previous lessons.

[186] Andrew Bowling, *yārē'*, TWOT #907; BDB 431d, "inspire reverence, godly fear, and awe, as an attribute of God." Deuteronomy 7:21; 10:17; Nehemiah 1:5; 4:8; 9:32; Daniel 9:4.

[187] "Awesome God," words and music by Rick Mullins, ©1988 BMG Songs, Inc. (ASCAP).

Q1. (Nehemiah 1:1-6) Why does Nehemiah pray day and night for four months? Why does he fast and weep? Isn't that excessive?
http://www.joyfulheart.com/forums/topic/1741-q1-continual-prayer/

Confession of Sins (Nehemiah 1:6b-7)

Now he comes to his confession of sins, placing himself among the sinners.

> "I confess the sins we Israelites, including myself and my father's house, have committed against you. We have acted very wickedly toward you. We have not obeyed the commands, decrees and laws you gave your servant Moses." (1:6b-7)

We examined confessing the sins of one's nation when we studied Ezra's prayer of confession in Lesson 5 (Ezra 9:6b-7). Both Ezra and Nehemiah place themselves with their people. They see themselves as part of this unrighteous people and confess the sins of the people on their behalf, a priestly role.

Reciting God's Promise to Moses (Nehemiah 1:8-9)

But let's go on to the basis for Nehemiah's prayer. He can't appeal to God on the basis of Israel's righteousness. What is his basis of appeal?

> "Remember the instruction you gave your servant Moses, saying, 'If you are unfaithful, I will **scatter** you among the nations, but if you return to me and obey my commands, then even if your exiled people are at the farthest horizon, I will **gather** them from there and bring them to the place I have chosen as a dwelling for my Name.'" (1:8-9)

These verses feature two common verbs: "to scatter" and "to gather."

The first verb, **"scatter,"** appears 64 times in the Old Testament – the scattering of an enemy's armies, the scattering of sheep, and most frequently of God scattering Israel (Leviticus 26:33; Deuteronomy 4:27; 28:64; 1 Kings 9:6). Hamilton observes, "It is not the Assyrians or Babylonians who scatter the people of God. They are simply instrumental. God himself is the scatterer." [188]

The second verb is "to **gather**." It is used of gathering food and of money, but most commonly of gathering people for social reasons, as an army, and for religious functions. The word is used many times for the gathering of God's people from their

---

[188] Victor P. Hamilton, *pûts*, TWOT #1745.

exile in Babylon (Ezra 1:1-4; Psalm 147:2; Jeremiah 32:37; Ezekiel 34:12-13; 36:24; Zechariah 8:7-8).[189] In the New Testament, ultimately, "gathering" refers to the gathering of the saints in the rapture (Matthew 3:12; 13:30; 24:31; 2 Thessalonians 2:1).

Now Nehemiah quotes back to God his own words and promises. He doesn't seem to have a single passage in mind, but draws his thoughts from several passages, particularly Deuteronomy 30:1-3. See the parallels between these:

The Curse of Scattering (Nehemiah 1:8)

"Remember the instruction you gave your servant Moses, saying, 'If you are unfaithful, I will scatter (*pûts*) you among the nations....'" (Nehemiah 1:8)

"When all these blessings and curses I have set before you come upon you and you take them to heart wherever the Lord your God disperses (*nādah*[190]) you among the nations...." (Deuteronomy 30:1)

The Blessings of Obedience (Nehemiah 1:9a)

"... But if you return to me and obey my commands, then even if your exiled people are at the farthest horizon...." (Nehemiah 1:9a)

"... And when you and your children return to the Lord your God and obey him with all your heart and with all your soul according to everything I command you today...." (Deuteronomy 30:2)

The Promise of Gathering (Nehemiah 1:9b)

"I will gather (*qābats*) them from there and bring them to the place I have chosen as a dwelling for my Name." (Nehemiah 1:9b)

"... Then the Lord your God will restore your fortunes and have compassion on you and gather (*qābats*) you again from all the nations where he scattered (*pûts*) you." (Deuteronomy 30:3)

God has scattered as he said he would, and he has gathered, according to his promise. There has been repentance and a renewed obedience among the returnees, Nehemiah is arguing.

---

[189] Leonard J. Coppes, *qābats*, TWOT #1983.
[190] Deuteronomy 30:1 uses the verb *nādah*, "impel, drive away, banish," the action of "forcibly driving or pushing something away."

The Dwelling Place of Your Name (Nehemiah 1:9b)

They have consequently been restored "to the place I have chosen as a dwelling for my Name" (Nehemiah 1:9). But Jerusalem's walls and gates are in ruins. The people are being oppressed in God's own city. You have a stake in the future of Jerusalem, Nehemiah contends, because it is the place where your Name dwells. When Jerusalem and God's people are in disgrace, it reflects on God's Name.

The Prayer of Your Servants (Nehemiah 1:10-11)

Nehemiah concludes his prayer by appealing to God for his servants:

"'They are your **servants** and your people, whom you redeemed by your great strength and your mighty hand. O Lord, let your ear be attentive to the prayer of this your **servant** and to the prayer of your **servants** who delight in revering your name. Give your **servant** success today by granting him favor in the presence of this man.' I was cupbearer to the king." (Nehemiah 1:10-11)

We might look upon being a servant as a lowly position. But it can also be looked at as an honor and a privilege. Nehemiah is a servant. As cupbearer to the king of Assyria, he is in a place of very high honor. In a society bound together by suzerain-vassal (king-servant) treaties, the servant has a duty towards the master, but the master also has a duty to protect the servant. It is a two-way covenant. Nehemiah makes two points about servants:

1. You redeemed your servants at great expense. (Nehemiah is probably referring to God delivering his people both from Egypt a thousand years before and from Babylon beginning in 539 BC.)
2. Your servants delight in honoring you.

Q2. (Nehemiah 1:7-11) What is the basis of Nehemiah's appeal? How does he argue his case before God? What do we learn from this about intercession?
http://www.joyfulheart.com/forums/topic/1742-q2-grounds-for-appeal/

Nehemiah's Two Petitions (Nehemiah 1:11)

On the basis of God's promise to restore his people to Jerusalem, and on the basis that God's servants are now calling upon his strength for protection, Nehemiah makes two petitions:

"**Let your ear be attentive to the prayer** of this your servant and to the prayer of your servants who delight in revering your name." (Nehemiah 1:11a)

"'Give your servant success today by **granting him favor in the presence of this man.**' I was cupbearer to the king." (Nehemiah 11:b)

Listen to our petition for Jerusalem, O God, and give me favor before the king, because I am *Your* servant.

The Danger of Nehemiah's Request

This second petition is no "slam-dunk." Artaxerxes' policy on Jerusalem had flip-flopped and there is no way to assess his current attitude toward Jerusalem.

As we have seen, in 458 BC Artaxerxes had ruled positively in favor of Ezra and given considerable money for the restoration of the temple and its sacrifices (Ezra 7:11-26). But recently, Artaxerxes' policy has turned against the Jews and Jerusalem, due to the court influence of their enemies (Ezra 4:17-23).

What Nehemiah is asking God is to give Nehemiah *so much favor* that the king will be willing to reverse himself yet again. That might be embarrassing for the king and make him look weak and inconsistent. Nehemiah is a trusted servant, granted, but he seems to be more of a personal servant in the role of cupbearer, than a secretary of state.

When he makes his request of the king, if the king is angry or offended, Nehemiah could quite easily lose his job or even his life! No king wants to feel manipulated, particularly by his servants, who might presume upon their position to ask for personal favors.

Parallels with Esther (Esther 4:13-16)

The situation sounds very much like the dilemma in which Esther found herself in this very palace some 35 to 40 years before. Haman, a high official in the court of the Persian king Xerxes (486-465/4 BC) and enemy of the Jews, has plotted to destroy the Jewish exile community living in the land. It "just so happened" that Xerxes' queen is Esther, a Jewess, but she can come into his presence only when she was summoned – upon pain of death – and she hasn't been summoned for the past 30 days (Esther 4:11). When a decree to annihilate the Jews is enacted, Esther's uncle Mordecai appeals to her to help her people:

"'Do not think that because you are in the king's house you alone of all the Jews will escape. For if you remain silent at this time, relief and deliverance for the Jews will arise from another place, but you and your father's family will perish. And who knows but that **you have come to royal position for such a time as this**?'

Then Esther sent this reply to Mordecai: 'Go, gather together all the Jews who are in Susa, and fast for me. Do not eat or drink for three days, night or day. I and my maids will fast as you do. When this is done, I will go to the king, even though it is against the law. **And if I perish, I perish**.'" (Esther 4:13-16)

Nehemiah's risk in bringing his request before the king is considerable. But he no doubt recognizes that God had elevated him to this position "for such a time as this." It is time for him to stand up and be counted with God's people. So Nehemiah prays fervently:

"'Give your servant success **today** by granting him favor in the presence of this man.' I was cupbearer to the king." (Nehemiah 1:11)

Today is the day he will make his request. Today he desperately needs God's help, for upon his success before the king hinges the success of God's people in far away Jerusalem.

> **Q3. (Nehemiah 1:11) In what way does Nehemiah's situation compare to Esther's? Why does God place his people in strategic positions today in the community, in business, in the military, in government? What responsibilities do we have to God that can cause danger to our positions and our lives? Has this ever happened to you? How do you pray in situations like this?**
> http://www.joyfulheart.com/forums/topic/1743-q3-strategic-witness/

Nehemiah prays for two things specifically: success[191] and favor.[192] He asks that some kind of bond of empathy or compassion will be formed between himself the king.

---

[191] "Success" (NIV, NRSV, ESV), "prosper" (KJV) is *tsālēah*, "prosper, succeed, be profitable," that is, "to accomplish satisfactorily what is intended" (2 Chronicles 26:5; 31:21; Joshua 1:8; Psalm 1:3; 118:25; Isaiah 55:11) (John E. Hartley, TWOT #1917).

[192] "Favor" (NIV) and "mercy" (KJV, NRSV) is *raḥămîm*, "tender mercy, compassion." The word can refer to the seat of one's emotions or the expression of one's deep emotion (Leonard J. Coppes, *rāḥam*, TWOT #2146).

In the Presence of the King (Nehemiah 2:1-4)

Nehemiah has humbled himself before God in weeping, mourning, and fasting. He has prayed. Now, four months after Nehemiah's initial receipt of the news about Jerusalem, the day has arrived. Nehemiah knows it.

Since the queen is present (Nehemiah 2:6), this probably isn't a public occasion, but likely the king and queen are being served in their apartment.

> "In the month of Nisan in the twentieth year of King Artaxerxes, when wine was brought for him, I took the wine and gave it to the king. I had not been sad in his presence before; so the king asked me, 'Why does your face look so sad when you are not ill? This can be nothing but sadness of heart.'" (Nehemiah 2:1-2)

Normally, servants are expected to mask their own personal feelings as they serve the monarch. But Nehemiah does not do this – purposely. Nehemiah isn't free to initiate any conversations with the king. He is a servant. But Nehemiah's countenance prompts a question from the king that Nehemiah is free to answer. In spite of the terror he feels, he says his piece, with respect, but with a clear boldness:

> "I was very much afraid, but I said to the king, "May the king live forever! Why should my face not look sad when the city where my fathers are buried lies in ruins, and its gates have been destroyed by fire?'" (Nehemiah 2:3)

Instead of apologizing for his sadness and covering up its causes as we so often do, he is open.

An Arrow Prayer (Nehemiah 2:4)

This is the crucial moment. The king can dismiss him from service and banish him forever from his presence. You must admit, his openness could be construed to put some blame on the king for Jerusalem's dire situation, since it resulted directly from the king's own policy.

> "The king said to me, 'What is it you want?'
> Then I prayed[193] to the God of heaven, and I answered the king...."
> (Nehemiah 2:4-5a)

The king asks what he wants, and – before he answers – Nehemiah prays a quick and silent prayer (sometimes called an "arrow prayer") to God for help. Then he answers the king.

---

[193] *Pālal*, the common verb for prayer is used both here and Nehemiah 1:4. The difference is quantitative, not qualitative.

You've prayed prayers like that. "Lord, help me! Lord, save me! Lord, give me strength!" But you may not have realized that "arrow prayers" are among the great prayers of the Bible prayed by God's servants for thousands of years when in dire straits.

It is important to observe, however, that Nehemiah's "arrow prayer" is not the *extent* of his prayer life, but rather the *overflow*. Nehemiah has agonized in prayer over this issue for days and months. The "arrow prayer" is but a continuation of Nehemiah's conversation and partnership with God about this issue.

> **Q4. (Nehemiah 2:4) What danger is Nehemiah in? Why does he pray quickly and silently before he answers the king? How does this quick "arrow prayer" relate to the four months of prayer he has just finished?**
> **http://www.joyfulheart.com/forums/topic/1744-q4-arrow-prayers/**

Request to Rebuild the City (Nehemiah 2:5-6)

The king has asked what he wants. Nehemiah's answer to the king is specific and well thought out:

> "And I answered the king, 'If it pleases the king and if your servant has found favor in his sight, let him send me to the city in Judah where my fathers are buried so that I can rebuild it.'
>
> Then the king, with the queen sitting beside him, asked me, 'How long will your journey take, and when will you get back?' It pleased the king to send me; so I set a time." (Nehemiah 2:5-6)

In the king's response, Nehemiah can sense that God has indeed given him favor. The king's concern is not whether he should go and rebuild Jerusalem, but how long he'll be gone.

Artaxerxes has just put down a rebellion in Egypt. He trusts Nehemiah to be loyal to him to increase Persia's military strength in an area close to Egypt, and to shore up Persian security in the region.

Request for Protection, Letters of Introduction, and Resources (Nehemiah 2:7-8)

But Nehemiah's prayer preparation about this matter means that he also knows what he needs from the king to have a successful outcome to his journey. Jerusalem's enemies must have a clear indication of the king's backing of Nehemiah's mission, since it signals a reversal in policy, so he spells it out.

> "7 I also said to him, 'If it pleases the king, may I have letters to the governors of Trans-Euphrates, so that they will provide me safe-conduct until I arrive in Judah? 8 And may I have a letter to Asaph, keeper of the king's forest, so he will give me timber to make beams for the gates of the citadel by the temple and for the city wall and for the residence I will occupy?'" (Nehemiah 2:7-8a)

At the crucial moment, Nehemiah is afraid, but through faith in the God of heaven he overcomes his fears, states the need, and makes his request of the king.

We aren't responsible for the result, only for our part. It is up to God to answer our prayer if we have prayed well and according to God's own will and purposes. In this case, Nehemiah reports:

> "And because the gracious hand of my God was upon me, the king granted my requests." (Nehemiah 2:8b)

It's interesting that while Ezra felt embarrassed to ask the king for a royal escort to protect from bandits during the dangerous journey (Ezra 8:22), Nehemiah doesn't. Faith differs, needs change, but God remains faithful.

Lessons for Disciples

When I reflect on Nehemiah's prayer, several lessons come to mind:

1. God can bring about reversal of the policies of superpowers to accomplish his purposes.
2. God has put on Nehemiah's heart the plight of his people. We can't solve the problems of every needy person in the world, but we are part of the solution for some. God will put some needs on our hearts. Sometimes we will feel God's sorrow and anguish for others and it may affect us deeply like it did Nehemiah – with weeping, sorrow, loss of appetite, fasting, humbling, and prayer.
3. Sometimes God sovereignly places us where we uniquely can help. He expects us to do our part where we're called.
4. As did Daniel, Nehemiah confesses the people's sins as his own.
5. Nehemiah appeals to God on the basis of his promises – in this case to restore his people to Jerusalem.
6. Nehemiah appeals to God on the basis of God's own Name and reputation.
7. Nehemiah appeals to God as a master on the basis of the needs of his servants.

8. Nehemiah prays for four months until it is time to bring the matter to the king. We must be patient in prayer and sensitive to the Lord's leading.
9. Nehemiah prays both at length in private and in brief spurts as the crisis unfolds.
10. Nehemiah acts on the basis of his prayer, willing to put himself in personal danger in order to see God's will accomplished.

Prayer

Lord, I pray for my brothers and sisters and me, that you would be able to trust us with the needs of others. That you would help us identify them. Give us vision, faith and courage. Help us not to be timid, but bold for you as we discern your will. Raise us up as your servants in every place and in every position of influence where you need your man or your woman to be faithful. And let us serve you there with faithfulness and in prayer. In Jesus' name, we pray. Amen.

Key Verses

"O Lord, let your ear be attentive to the prayer of this your servant and to the prayer of your servants who delight in revering your name. Give your servant success today by granting him favor in the presence of this man." (Nehemiah 1:11)

"Then I prayed to the God of heaven, and I answered the king...." (Nehemiah 2:4b-5a)

7. Restoring the Wall (Nehemiah 2:9-7:73)

God has answered Nehemiah's prayer and helped the Jews. And so Nehemiah begins the arduous journey along the Euphrates, across the desert to Syria, then south to Jerusalem.

He is a devout believer – and, as wine steward of the king, understands the world of palace intrigue. But does he have the skills to lead people? Yes. God, the ultimate Personnel Manager, has selected well. Nehemiah travels to Judah (the Persian province of Yehud (Judah) as the king's newly-appointed governor.

Consternation among Judah's Enemies (Nehemiah 2:9-10)

> "So I went to the governors of Trans-Euphrates and gave them the king's letters. The king had also sent army officers and cavalry with me." (Nehemiah 2:9)

James J. Tissot, 'Nehemiah Sees the Rubble in Jerusalem' (1896-1903), gouache on board, The Jewish Museum, New York.

Nehemiah's appearance, arriving in the cities of the Satrapy of Abar-Nahara ("Beyond the River") with royal cavalry escorting him, carrying letters from the king, has a devastating effect on Judah's enemies. Artaxerxes had approved their anti-Jewish building ban, but now that has been completely reversed. The Jews have royal authority to proceed with rebuilding Jerusalem's walls. Any interference could be construed as obstructing the king's command, so you'll notice in this lesson that most of their opposition amounts only to bluffs, rather than actual physical interference.

> "When Sanballat the Horonite and Tobiah the Ammonite official heard about this, they were very much disturbed that someone had come to promote the welfare of the Israelites." (Nehemiah 2:10)

More on Nehemiah's enemies shortly.

Nehemiah Inspects Jerusalem's Walls (Nehemiah 2:11-16)

Notice carefully Nehemiah's strategy. He is being closely watched, so he doesn't do much for his first three days in the city. Then he acts in secret.

> "[11] I went to Jerusalem, and after staying there three days [12] I set out during the night with a few men. I had not told anyone what my God had put in my heart to do for Jerusalem. There were no mounts with me except the one I was riding on.
>
> [13] By night I went out through the Valley Gate toward the Jackal Well and the Dung Gate, examining the walls of Jerusalem, which had been broken down, and its gates, which had been destroyed by fire. [14] Then I moved on toward the Fountain Gate and the King's Pool, but there was not enough room for my mount to get through; [15] so I went up the valley by night, examining the wall. Finally, I turned back and reentered through the Valley Gate." (Nehemiah 2:11-15)

Jerusalem in Nehemiah's Time
©2017, Ralph F. Wilson <pastor@joyfulheart.com>

We can't be sure about all the locations. However, the Valley Gate seems to open on the west into the Hinnom Valley.[194] The Dung Gate is about 500 yards south of the Valley Gate,[195] at the southwest corner of the wall, probably opposite the refuse heap of Jerusalem.[196] Perhaps it was a place of perpetual burning as garbage was burned there outside the city.[197] Dung Gate is probably an alternative name for the Potsherd (rubbish)

---

[194] The Valley Gate is also mentioned in 2 Chronicles 26:9.

[195] Nehemiah 3:13 says the two gates are separated by 1,000 cubits. A cubit is the distance from the finger tips to the elbow, usually about 18 inches or half a yard.

[196] J.A. Patch, "Dung," ISBE 1:996.

Gate of Jerusalem (Jeremiah 19:2). The Fountain Gate seems to have led to the spring En Rogel, while the Water Gate, farther north along the east wall of the city led to the Gihon spring. The King's Pool probably refers to what was later called the Pool of Siloam.[198]

> "The officials did not know where I had gone or what I was doing, because as yet I had said nothing to the Jews or the priests or nobles or officials or any others who would be doing the work." (Nehemiah 2:16)

Though it is often wise to work in collaboration with others where there is an agreed upon objective, in this case, Nehemiah doesn't yet have people in the city that he can trust. He must do his homework. If he presents his plan for rebuilding without careful study, it will be rejected out of hand. The response might be, "Who is this who comes from Susa to tell us what to do? What does he know?"

Nehemiah Reveals His Plan (Nehemiah 2:17-18)

So Nehemiah studies and plans in secret. Only when he is ready does he reveal his plan and work to get the local residents excited about it.

> "Then I said to them, 'You see the trouble we are in: Jerusalem lies in ruins, and its gates have been burned with fire. Come, let us rebuild the wall of Jerusalem, and we will no longer be in disgrace.'" (Nehemiah 2:17)

He begins with the obvious problem, then provides a solution, and explains the resources at his disposal.

> "I also told them about the gracious hand of my God upon me and what the king had said to me. They replied, 'Let us start rebuilding.' So they began this good work." (Nehemiah 2:18)

Nehemiah explains:

1. **Enemies**. King Artaxerxes has reversed his anti-building edict, and has sent Nehemiah with the specific task of rebuilding the walls. They now have the king's protection.

---

[197] D.J. Wieand, ("Hinnom, Valley of," ISBE 2:718) attributes this speculation to Lightfoot. The New Testament word *gehenna* comes from this, associated with the idea of fire and judgment. The Valley of Hinnom was to be a place of judgment (Jeremiah 19:6-7), and came to represent the eschatological place of judgment.

[198] Nehemiah 3:15 mentions "the pool of Shelah of the king's garden," a related Hebrew word (Kidner, *Ezra and Nehemiah*, p. 90).

2. **Leadership**. Nehemiah has been appointed governor of the province. As we'll see, he is a skilled leader.

3. **Materials**. The king has provided for the timbers necessary to rebuild the gates, as the original timbers had been destroyed when the city was burned by the Babylonians. Many other repairs can be made with the cut stones recoverable from the rubble of the previous walls.

4. **Labor**. As we'll see in Nehemiah 3, he presents a plan to divide up the huge project among the locals, so that the project doesn't seem as overwhelming.

Enemy Reactions (Nehemiah 2:19-20)

The enemies of the Jews don't take long to respond with an accusation.

"But when Sanballat the Horonite, Tobiah the Ammonite official and Geshem the Arab heard about it, they mocked and ridiculed us. 'What is this you are doing?' they asked. 'Are you rebelling against the king?'" (Nehemiah 2:19)

The enemies initially come with two responses: (1) ridicule, and (2) a renewed accusation of rebellion against Artaxerxes. At this time, Nehemiah doesn't waste time answering or defending their mocking. They know he has the king's authorization, so they are powerless to bring a new charge of rebellion, as they had previously (Ezra 4:7-23). Instead, he points to God's help and blessing.

"The God of heaven will give us success. We his servants will start rebuilding, but as for you, you have no share in Jerusalem or any claim or historic right to it." (Nehemiah 2:20)

As the king's governor of the province, Nehemiah denies them any role in the rebuilding project, as had Zerubbabel and Jeshua when the temple was rebuilt (Ezra 4:3). He knows that any offer to help that they make is insincere. Their real desire is to stop the project any way they can. So he excludes them from being part of the project.

Which Walls Were Rebuilt in Nehemiah's Time?

It is not clear exactly which walls were in place in Nehemiah's day. There is some attempt to repair the walls and gates when Ezra comes (Ezra 4:12-13), but that effort is stopped when Jerusalem's enemies complain to the king.

Some mapmakers in our day show a larger city in Nehemiah's time, but it had shrunk since its heyday under David and his descendants, and had few residents (Nehemiah 11). Apparently walls farther west had been abandoned, and the west wall of the city was now just east of the Hinnom Brook. At the top of the eastern ridge of the City of David, Nehemiah and the returned exiles build a new city wall. Although they simply repair the pre-existing walls elsewhere in the city, the wall just above the steep Kidron Valley is too damaged and too difficult to mend. So they relocate the eastern wall higher up the slope and, according to Eilat Mazar, build it directly on top of a ruined wall of King David's palace and its massive rampart.[199]

Builders of the Wall (Nehemiah 3)

Nehemiah 3 details how the wall is rebuilt. Nehemiah divides the task into 41 different sections, some larger, some smaller, according to the number and wealth of those recruited for the task.

Read this chapter, skipping all the hard-to-pronounce names. You'll see a number of wealthy individuals who take a section, involve their offspring in the task, or pay workmen to repair it. Mashullum son of Berechiah repair two sections (4:3, 30). In other cases, various organized groups take their parts.

- Priests from Jerusalem (verses 1, 22) and the surrounding region (verse 28)
- Goldsmiths (verses 8, 31-32)
- Perfume-makers (verse 9)
- Levites (verse 17)
- Temple servants (verse 26)
- Guard of the East Gate (verse 29)
- Merchants (verse 32)

Leaders from surrounding towns where the Jews lived, make their section a community project. They bring workers from their towns to complete their assigned portions. We see workers from:

---

[199] Leen and Kathleen Ritmeyer, *Jerusalem in the Time of Nehemiah* (Second Edition; Jerusalem: Carta, 2005, 2015); Etgar Lefkovits, "Nehemiah's wall uncovered," *Jerusalem Post*, November 28, 2007; Eilat Mazar, "The Wall That Nehemiah Built," *Biblical Archaeology Review* (Vol. 35, No. 2), March/April 2009.

- Jerusalem (verses 9, 12)
- Jericho (verse 2)
- Tekoa (verses 5, 27)
- Gibeon (verse 7)
- Mizpah (verses 7, 15, 19)
- Zanoah (verse 13)
- Beth Hakkerem (verse 14)
- Ben Zur (verse 16)
- Keilah (verses 17-18)

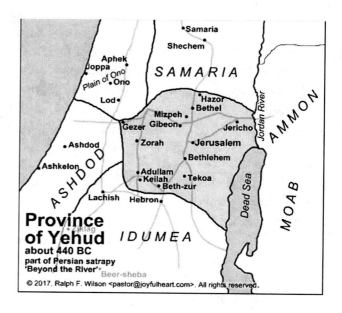

A number of people repair sections of the wall next to their houses (verses 23, 28-30). You can be sure they didn't want the sections of the wall close to their home to fail under attack!

We see a couple of interesting comments:

- "The nobles [of Tekoa] would not put their shoulders to the work under their supervisors" (verse 5). The nobles felt they were too good to work under a mere foreman. Pride.
- "Shallum … repaired the next section with the help of his daughters" (verse 12). Building isn't considered "woman's work," but Shallum's daughters are heavily involved in their father's project.

Rebuilding the Gates

Several times we read about the rebuilding of a gate.

"They laid its beams and put its doors and bolts[200] and bars in place" (Nehemiah 3:3, 6, 13-15).

Gates are the most vulnerable parts of a city's fortifications. Jerusalem in Nehemiah's time has nine gates. If one of these fails, the entire city can be taken. So they are built carefully.

---

[200] "Bolt" (NIV, ESV, NRSV), "lock" (KJV) is *man'āl*, "lock, bolt for gate" (Holland, p. 202). Used in Nehemiah 3:3, 6, 13, 14, 15.

A gate system would have a beam that supports the masonry above the gate opening. A pair of doors swing on projections that fit into sockets in the sill and lintel. The gates are made of heavy planks, perhaps plated with metal to keep them from burning (Psalm 107:16; Isaiah 45:2). The gate is locked at night with one or two large bars that are fitted into clamps on the doors. Above each gate are towers where defenders can rain down arrows, rocks, and perhaps fire upon attackers. [201]

Project Management

If you've ever managed a large project, you can understand that Nehemiah doesn't begin to rebuild three days after he arrives. Here's what Nehemiah's task entails:

1. **Assessing the task.** This begins with Nehemiah's night reconnaissance of the wall (Nehemiah 2:11-16).

2. **Communicating his vision of the completed wall.** Most of the Jews have lived in Judah for 10 to 70 years by the time Nehemiah comes. They are used to the status quo. Many are discouraged from previous setbacks. Others owe political favors to Nehemiah's enemies, especially Tobiah (Nehemiah 6:17-19). Nehemiah helps them understand the advantages of a completed wall and a secure city.

3. **Dividing the task into manageable sections.** This probably works in tandem with how many leaders he can recruit.

4. **Recruiting leaders** for each section, 41 in all. These are individuals who lead groups of men, or are wealthy enough to pay for workers to help. Nehemiah needs to convince them to take on such a project at their own expense! This must have taken some time, but has to be completed before construction begins so that work can take place simultaneously all around the city.

5. **Gathering materials** for the task includes ordering timber from Lebanon for the beams of the gate structures. Everything has to be on site before construction begins. Quarries supply stones to replace those that are unusable from the existing rubble.

6. **Training and Direction.** Nehemiah provides instruction and training for each of the 41 sectional teams. One of the first tasks, for example, is to clear the heaps of burned rubble and identify usable stones to place in the rebuilt wall (Nehemiah 4:2, 10). That alone takes a great deal of labor. Each team needs instruction in how

---

[201] Burton Scott Easton, Ralph W. Vunderink, "Gate, ISBE 2:408; Keith N. Schoville, "Fortification," ISBE 2:346-354.

to move and set huge stones. Some teams have to reconstruct complex gates and towers.

7. **Building a Management Team.** Nehemiah doubtless assembles a management team to handle different aspects of the project. He probably appoints several leaders, each of whom manages several of the 41 wall construction teams, as well as logistics manager and military commanders to organize the defense.

We're not told how long these preparations take. But when they begin, the people work with all their heart and the entire project is completed in under two months.

> "The wall was completed on the twenty-fifth of Elul, in fifty-two days." (Nehemiah 6:15-16)

But we're getting ahead of ourselves. During construction Nehemiah is working hard as well.

8. **Ongoing management of people and problems.** When you have 41 teams working simultaneously, you are required to manage personalities and problems, competition for resources, and unanticipated needs that occur.

9. **Security.** We see in Nehemiah 4:16-21 that partway through the rebuilding project Nehemiah had to assign half his workforce to defense. This slows completion, but is necessary. Since the workforce is made up of 41 teams, managing defense is a complex task.

Where does Nehemiah get the experience and ability to lead such a huge task? We're not sure of all the roles required of a cupbearer to the Persian king. Did he lead a staff in the palace? Perhaps. Certainly he observed how the king organized and delegated authority. It's obvious that Artaxerxes has confidence in his abilities, or he wouldn't have sent him with the authority of governor. No doubt, Nehemiah is a remarkable leader.

As governor, Nehemiah supervises the entire project, but it could have been completed in less than two months *only* if it were superbly organized and supervised.

Why try to build the wall all at once rather than in pieces, one at a time? I see two main reasons:

1. **Security.** The city needs immediate security. A years-long wall construction process would have given many opportunities for military attacks by Jerusalem's enemies. A quick construction gives the enemy only a narrow window of time to attack, and Nehemiah's heavy guard forestalls such an attack until the wall is complete.

2. **Forestalling appeals.** Jerusalem's enemies have a history of stopping wall repair by appeals to the Persian king (Ezra 4:5-23; 5:1-17). With a two-month construction period, there isn't enough time to send a message to Mesopotamia and then get back a reply before the wall is fully repaired. At that point, any order to cease repair is moot.

Q1. (Nehemiah 3) Why does Nehemiah need to build the walls quickly? Why does he assign so many teams? What motivates these teams? What kinds of problems would Nehemiah need to solve with so many teams working simultaneously? http://www.joyfulheart.com/forums/topic/1745-q1-team-building/

Opposition to Rebuilding (Nehemiah 4)

The Scripture lists three primary enemy leaders.

1. **Sanballat the Horonite.** Sanballat leads the Samaritan opposition. According to an Aramaic papyri from Elephantine, he is governor of the Persian province of Syria. Sanballat I is contemporary with Nehemiah, about 444 BC. Later, the son of Jehoiada marries his daughter (Nehemiah 13:28).[202]

2. **Tobiah the Ammonite official.** He may have had the status of governor over Ammonite territory, east of Judah. A family by his name is prominent in Ammon during the Persian period. Tobiah seems be of Jewish descent and has close ties to the temple and Jewish nobility. Many influential people are bound to him by oaths (Nehemiah 6:17-19), making him particularly dangerous, since he has a lot to lose from Nehemiah's reforms. He also occupies a chamber in the temple precincts during Nehemiah's absence from Jerusalem (Nehemiah 13:4-9), threatens military raids against Jerusalem while the walls were being built (Nehemiah 4:7-9), and seeks to lure Nehemiah out of the city to assassinate him (Nehemiah 6:1-3). [203]

3. **Geshem the Arab** seems to be the chief of an Arabian tribe that has settled in the area (Nehemiah 2:19; 6:1-2, 6). His name appears on a silver vessel about 40 years after Nehemiah's time. Apparently, Geshem and his son rule a league of Arabian

[202] William S. LaSor, "Sanballat," ISBE 4:321.
[203] A.E. Hill, "Tobiah," ISBE 4:865.

tribes that have taken control of Moab and Edom, to the south and east of Judah.[204]

Taunts from the Enemies (Nehemiah 4:1-6)

Certainly the surrounding province leaders are worried as the project begins. In chapter 4 we meet Sanballat and his associate Tobiah.

> "When Sanballat heard that we were rebuilding the wall, he became angry and was greatly incensed."[205] (Nehemiah 4:1a)

Sanballat is extremely upset. The defenseless city over which could previously exercise some control, is repairing its fortifications. Soon it will be impregnable – and independent from his domination. So he and his associate resort to mocking and jeering.

> "[1b] He ridiculed the Jews, [2] and in the presence of his associates and the army of Samaria, he said, 'What are those feeble Jews doing? Will they restore their wall? Will they offer sacrifices? Will they finish in a day? Can they bring the stones back to life from those heaps of rubble – burned as they are?'
>
> [3] Tobiah the Ammonite, who was at his side, said, 'What they are building – if even a fox climbed up on it, he would break down their wall of stones!'" (Nehemiah 4:1b-3)

The Jews have tried to rebuild the walls before and failed. Again, Sanballat and Tobiah try to undermine their confidence. The reference to sacrifice may mean something like, "Do you expect to pray the wall into existence?" They point out the huge amount of work involved in recovering the stones from the piles of rubble – and indeed it was hard, tiring work (Nehemiah 4:10).

When we seek to serve the Lord, sometimes our friends mock us and tell us that we can't do it, that we'll fall back into our old ways. Sometimes, when we sin, Satan mocks us. "What a hypocrite you are! You claim to be a Christian, but you keep doing the same sins." But with God, we can rise above failure. The answer is to look to God for help.

---

[204] Kidner, *Ezra and Nehemiah*, pp. 83-84; J.J. Reeve, "Geshem," ISBE 2:449.

[205] "Become angry" (NIV, ESV), "furious" (NRSV), "wroth" (KJV) is the verb *ḥārâ*, "burn, be kindled (of anger)." The root is related to an Aramaic root, "to cause fire to burn." In Hebrew it's always used to refer to anger. (TWOT #736). "Was greatly incensed" (NIV), "very angry" (NRSV), "greatly enraged" (ESV), "took great indignation" (KJV) is the adverb *rābâ*, "great, much, numerous" plus the verb *kāʿas*, "to vex, agitate, stir up, or provoke the heart to a heated condition which in turn leads to specific actions" (Gerard Van Gronigen, TWOT #1016)

Instead of wasting time answering the insults[206] of the enemy, or demanding a duel or battle to vindicate the Jews, Nehemiah calls upon God to vindicate their cause (Nehemiah 4:4-5) – just as Jesus did not answer his accusers and those who mocked him (1 Peter 2:23).

The Jews ignore the insults and keep working. Good morale and diligent leadership keep them moving forward.

> "So we rebuilt the wall till all of it reached half its height, for the people worked with all their heart." (Nehemiah 4:6)

As other translations put it, "the people had a mind to work" (NRSV, ESV, KJV).[207] This refers to the Jews' morale, vision, hope, and will. They enthusiastically build until all the gaps are closed – at least to half the height. Now any would-be attackers will be forced to scale some height of wall at the very least.

Threat of Attack (Nehemiah 4:7-9)

But morale is a fickle thing. It can turn to despair and discouragement. It is that morale that Judah's enemies try to attack next, this time with fear.

> "7 But when Sanballat, Tobiah, the Arabs, the Ammonites and the men of Ashdod heard that the repairs to Jerusalem's walls had gone ahead and that the gaps were being closed, they were very angry. 8 They all plotted together to come and fight against Jerusalem and stir up trouble against it." (Nehemiah 4:7-8)

Those who want to keep Judah weak are upset at the Jews' progress. If they're going to stop the Jews with military force, they need to do it before the wall gets any higher.

We've met most of these enemies before – Sanballat, Tobiah, and Gesher. But "the men of Ashdod" is a new threat. Ashdod is an old Philistine city on the Mediterranean, about 40 miles (62 kilometers) west of Jerusalem. Ashdod still has interests in the area, and later intermarries with the Jews – against God's command (Nehemiah 13:3-4).

---

[206] "Despised" (verse 4a) is the noun *bûzâ*, "contempt," from *bûz*, "despise, hold as insignificant" (Elmer A. Martens, TWOT #213b). In verse 4b, "insults" (NIV), "reproach" (NRSV), "taunt" (ESV), "despised" (KJV) is the noun *ḥerpâ*, from *ḥārap*, "to reproach," with the specific connotation of casting blame or scorn on someone (Thomas E. McComiskey, TWOT #749).

[207] The noun is *lēb*, "heart, understanding, mind." It is "the richest biblical term for the totality of man's inner or immaterial nature ... either to the inner or immaterial nature in general or to one of the three traditional personality functions of man; emotion, thought, or will" (Andrew Bowling, TWOT #1071a).

Sanballat seems to have organized this military alliance[208] to attack Jerusalem.[209] Nehemiah responds with a two-fold strategy:

> "But we prayed to our God and posted a guard day and night to meet this threat." (Nehemiah 4:9)

Nehemiah begins with prayer. God is the nation's ultimate Protector. First, Nehemiah seeks Him. Then he responds with practical action by posting a 24-hour guard to protect the city, soon to be strengthened further by arming the workers themselves (verses 13-23).

Sometimes people think that if you pray, you shouldn't take any action yourself. To do so would indicate distrust in God, they say. But the Biblical pattern is to pray and then to take whatever action God seems to show you. We pray that God will meet all our needs, but we also seek a job. These are not incompatible.

Discouragement and Fear (Nehemiah 4:10-13)

Nehemiah faces an external threat from Judah's enemies, but also twin internal threats: discouragement and fear.

The wall is half its height, but the workers are exhausted. Can they keep up the pace that Nehemiah has set to complete the project? There are the inevitable complainers and whiners.

> "The strength of the laborers is giving out, and there is so much rubble that we cannot rebuild the wall." (Nehemiah 4:10)

In addition to exhaustion, there is fear, which can be contagious. The enemies' fear campaign is having an effect on morale.

> "[11] Also our enemies said, 'Before they know it or see us, we will be right there among them and will kill them and put an end to the work.' [12] Then the Jews who lived near them came and told us ten times over, 'Wherever you turn, they will attack us.'" (Nehemiah 4:11-12)

It sounds like some were panicking and spreading their fears.

---

[208] "Plotted" (NIV, ESV), "conspired" (NRSV, KJV) is the Qal stem of *qāshar*, "bind, conspire." The basic idea is to bind or tie something to something else. Here it refers to people binding together in a pact or military alliance (Leonard J. Coppes, TWOT #2090).

[209] "Fight" is *lāḥam*, "fight, do battle." "Stir up trouble" (NIV), "cause a disturbance" (NRSV), "cause confusion" (ESV), "hinder" (KJV) is the verb "to make" plus the noun, *tôʿâ*, "error," from the noun "err, stagger, stray, wander." Holladay (*Hebrew Lexicon*, p. 388) defines the noun as "confusion, chaos, perversion."

Whether or not the fear is warranted, Nehemiah realizes that even the *perception* of danger can derail the rebuilding project. So he develops a two-fold plan to provide a defense: (1) reinforce the most vulnerable places in the wall, and (2) arm the workers so as to provide security even while they are working.

Reinforcing the Low Points, Encouraging Faith (Nehemiah 4:13-14)

Nehemiah gives orders to reinforce the guard at the weakest parts of the wall.

> "13 Therefore I stationed some of the people behind the lowest points of the wall at the exposed places, posting them by families, with their swords, spears and bows. 14 After I looked things over, I stood up and said to the nobles, the officials and the rest of the people, 'Don't be afraid of them. Remember the Lord, who is great and awesome, and fight for your brothers, your sons and your daughters, your wives and your homes.'" (Nehemiah 4:13-14)

Nehemiah makes sure the defense force is well-armed and placed strategically. This is not a professional army; none is available. Rather, he uses family groups, knowing that family members will fight ferociously for each other. Then he gives them a pep-talk:

1. Don't be afraid.
2. Remember the Lord's awesome power.
3. Fight for your families. He reminds them that they're not defending Jerusalem because they've been conscripted. He makes it personal. This is a personal battle for your family's survival. And to underscore the point, he has family groups and clans fighting alongside each other.

Nehemiah takes prudent actions to defend the city and rebuild it, but he is fully aware that it is the Lord who is the real Defender and Builder.

> "Unless the LORD builds the house,
> its builders labor in vain.
> Unless the LORD watches over the city,
> the watchmen stand guard in vain." (Psalm 127:1)

Nehemiah's response is effective.

> "When our enemies heard that we were aware of their plot and that God had frustrated it, we all returned to the wall, each to his own work." (Nehemiah 4:15)

Judah's enemies see Jerusalem's walls bristling with armed men and they know they have lost the element of surprise. God has "frustrated" their plot.[210] Even more important, the Jews feel secure enough to return to the task of rebuilding. Rather than giving up the work in panic and confusion, they resume the task with even greater focus, because they realize of the consequences if they fail to complete the wall.

Guarding the Builders (artist unknown)

Citizen Soldiers (Nehemiah 4:16-23)

Nehemiah doesn't relax his vigilance once the immediate threat has been overcome. Rather, he directs that each group of workers has its own armed guard – half guarding, half working.

> "16 From that day on, half of my men did the work, while the other half were equipped with spears, shields, bows and armor. The officers posted themselves behind all the people of Judah 17 who were building the wall. Those who carried materials did their work with one hand and held a weapon in the other, 18 and each of the builders wore his sword at his side as he worked." (Nehemiah 4:16-18a)

The result of this is a sudden drop in productivity, since defense takes a great investment in personnel. But it is necessary.

Nehemiah arranges a signal: "When you hear the sound of my trumpet, gather to me and fight" (Nehemiah 4:18b-21).

As part of the defense, Nehemiah has all the workers stay inside the city at night rather than returning to their villages outside the city. Moreover, Nehemiah and his

---

[210] "Frustrated their plan" (NIV, NRSV, ESV), "brought their counsel to naught" (KJV) uses the verb *pārar*, "break, destroy, frustrate, invalidate…. *Pārar* has a moral overtone. It does not mean 'to break' in the sense of an exhibition of physical strength, but to violate or renege on revealed truth" (Victor P. Hamilton, TWOT #1829) In this case the enemy's "plot" (NIV), "plan" (NRSV, ESV), or "counsel" (KJV) has been revealed. The noun is *ēṣâ* (TWOT #887a).

bodyguards set the personal example of constant preparedness. What the people see their leaders doing, they are likely to emulate (Nehemiah 4:1-23).

When all is said and done, the huge personnel commitment to defense has the result that Jerusalem's enemies are afraid to attack. And so the restoration continues to completion – more slowly, yes, but safely.

Rebuilding the Walls of Our Lives

Bible expositor Ray Stedman (1917-1992) observes,

> "You will never build the walls of your life until you have first become greatly concerned about the ruins. Have you ever taken a good look at the ruins in your own life?"[211]

Leaning to protect ourselves from Satan's attacks is vital. If we are so vulnerable to temptation that Satan can savage our lives at will, we find it difficult to grow. Sometimes we blithely go through our lives without understanding of the enemy's plots and devices (2 Corinthians 2:10-11). We don't take the devil's power seriously, and fail daily to arm ourselves. We identify triggers that lead to sin, for example, and take steps to avoid those situations.

Paul issues a militant command:

> "[10] Finally, be strong in the Lord and in his mighty power. [11] Put on the full armor of God so that you can take your stand against the devil's schemes. [12] For our struggle is not against flesh and blood, but against the rulers, against the authorities, against the powers of this dark world and against the spiritual forces of evil in the heavenly realms. [13] Therefore put on the full armor of God, so that when the day of evil comes, you may be able to stand your ground, and after you have done everything, to stand." (Ephesians 6:10-13)

When we live our days prepared for battle, we're much less likely to be attacked in our areas of weakness. Time invested in our own spiritual preparedness and defense allows us to continue our work on God's priorities without being distracted so easily by sin.

> **Q2. (Nehemiah 4) How does Nehemiah respond to his enemies' ridicule? How does Nehemiah respond to military threats? What effect does this have on construction? How does Nehemiah respond to discouragement and fear in the people? How do you respond to discouragement and fear? What "walls" need to be rebuilt**

---

[211] Ray C. Stedman, "Reading Nehemiah," RayStedman.org

in your life to protect you from temptation and sin?
http://www.joyfulheart.com/forums/topic/1746-q2-threat-response/

Dealing with Greed and Disregard for the Poor (Nehemiah 5:1-18)

But now another problem comes to Nehemiah's attention – greed and disregard for the poor. This isn't directly related to the effort to build the wall – but it may have been addressed during this period. The wall rebuilding project takes a great deal of men away from tending the crops.

Under normal conditions, the people are surviving and even prospering. But now, drought and resulting famine stress the entire economy.

> "¹ Now the men and their wives raised a great outcry against their Jewish brothers. ²
> Some were saying, 'We and our sons and daughters are numerous; in order for us to
> eat and stay alive, we must get grain.' ³ Others were saying, 'We are mortgaging our
> fields, our vineyards and our homes to get grain during the famine.' ⁴ Still others
> were saying, 'We have had to borrow money to pay the king's tax on our fields and
> vineyards. ⁵ Although we are of the same flesh and blood as our countrymen and
> though our sons are as good as theirs, yet we have to subject our sons and daughters
> to slavery. Some of our daughters have already been enslaved, but we are power-
> less, because our fields and our vineyards belong to others.'" (Nehemiah 5:1-5)

Their crops fail and they are forced to purchase food. Demand causes food prices to skyrocket. To pay the high prices, people have to borrow at high interest rates to be able to feed their families. If farmers want to plant, the price of seed is high, and any future crop may be lost due to the drought. An economic and social disaster is going on. And through it all, the rich are getting richer and the poor are getting poorer. It reminds me of all the people who lost their farms in the Dust Bowl and Depression in 1930s America.

The results of this inflationary cycle are heartbreaking.

1. **Slavery**. Those without lands are being sold into slavery to repay the money they
   borrowed to buy food. Moreover, to avoid restrictions on slavery within Judaism,
   some are being sold to Gentiles whose law offers less legal protection for the
   slaves (Nehemiah 5:5-6). Families are being torn apart.

2. **Mortgage Defaults**. Landowners use their lands for collateral, and forfeit them when they can't repay the mortgage fast enough.[212] Some who have had to sell their property, now find no way to repay their loans. Slavery is next.
3. **High taxes**. Landowners suffer under high Persian taxation.
4. **Lack of compassion**. The rich don't care about their poor countrymen, only about taking advantage of the situation to increase their own fortunes.

Loans and Usury in Mosaic Law

High interest rates seem to be at the root of the problem – which are clearly contrary to Mosaic Law.

> "If you lend money to one of my people among you who is needy, do not be like a moneylender; charge him no interest." (Exodus 22:25; cf. Leviticus 25:35-37; Deuteronomy 15:7-8; 23:19-20a)

The Mosaic Law isn't talking about interest on a loan to expand a business, purchase a house, buy an automobile, or increase one's standard of living. It's talking about lending money needed for the poor to survive – for basic food. Throughout the Scripture, God is portrayed as One who has compassion for the widow and orphan, as the Defender of the poor; He commands his people to have the same attitude.

Nehemiah calls a large general meeting to deal with the situation. In it he publicly exposes the heartlessness of the rich and demands change.

> "6 When I heard their outcry and these charges, I was very angry. 7 I pondered them in my mind and then accused the nobles and officials. I told them, 'You are exacting usury from your own countrymen!'" (Nehemiah 5:6-7)

Nehemiah uses his authority as governor to severely and publicly reprimand the rich who are taking advantage of the poor. They are embarrassed and have nothing to say in their defense. Then Nehemiah:

1. **Buys back Jews sold into slavery to Gentiles** and forbids the sale of other Jews to pay their debts (verses 8-9).

2. **Demands the end of high interest rates**, exacting usury.[213] Verse 11 is difficult, but it seems that Nehemiah is limiting interest rates to 1% per month. He asserts

---

[212] "Mortgaging" is 'ārab, "to be / become surety, mortgage, pledge" (Ronald B. Allen, TWOT #1686).

[213] "Exacting usury" (NIV, NRSV, cf. KJV), "exacting interest" (ESV) in verses 7 and 10 is maśśā', "Load, burden, lifting, bearing, tribute," from nāśā', "lift, carry, take" (TWOT #1421d). Holladay sees this as "burden = hardship." This isn't the Hebrew word for usury, but that seems to be the meaning. See Kidner, *Ezra and Nehemiah*, pp. 95-96.

that he and his people have made loans to people so they can buy food to eat, but they too will abide by the new limited interest rates (verse 10).

3. Demands the **return of confiscated lands** to their original owners (verse 11a).

4. Demands the **refund of excessive interest** – or of income derived from the confiscated lands[214] (verse 11b).

5. **Cuts taxes** required to support the governor (verses 14-19).

6. **Pronounces a curse** on those who don't comply (verse 13a).

In the public meeting, the shamed nobles and officials agree to Nehemiah's demands. Not taking them at their word, he calls for the priests and administers oaths that will legally bind them to their promises (similar to Ezra demanding oaths from leaders in Ezra 10:5).

Foregoing the Governor's Rights (Nehemiah 5:14-19)

For his part, Nehemiah refuses to tax the people to pay for his maintenance as Persian governor of the province. He notes that previous governors have taken advantage of their office, but he refuses to. And he asks God to remember his good deeds. His prayer may sound a bit self-serving – but then so do some of mine.

> **Q3. (Nehemiah 5) Why doesn't Nehemiah wait until he isn't so busy to deal with the complaints of the poor who are being oppressed? What is the chief motivation of their oppressors? How does Nehemiah deal with the issue? Why are church leaders sometimes quicker to deal with the complaints of the wealthy than those of the poor? What motivates these leaders?**
> **http://www.joyfulheart.com/forums/topic/1747-q3-oppressing-the-poor/**

A Plan to Assassinate Nehemiah (Nehemiah 6:1-9)

The wall is almost finished and Nehemiah's enemies are desperate.

"¹ When word came to Sanballat, Tobiah, Geshem the Arab and the rest of our enemies that I had rebuilt the wall and not a gap was left in it – though up to that time I had not set the doors in the gates – ² Sanballat and Geshem sent me this message: 'Come, let us meet together in one of the villages on the plain of Ono.'

---

[214] So Kidner, *Ezra and Nehemiah*, p. 105; and the New English Bible.

But they were scheming to harm me; [3] so I sent messengers to them with this reply: 'I am carrying on a great project and cannot go down. Why should the work stop while I leave it and go down to you?' [4] Four times they sent me the same message, and each time I gave them the same answer." (Nehemiah 6:1-4)

Sanballat and his fellow conspirators ask Nehemiah to attend a meeting on the "plain of Ono," a location about 37 miles (60 km) northwest of Jerusalem near the coast, a day's journey away.[215] This is a substantial distance from the safety of Jerusalem, and would expose Nehemiah to considerable danger. Perhaps they sweeten the offer by including him in a kind of regional summit with other leaders – something that would appeal to his ego. But Nehemiah sees through it and says, "I'm too busy." "A great work" (NRSV, ESV, KJV), which suggests self-praise, is probably better translated "a great project" (NIV) or "task."[216]

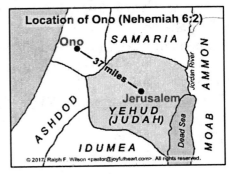

So they try another tactic. They threaten to tell the king that Jerusalem intended to rebel from Persian control. "Come," they said, "let's negotiate this." Nehemiah refuses that invitation as well (verses 5-7).

"I sent him this reply: 'Nothing like what you are saying is happening; you are just making it up out of your head.'" (Nehemiah 6:8)

Judeans would be afraid, since such a threat had been carried out successfully by previous enemies (Ezra 4:6-23). But Nehemiah realizes that delaying out of fear plays into his enemies' hands. If the Jews keep working the walls and gates, they will be completed long before any order from the king can be received.

"They were all trying to frighten us, thinking, 'Their hands will get too weak for the work, and it will not be completed.' [But I prayed,] 'Now strengthen my hands.'" (Nehemiah 6:9)

The Jews remain at work, putting the finishing touches on the walls and gates.

---

[215] Ono is the site of the present day town of Kafr 'Anam (Hebrew, Or Yehuda), an eastern suburb of Tel Aviv.

[216] Kidner, *Ezra and Nehemiah*, p. 107.

A Plot to Lead Nehemiah into Sin (Nehemiah 6:10-14)

When these conspiracies fail to sidetrack Nehemiah, his enemies try something much more subtle – prophecies intended to frighten[217] Nehemiah and lead him into sin. The conspirators are the prophet Shemaiah (Hebrew, "Yahweh has heard") and a prophetess named Noadiah (Hebrew, "appointed by Yahweh") and others, paid by Tobiah and Sanballat to prophesy falsely. These leaders among the prophets are people of influence who have been corrupted by bribes.

The prophet Shemaiah is confined to his house – perhaps for some kind of ritual defilement.[218] He calls for Nehemiah to visit him, and, in the privacy of his home, he prophesies that Nehemiah is in danger of an assassination plot and should take refuge from his enemies in the temple in order to preserve his life. He tries to frighten[219] Nehemiah so he'll panic and sin, but Nehemiah sees through the ruse.

Corrupt Prophets

It's a heavy thing when a prophet of God speaks a word to you. But God helps Nehemiah discern that it isn't God motivating this prophet, but Satan. Shemaiah, once one who listened to God, now listens to those who pay him.

Dear friends, this happens today. A man or woman of God – maybe you – begins sincerely following God, listening for his voice, and being obedient. But somewhere along the line, perhaps out of fear of not having enough, or valuing too much what money will buy (greed), he or she stops listening to God so closely and starts following the money. The wealthy people in the church or ministry have a louder voice. The church board succeeds in controlling their spiritual leader by the salary they pay (or don't pay). And the servant of God becomes corrupted by money. He or she will do whatever is necessary to secure a living, an income. The leader is now corrupt, serving Mammon (Matthew 6:24).

Shemaiah is corrupted by money. He is paid to try to manipulate Nehemiah through fear to induce him to commit sin by going into the temple building.

---

[217] "Discredit" (NIV), "reproach" (NRSV, KJV), "taunt" (ESV) is the Piel stem of *ḥārap*, "taunt, reproach" (Holladay, *Hebrew Lexicon*, p. 117).

[218] For example, see Numbers 19:11-13.

[219] "Intimidate" (NIV) in verses 13 and 14 is "become frightened" (NRSV), "be afraid" (ESV, KJV) is the Qal stem (vs. 13) *yārē'*, "fear, be afraid." The Piel stem in vs. 9, 14, 19 means "to overawe, alarm" (Holladay, *Hebrew Lexicon*, p. 142-143).

Attempt to Compromise Nehemiah's Integrity (Nehemiah 6:13)

Nehemiah, though governor of the province of Judah, is not allowed to go into the temple building for two reasons: (1) he has probably been castrated as a eunuch, and thus seems to be excluded from temple worship by Mosaic Law (Deuteronomy 23:1), and (2) he is not a priest or Levite. The Scripture instructs Aaron and his sons:

> "Let no one enter the house of the LORD except the priests and ministering Levites. They may enter, for they are holy...." (2 Chronicles 23:6a; also Numbers 18:7)

Kidner observes, "King Uzziah trespassing, had been fortunate to escape with no more than leprosy (2 Chronicles 26:16-21)."[220]

The Jews' enemies can't get Nehemiah in a vulnerable place to assassinate him. And as the Persian governor, he is politically untouchable. But if they can get him to break the Mosaic Law, his enemies have cause to discredit him among the Jews, destroying his reputation and ability to lead, and thus derailing the wall-building project just before it can be completed. Paying for the corrupt prophet's false words is Sanballat's and Tobiah's last attempt to stop Jerusalem from becoming secure. They fail.

Nehemiah prays for justice against his enemies:

> "Remember Tobiah and Sanballat, O my God, because of what they have done; remember also the prophetess Noadiah and the rest of the prophets who have been trying to intimidate me." (Nehemiah 6:14)

Q4. (Nehemiah 6:1-14) Why do Nehemiah's enemies want him to travel away from Jerusalem? Why do his enemies bribe the prophets? How are they hoping to hurt Nehemiah's integrity, will, and authority? How is your enemy trying to make you stumble?
http://www.joyfulheart.com/forums/topic/1748-q4-subtle-temptations/

Completion of the Wall (Nehemiah 6:15-16)

Now the text states an astounding achievement:

> "So the wall was completed on the twenty-fifth of Elul, in fifty-two days." (Nehemiah 6:15)

Elul (August/September) is the sixth month of the year.

---

[220] Kidner, *Ezra and Nehemiah*, p. 109

Considering all the obstacles they have faced, what are the odds of a 52-day completion? Has Nehemiah been the target of spiritual warfare? Undoubtedly. Yes, the warfare is manifested in real-time circumstances by flesh-and-blood enemies. But behind it all is Satan, who does not want the people to return to God with their hearts, to be secure, to be "a light to the Gentiles." Paul reminds the Ephesian church about the true nature of their enemy:

> "Our struggle is not against flesh and blood, but against the rulers, against the authorities, against the powers of this dark world and against the spiritual forces of evil in the heavenly realms." (Ephesians 6:12)

The result of the wall's completion is a victory both in the heavenly realm and over the Persian provinces adjoining Judah.

> "When all our enemies heard about this, all the surrounding nations were afraid and lost their self-confidence, because they realized that this work had been done with the help of our God." (Nehemiah 6:16)

Who gets the glory? God!

Tobiah's Ongoing Influence among the Nobility (Nehemiah 6:17-19)

The victory is complete, but in spite of that, the spiritual battle continues. Nehemiah tells us of behind-the-scenes correspondence and divided loyalties among the wealthy and powerful in Judah.

Tobiah, an Ammonite with Jewish roots, has powerful ties. Tobiah's father-in-law is Shecaniah, a Jewish noble. And Tobiah's son marries the daughter of Meshallam son of Berekiah, a noble who had helped build two sections of the wall of Jerusalem (Nehemiah 3:4, 30). Tobiah also has close ties to the high priestly family (Nehemiah 13:3-4), which show up after Nehemiah has returned to Susa for a time.

These families of the "Tobiah party" keep promoting Tobiah's cause to Nehemiah and providing intelligence to Tobiah – an act which is best called treason! Tobiah's threats kept coming even after the wall is completed.

A Summary of Opposition Tactics

We've looked at the various opposition tactics. A comprehensive list helps us appreciate the determination of Nehemiah's enemies – and the greatness of our God who gives him wisdom to deal with each of the threats. It also provides a checklist that modern-day leaders might consider:

1. False accusations (Nehemiah 2:19; 6:5-9).
2. Ridicule (Nehemiah 4:1-3).
3. Devious attempts to be included in the project so they can subvert it from within (Ezra 4:1-3; Nehemiah 2:20).
4. Appeal to higher authorities to stop the project (Ezra 4:5).
5. Bluffs.
6. Rumors to instill fear (Ezra 4:4; Nehemiah 4:11-12).
7. Temptations to sin in order to undermine moral authority (Nehemiah 6:10-11).
8. False prophecies or supposed "words from God" (Nehemiah 6:12-14).
9. Threats and plots to physically incapacitate Nehemiah (Nehemiah 4:7-8; 6:1-4).
10. Plots to distract his attention (Nehemiah 6:3).
11. Disloyalty among Nehemiah's own team (Nehemiah 6:17-19).

Securing Jerusalem (Nehemiah 7:1-3)

Chapter 7 begins with actions Nehemiah takes to regularize life in a secure Jerusalem. Nehemiah appoints:

1. **Temple servants** – gatekeepers, singers, and Levites who are to keep temple worship in order.
2. **Mayor of Jerusalem** – his brother Hanani, who had first brought word of Jerusalem's problems to Nehemiah while in Susa (Nehemiah 1:2-3).
3. **Commander of Jerusalem's Defense**, Hananiah, a God-fearing man of integrity. This fortress or citadel seems to have been located adjacent to the temple (Nehemiah 2:8), perhaps the Tower of Hananel (Nehemiah 3:1).
4. **Gate-Keepers.** The gatekeepers are given instructions not to open the doors at night and to guard them to make sure no one gets in or out at night.
5. **Guards.** Some of these have regular posts during the daytime to prevent against attack. Others seem to be some kind of Neighborhood Watch guards, who post someone to guard the area around their homes.

List of the Exiles Who Returned (Nehemiah 7:4-73)

"⁴ Now the city was large and spacious, but there were few people in it, and the houses had not yet been rebuilt. ⁵ So my God put it into my heart to assemble the nobles, the officials and the common people for registration by families. I found the genealogical record of those who had been the first to return. This is what I found written there." (Nehemiah 7:4-5)

Notice the phrase, "God put it into my heart...." (verse 5a). Nehemiah, a man of prayer, is sensitive to God's leading.

Nehemiah has provided for Jerusalem's government, worship, and security. Now he tackles the problem of its small population, which we'll consider when we look at Nehemiah 11 in Lesson 8. The remainder of Nehemiah 7 is comprised of a list of the first to return to Judah. The list is almost an exact transcription of the list found in Ezra 2.

Lessons for Disciples

This passage is rich in lessons for modern-day disciples.

1. Nehemiah inspects the wall and prepares his strategy prior to announcing his plans. We learn from this to keep our own counsel (or with a small group of advisors) until our plans are complete. Only then should we share them with the larger group. If we share half-baked plans, it gives our opposition all they need to stop us (Nehemiah 2:11-16). This is especially true of leaders new to an organization.

2. In any great God-inspired work we can expect opposition. Having enemies doesn't mean you're out of God's will; rather, it may even be an indication that you *have* heard from God.

3. Nehemiah involves people in the project who will be motivated by their own self-interest. We need to build coalitions of people to implement projects. This often takes time, but is essential to success (Nehemiah 3).

4. In any God-inspired project we can expect some people in our organizations to be opposed or to refuse to help (Nehemiah 3:5). Don't wait to act until you have complete unanimity; find God's will and then go forward.

5. Prayer should be combined with action, whenever possible. Taking God-guided action, doesn't mean you lack faith in God's ability to answer prayer. Rather, it is a willingness to allow God to use you as part of the answer (Nehemiah 4:9).

6. In any great God-inspired project we can expect discouragement and apprehension among our workers, and will need to deal with it (Nehemiah 4:10-15).

7. Leaders must be willing to adapt their original plans to meet unforeseen circumstances (Nehemiah 4:16-18). German military strategist Helmuth von Moltke (1800-1891) famously said, "No battle plan survives contact with the enemy."

8. Every great God-inspired work needs to take into account security (Nehemiah 4:16-21). Since we are in a spiritual battle, this probably means intercessory prayer teams and the like.

9. Rebuilding Jerusalem's defenses so the enemy cannot control us is analogous to us building up spiritual defenses against Satan's temptations, so he cannot keep us weak (Ephesians 6:10-13).

10. God opposes anything that oppresses the poor – including high interest rates and injustice. We must resist the temptation to greed (unjust gain) at the expense of others (Nehemiah 5:1-18). The underlying issues are injustice and a lack of compassion.

11. Nehemiah uses public shaming to force greedy Jews to change their ways (Nehemiah 5:7-12). This can work if the leader has enough influence, but we must be very careful in adopting this tactic so that it will not backfire.

12. Nehemiah sets an example by foregoing his rights to financial support (Nehemiah 5:14-19), just as does the Apostle Paul centuries later (1 Corinthians 9:3-23). Leaders should set an example of self-sacrifice, not of privileged rights and luxury. Unfortunately, some proponents of the Prosperity Gospel neglect this principle.

Prayer

Father, as I read about Nehemiah's struggles, I remember that Paul and Barnabas cautioned Christian leaders, "We must go through many hardships to enter the kingdom of God" (Acts 14:22). But constant warfare is wearing. We get tired. We get discouraged. I ask you, O Almighty God, strengthen the hands of your people. Lift us up. Help us. Increase our faith. Help us to see your mighty power to achieve your goals. And help us to align ourselves with your goals – and with your strength. In Jesus' name, we pray. Amen.

Key Verses

"They said to me, 'Those who survived the exile and are back in the province are in great trouble and disgrace. The wall of Jerusalem is broken down, and its gates have been burned with fire.' When I heard these things, I sat down and wept. For some days I mourned and fasted and prayed before the God of heaven." (Nehemiah 1:3-4, NIV)

"Then I said to them, 'You see the trouble we are in: Jerusalem lies in ruins, and its gates have been burned with fire. Come, let us rebuild the wall of Jerusalem, and we will no longer be in disgrace.' I also told them about the gracious hand of my God upon me and what the king had said to me. They replied, 'Let us start rebuilding.' So they began this good work." (Nehemiah 2:17-18, NIV)

"So we rebuilt the wall till all of it reached half its height, for the people worked with all their heart." (Nehemiah 4:6, NIV)

"Don't be afraid of them. Remember the Lord, who is great and awesome, and fight for your brothers, your sons and your daughters, your wives and your homes." (Nehemiah 4:14b, NIV)

"Those who carried materials did their work with one hand and held a weapon in the other, and each of the builders wore his sword at his side as he worked." (Nehemiah 4:17b-18a, NIV)

"They were all trying to frighten us, thinking, 'Their hands will get too weak for the work, and it will not be completed.' [But I prayed,] 'Now strengthen my hands.'" (Nehemiah 6:9, NIV)

"So the wall was completed on the twenty-fifth of Elul, in fifty-two days. When all our enemies heard about this, all the surrounding nations were afraid and lost their self-confidence, because they realized that this work had been done with the help of our God." (Nehemiah 6:15-16, NIV)

8. Repentance and Revival (Nehemiah 8-13)

So far, the books of Ezra and Nehemiah have talked about how God helps the Jews return to Jerusalem, rebuild the temple, and then restore the wall around the city. However, this final section of Nehemiah recounts a genuine spiritual revival that takes place under Ezra's ministry after the wall is completed.

Ezra Reads the Law (artist unknown)

Prior to the completion of the wall there is no secure location where a large gathering could be held, not to mention for an extended time of feasting and worship. But now a large number can safely assemble within the city.

Ezra Reads the Law (Nehemiah 7:73b-8:18)

"73 The priests, the Levites, the gatekeepers, the singers and the temple servants, along with certain of the people and the rest of the Israelites, settled in their own towns. When the seventh month came and the Israelites had settled in their towns, 1 all the people assembled as one man in the square before the Water Gate. They told Ezra the scribe to bring out the Book of the Law of Moses, which the LORD had commanded for Israel." (Nehemiah 7:73b-8:1)

The occasion of this revival is the first day of the month of Tishri, our September/October, a holy day then known as the "Feast of Trumpets."[221] The Law directs:

"On the first day of the seventh month you are to have a day of rest, a sacred assembly[222] commemorated with trumpet blasts." (Leviticus 23:24-25a; cf. Numbers 29:1)

---

[221] By the second century BC, the Feast of Trumpets had became known as Jewish New Year, Rosh Hashanah (literally "beginning/head of the year"). Now it is considered the first of the High Holidays, followed by Yom Kippur (the Day of Atonement) and the Sukkoth (Feast of Tabernacles) later in the month.

The public reading of the Law is normally commanded during the Feast of Tabernacles, which takes place a few days after the Feast of Trumpets. But neither of these events have been held for many years (Ezra 3:4) – perhaps never in the lifetime of those present. That Ezra is asked to read the Law is an indication of the people's willingness to reinstate God's commandments in Judah's public life.

> "Ezra the scribe stood on a high wooden platform[223] built for the occasion." (Nehemiah 8:4)

Ezra is flanked by thirteen leaders who are named – though many of the names are so common we can't be sure they refer to individuals named elsewhere in Nehemiah. The people are all gathered. And so Ezra brings out the "book" of the Law and lays it on a reading table. This isn't a bound book, but a scroll.[224]

> "5 Ezra opened the book. All the people could see him because he was standing above them; and as he opened it, the people all stood up. 6 Ezra praised the LORD, the great God; and all the people lifted their hands and responded, 'Amen! Amen!' Then they bowed down and worshiped the LORD with their faces to the ground." (Nehemiah 8:5-6)

Notice the reverence of the people for the Scripture. They stand up from where they had been seated in the square. Ezra praises the Lord, then all the people lift their hands – a sign of prayer and blessing – and say "Amen!" (which we saw in Nehemiah 5:13). The Hebrew word ('āmēn) comes from the verb 'āman, "to be certain, to believe in." "Amen" means "verily, truly," and expresses a certain affirmation in response to what has been said.[225]

---

[222] "Assembly" (NIV), "convocation" (NRSV, ESV, KJV), is miqrā', "convocation, reading," from qārā', "call out, recite." Holladay gives two definitions: "convocation, assembly," and "reading (aloud)" (Nehemiah 8:4; Holladay, *Hebrew Lexicon*, p. 213).

[223] "Podium" (NRSV), "platform" (NIV, ESV), "pulpit" (KJV) is migdāl, "tower."

[224] "Book" is sēper, "writing, book." It is closely related to sōpēr, "scribe." This doesn't mean a bound book, later called a codex. During this era documents were written on scrolls, with pages sown successively to each other to be rolled up, not stacked up and bound together at one edge.

[225] Jack B. Scott, 'āmēn, TWOT #116b. The word is used after the pronouncement of solemn curses, and after prayers and hymns of praise.

After this the people, who are now standing, bow down,[226] and then get down on their knees with their faces to the ground, as you sometimes see Muslims do in their call to prayer. It is a position of abject humility before a superior.[227]

This could all be a formal, pre-planned response to emphasize the superiority of Scripture as the Word of God. But I think something more is happening here, something spiritual, something life-giving.

> "He read it aloud from daybreak till noon... And all the people listened attentively to the Book of the Law." (Nehemiah 8:3)

If you take these words at face value, something amazing is taking place. Ezra (and probably others) read for six hours or so, and the people "listened attentively" (NIV).[228] Normally, people listen to a reading for a few minutes, perhaps, and then tune out. But these people in the September morning sun listen for hours on end. Why?

Communicating Understanding (Nehemiah 8:7-8)

Our text shows a strong emphasis on understanding. The whole occasion is designed to help the people grasp what the Law teaches.

> "7 ... The Levites, helped the people to understand the Law, while the people remained in their places. 8 They read from the book, from the Law of God, clearly, and they gave the sense, so that the people understood the reading." (Nehemiah 8:7-8)

Two teams of thirteen people each are ready. One team reads from the platform; the other mingles among the people to explain what they are hearing.

Look at these indications in the text that indicate actual learning and understanding is taking place.

- "All who were able to **understand**"[229] (verse 2).

---

[226] "Bowed down" (NIV), "bowed low" (NRSV), "bowed their heads" (ESV, KJV), is *qādad*, "bow down." This root refers to the bowing of one's head accompanying and emphasizing obeisance (Leonard J. Coppes, TWOT #1985).

[227] They "worshipped" (NIV, NRSV, ESV, KJV), is literally "prostrated themselves" (New English Bible, New Jerusalem Bible). The verb is the Eschtaphal stem of *hāwâ*, "to prostrate oneself, to worship" (Edwin Yamauchi, TWOT #619), though it was once analyzed as a Hithpael of *shāhâ*, "bow down."

[228] "Listened attentively" (NIV), "were attentive" (NRSV, ESV), is literally "the ears" (KJV). Our corresponding slang expression is, "They were all ears."

[229] "Understand" in verses 2, 3, 7a, 9a, 12b is the Hiphil stem of *bîn*. Vs. 8 has the Qal stem. "The background idea of the verb is to 'discern.' The verb refers to knowledge which is superior to the mere gathering of data. It is necessary to know how to use knowledge one possesses. It is possible to hear without perceiving. The Hiphil stem especially emphasizes ability to understand (Louis Goldberg, TWOT #239).

- "Others who could **understand**" (verse 3b).

- "All the people **listened attentively** (verse 3c).

- The Levites … helped the people **to understand**[230] the Law (verse 7a, ESV, cf. verse 9a).

- "**Making it clear**[231] and **giving the meaning**[232] so that the people could **understand**[233] what was being read" (verse 8).

- "They now **understood** the words that had been made known to them" (verse 12b).

Exactly what the procedure is, we're not sure. Apparently the thirteen people on the platform with Ezra each read in turn throughout the morning with a loud, clear voice. Probably, during breaks in the public reading, the team of thirteen Levites fan out among the people to help answer questions. This might have involved translating the Hebrew of the Biblical text into the Aramaic language that the people commonly spoke.[234]

The point of the elaborate preparations for readers and interpreters is so that the people might understand the Law. And it becomes clear that for many – perhaps most – of the people, this was the first time they really understand God's word in the first five books of the Bible.

---

[230] "Instructed" (NIV), "explained" (NRSV), "helped to understand" (ESV), "caused to understand" (KJV) is the Hiphil stem of *bîn*, which we saw in verse 3. The Hiphil emphasizes the ability to understand (Louis Goldberg, TWOT #239).

[231] "Making it clear" (NIV), "translating" (NRSV), "clearly" (ESV), "distinctly" (KJV) is the Pual stem of *pārash*, "make distinct, declare." The basic meaning is, "to make/be made clear" by revelation, explication, or translation (Victor P. Hamilton, TWOT #1833).

[232] "Giving the meaning" (NIV), "to give the sense" (NRSV, ESV, KJV) is *śûm*, "put, place, set, appoint, make," plus the noun *śekel*, "understanding," from *śākal*, "wisely, understand, prosper." While *bîn* indicates "distinguishing between," *śākal* relates to an intelligent knowledge of the reason. There is the process of thinking through a complex arrangement of thoughts resulting in a wise dealing and use of good practical common sense. Another end result is the emphasis upon being successful (Herbert Wolf, TWOT #2263a).

[233] "Could understand" is the Qal stem of *bîn*, "understand."

[234] Aramaic was the language of Babylon. While Aramaic is similar to Hebrew, it has differences. You find Aramaic in the Old Testament in passages related to the people's sojourn in Babylon – primarily Daniel 2:4b-7:28 and Ezra 4:8-6:18 and 7:12-26. Aramaic was also the common language spoken in Galilee and Judea in New Testament times, though Jewish men learned Hebrew in the synagogue schools (see Mark 5:41; 7:34; John 1:42; Acts 9:36, 40; 1 Corinthians 1:12; 16:22, etc.).

Understanding, Sorrow, and Repentance (Nehemiah 8:9-11)

> "All the people had been weeping as they listened to the words of the Law." (Nehemiah 8:9b)

As they begin to understand the commandments – and the grievous way that God's people have broken these commandments – their hearts are broken. All over the crowd you can hear the weeping and wailing characteristic of Near Eastern mourning.[235]

Their reaction is similar to that of King Josiah when the Book of the Law is found in a temple restoration project.

> "When the king heard the words of the Book of the Law, he tore his robes.... 'Great is the LORD's anger that burns against us because our fathers have not obeyed the words of this book; they have not acted in accordance with all that is written there concerning us.'" (2 Kings 22:11, 13b)

In a similar way, the returned exiles are beginning to understand how far Israel has strayed from God's plan. Why God has allowed Jerusalem to be destroyed by the Babylonians. The justice of the 70-year exile in Babylon. And how they even now are breaking God's commandments for how they should live.

Previously, this knowledge had been the focus of the scribes and Levites, but the common people only knew what their leaders told them.

Now they are hearing it for themselves. And – to use a New Testament phrase – they are cut to the heart (Acts 2:37). The tears and mourning are a clear indication that the Holy Spirit is at work bringing a revival, a renewal to the people. Without the Holy Spirit, after several hours in the sun they would have been complaining, murmuring, and talking to their neighbors. Instead, there is a holy hush – words being read from the platform and weeping is everywhere.

Paul exhorts Timothy not to neglect reading and teaching.

---

[235] "Mourn" in vs. 9 is 'ābal, "mourn, lament." 'Ābal, which emphasizes the formal mourning for the dead (expressed by 'ābal, sāpad, etc.), involved emotion, usually expressed audibly (TWOT #6). "Grieve" (NIV, NRSV, ESV), "be sorry/be grieved" (KJV), vss. 10-11, is the Niphal stem of 'āṣab. It relates to physical pain as well as to emotional sorrow, a term of physical and mental discomfort. The Niphal of 'āṣab is found seven times, usually mental and spiritual anguish (Ronald B. Allen, TWOT #1666). "Weep" in vs. 9 is bākâ, "to weep, cry, shed tears." To weep by reason of joy or sorrow, the latter including lament, complaint, remorse or repentance. The root is commonly paralleled with dāmac "to shed tears" and with sāpad "to mourn." But, whereas tears are associated with the eyes, weeping is associated with the voice, Semites do not weep quietly, but aloud. Throughout the Old Testament, weeping is the natural and spontaneous expression of strong emotion (John N. Oswalt, TWOT #243).

"Until I come, devote yourself to the public reading of Scripture, to preaching and to teaching." (1 Timothy 4:13)

If you've studied the history of revivals in the last two or three hundred years, you recognize this as evidence of a true spiritual revival, where God softens the hearts of men and women and brings deep repentance. To learn more, I encourage you to google "The Great Awakening" (Britain and America, 1730-1750), the "Welsh Revival" (Wales, 1904-1905), the "East Africa Revival" (1929-1950s), the "Azusa Street Revival" (Los Angeles, 1906), etc.

Here in the city square inside the Water Gate, God is powerfully at work among his people.

Repentance and Joy (Nehemiah 8:9-11)

But the mourning and tears upset the leaders. They haven't planned on God doing a deep revival in hearts; rather they have planned a festive day.

"9 Then Nehemiah the governor, Ezra the priest and scribe, and the Levites who were instructing the people said to them all, 'This day is sacred to the LORD your God. Do not mourn or weep.' For all the people had been weeping as they listened to the words of the Law.

10 Nehemiah said, 'Go and enjoy choice food[236] and sweet drinks,[237] and send some to those who have nothing prepared. This day is sacred[238] to our Lord. Do not grieve, for the joy of the LORD is your strength.' 11 The Levites calmed all the people, saying, 'Be still,[239] for this is a sacred day. Do not grieve.'" (Numbers 8:9-11)

I think God is extremely gracious as the leaders try to intervene in what God is sovereignly doing. Sometimes we leaders are clueless to what God wants to do.

But in spite of the leaders, God works powerfully. First, he works in them the sorrow that leads to repentance (2 Corinthians 7:10). Then, he works in them the joy that comes from knowing God's love and forgiveness and grace (1 Peter 1:8b).

---

[236] "Choice food" (NIV), "the fat" (NRSV, ESV, KJV) is *mashmān*. Holladay defines it as "delicious, festive food prepared with much fat" (*Hebrew Lexicon*, p. 220). Austel defines it as "richly prepared food." It is similar to *mashmān*, "fatness," from *shāmēn*, "to be(come) fat" (Hermann J. Austel, TWOT #2410f).

[237] "Sweet drinks" (NIV), "the sweet" (NRSV, KJV), "sweet wine" (ESV) is *mamtaqqîm*, "sweetness," from *mātōq*, "be sweet" (TWOT #1268d).

[238] "Sacred" (NIV), "holy" (NRSV, ESV, KJV) is *qādôsh*, "holy," from the verb *qādash*, "the state of that which belongs to the sphere of the sacred." (TWOT #1990).

[239] "Be silent" is *hāshâ*, "to keep quiet," that is, to be inactive, especially with reference to speaking (Leonard J. Coppes, TWOT #768).

"Then all the people went away to eat and drink, to send portions of food and to celebrate with great joy, because they now understood the words that had been made known to them." (Nehemiah 8:12)

Now, in place of the weeping, there begin to be shouts of joy among the people. Praise breaks out. And as they eat the refreshments that many families have prepared for the occasion, they praise God, and share with families that have nothing.

The Joy of the Lord Is Your Strength (Nehemiah 8:10b)

Nehemiah the governor intervenes, along with the other leaders, to try to turn the mourning into joy. He says:

"Do not grieve, for the joy of the LORD is your strength." (Nehemiah 8:10b)

In what way is the joy of the Lord our strength? To understand, let's first look at the words in this short saying.

"Grieve" (NIV), "be grieved" (NRSV, ESV), "be sorry" (KJV) refers to mental and spiritual anguish.[240]

"Strength" refers to a "place or means of safety, protection, stronghold, fortress."[241] This word is used often for "refuge, stronghold" in the Old Testament, especially in the Psalms and Prophets. For example:

"You have been a **refuge** (*mā'ōz*) for the poor,
a **refuge** (*mā'ōz*) for the needy in his distress,
a shelter from the storm and a shade from the heat." (Isaiah 25:4)

"The LORD is good,
a **refuge** (*mā'ōz*) in times of trouble." (Nahum 1:7a)

"Joy" (*ḥedwâ*) is the opposite of grief – "gladness, joy."[242] Occasionally, we see passages where sorrow is turned into joy (Jeremiah 31:13), such as a familiar passage from Isaiah that prophesies joy at the return from exile.

---

[240] Ronald B. Allen, *'āṣab*, TWOT #1666, the Niphal stem.

[241] Carl Schultz, *mā'ōz*, TWOT #1578a. The verb has a sense of urgency, with the concept of taking shelter quickly. From the verb *'ûz*, "take refuge, bring to a refuge."

[242] "Joy" is *ḥedwâ*, "gladness, joy," from the verb *ḥādâ*, "rejoice" (Qal), "make glad, gladden" (Piel) (TWOT #607a). The Hebrew word for "joy" used in our passage is fairly rare in the Old Testament, used only once elsewhere, though a couple of synonyms are used more frequently – *śāśôn*, "joy, gladness," and *śimḥâ*, "joy, mirth." The related verb *ḥādâ*, "rejoice," is a bit more common, used three times in the Old Testament.

"And the ransomed of the LORD shall return
and come to Zion with singing;
everlasting joy[243] shall be upon their heads;
they shall obtain gladness[244] and joy,[245]
and sorrow and sighing shall flee away." (Isaiah 51:11, ESV)

I think Nehemiah is saying: Don't continue in your state of grief for your sins. Rather, turn to Yahweh, who is a place of refuge for you in your weakness. It is he who can give you joy to replace your sorrow.

Repentance is good. A deep realization that we are at our root sinners is good. But if we are continually confessing that we are sinners, that doesn't bring much glory to God, even if it's true. He would much rather that we take refuge in his grace, and move on to the joy that he would give us – a fruit of his Spirit within us (Galatians 5:22-23). We can wallow in our sinfulness (negative), or we can move on to the joy that we find in God's grace and love (positive).

My dear friend, it's time for you to let the past go, with all its failings and "should-have-beens," and instead take hold of God's healing future for you, for this is your refuge and your place of joy.

Even in the midst of great sorrow we can experience joy in the Lord. He is the refuge we go to when the world is falling apart around us. And in him is joy, because of his promises, his love, his care, his great and everlasting grace. My friend, step beyond your overwhelming sorrow into his refuge, and find his joy to lift you up.

Celebrate with Great Joy (Nehemiah 8:12)

The people *did* heed Nehemiah's exhortation and found joy in the Lord.

"Then all the people went away to eat and drink, to send portions of food and to **celebrate with great joy**, because they now understood the words that had been made known to them." (Nehemiah 8:12)

How do you move from great sorrow to celebrating with great joy? I like this phrase, "celebrate with great joy." The root of the noun *śimḥâ*, "joy, mirth," denotes "being glad

---

[243] *Śimḥâ.*
[244] *Śāśôn.*
[245] *Śimḥâ.*

or joyful with the whole disposition, as indicated by its association with the heart, the soul, and with the lighting up of the eyes."[246]

How do the people get to "celebrating with great joy"? Through understanding God's word. It takes teachers to explain it – which should be an encouragement for those who have a gift of teaching. As you help expound the Scripture, the lights come on in your hearers. They begin to understand. They "get it." They become excited about it. Their faith increases and they open up in faith to the Spirit who gives joy as his fruit. Keep teaching faithfully; God uses you.

> **Q1. (Nehemiah 8:1-12) Why does the reading of Scripture bring such sorrow to the people? Why is Scripture reading so important in personal spiritual revival? What place does the Spirit have in this? What is the relationship between joy and faith in God's compassion and love?**
> http://www.joyfulheart.com/forums/topic/1749-q1-revival-and-joy/

Celebrating the Feast of Booths (Nehemiah 8:13-18)

As mentioned above, the month of Tishri, the seventh month in the Jewish calendar, ushers in what are now known as the Jewish high holy days:

- Day 1 – **Feast of Trumpets** (later Rosh Hashanah, Leviticus 23:23-25)
- Day 10 - **Yom Kippur**, the Day of Atonement (Leviticus 23:26-32)
- Days 15-23 – **Feast of Booths** (or Tabernacles, Leviticus 23:33-36)

As we'll see, on Day 24, before the people return to their everyday lives, Ezra institutes a special day of confession and covenant, unparalleled in the Law.

Begun on the Feast of Trumpets, the marathon Bible reading continues for a second day, though with a smaller group – heads of the families, priests, and Levites (Nehemiah 8:13-15). They are probably reading Leviticus 23 that talks about the various festivals. Curiously, the Day of Atonement (that is to be observed on the 10th day of Tishri) isn't mentioned in our text (though on the 24th day of Tishri the people observe a time of

---

[246] "Celebrate with great joy" (NIV), "celebrate a great festival" (NRSV), "make great mirth" (KJV) is literally, "make great rejoicing" (ESV), also in Nehemiah 12:27. The phrase is made up of three words: 'āśâ, "do make"; plus śimḥâ, "joy, mirth" (from śāmēaḥ, "rejoice"); and gādôl, "great." The Lord and his salvation are cited most frequently as the reason for joy (Bruce K. Waltke, śimḥâ, TWOT #2268b). Śimḥâ is also used to describe their celebration at the Feast of Booths in verse 17.

fasting and confession of sin). Perhaps the author skips mention of the Day of Atonement so he can move from one joyful celebration (Feast of Trumpets) to talk about another joyful celebration (Feast of Booths).

What draws the people's attention is the Feast of Booths (or Tabernacles) that hadn't been celebrated by the whole people for a long, long time. Yes, it had been observed in the temple (Ezra 3:4), but not by the extensive camping-out element that catches the imagination of the common person and turns it into a joyful feast. So preparations are made for this feast that comes up later in the month.

God designs the Feast of Booths to remind these city and town dwellers that their forefathers lived in temporary dwellings (tents) in the desert.

> "[42] You shall dwell in booths for seven days. All native Israelites shall dwell in booths, [43] that your generations may know that I made the people of Israel dwell in booths when I brought them out of the land of Egypt: I am the LORD your God." (Leviticus 23:42-43)

Jesus celebrates this festival when he is on earth (John 7:2-14), and pious Jews celebrate it to this day, a kind of national camp-out when families sleep outside their houses in temporary dwellings made with wooden poles covered with leafy branches. The feast is marked by great joy and celebrated at the conclusion of harvest (Deuteronomy 16:14-15).

So in Ezra and Nehemiah's day, inspired by Scripture, the people celebrate the Feast of Booths wholeheartedly, "and their joy was very great" (vs. 17b).

> "[16] So the people went out and brought back branches and built themselves booths on their own roofs, in their courtyards, in the courts of the house of God and in the square by the Water Gate and the one by the Gate of Ephraim. [17] The whole company that had returned from exile built booths and lived in them. From the days of Joshua son of Nun until that day, the Israelites had not celebrated it like this. And their joy[247] was very great." (Nehemiah 8:16-17)

During the feast, Ezra's Scripture reading program continues unabated, in accordance with God's command (Deuteronomy 31:10-12). And so Ezra and his team read the Scripture throughout this seven-day festival.

---

[247] "Joy" (NIV), "rejoicing" (NRSV, ESV), "gladness" (KJV) is *śimḥâ*, which we saw in verse 12.

"Day after day, from the first day to the last, Ezra read from the Book of the Law of God. They celebrated[248] the feast for seven days, and on the eighth day, in accordance with the regulation, there was an assembly."[249] (Nehemiah 8:18)

The Israelites Confess Their Sins (Nehemiah 9:1-37)

So far the Tishri revival has included Scripture reading, repentance, and the joyful celebration of the Feast of Tabernacles. But the revival of Yahweh worship isn't over yet. The day after the concluding assembly of the Feast of Booths (on Tishri 23), while people are still in Jerusalem and before they return to their home villages, Ezra calls a day of repentance and fasting (Tishri 24).

Kidner notes that Nehemiah has been eager to associate God's will with delight and joy (Nehemiah 8:9-12), but now it is equally important to set this delight firmly in contrast to the gall of sin, so that when the people return home, the revival that has taken place has a lasting effect, one sealed by covenant.[250]

"On the twenty-fourth day of the same month, the Israelites gathered together, fasting and wearing sackcloth and having dust on their heads." (Nehemiah 9:1)

The people gather for this occasion in great humility and abasement. Sackcloth, or sacking is the material used to make the rough cloth that bags that were used to carry items by donkey, or perhaps store goods. Sackcloth is made of goat or camel hair and worn especially during times of mourning (Joel 1:13).[251] As we have seen, fasting is a way of humbling oneself before God. Sprinkling dust on one's head is symbolic of deep humiliation, abasement, or grief.[252]

---

[248] "Celebrated" (NIV) in verse 17 is literally "done so" (NRSV, ESV, KJV).

[249] Vs. 18, "Assembly" (NIV), "solemn assembly" (NRSV, ESV, KJV) is *aṣārâ*, "solemn assembly," from *'āṣar*, "restrain, refrain, withhold, close up." Holladay (*Hebrew Lexicon*, p. 281) translates it, "festive assembly," with the idea of refraining from work that day. Another approach is to see its derivation from *'āṣar* ("restrain" or "close up") and from the contexts in which it occurs, to suggest an occasion of fasting and abstention from work and other profane activities. The NEB renders it "closing ceremony" (Gary Chamberlain and Nola J. Opperwall-Galluch, "Solemn," ISBE 4:566). "This word generally refers to the final, or closing, day of an extended feast, though elsewhere it may simply designate a religious assembly, whether approved by Yahweh or not. Semantically, the word ranges from simply a pious assembly of any sort to something approximating the *miqrā' qōdeš* that brought a period of feasting to an end" (Carl E. Amerding, "Festivals and Feasts," T. Desmond Alexander and David W. Baker (eds.), *Dictionary of the Old Testament: Pentateuch* (InterVarsity, 2003).

[250] Kidner, *Ezra and Nehemiah*, p. 120.

[251] Larry G. Herr, "Sackcloth," ISBE 4:256.

[252] Joshua 7:6; Job 2:12; Lamentations 2:10; Ezekiel 27:30; Revelation 18:19.

"Those of Israelite descent had separated themselves from all foreigners." (Nehemiah 9:2a)

One of the problems the exiles face is their close association with and intermarriage between non-Israelites, particularly the half-breed Samaritans who live close by. Separation is not some kind of ethnic purity ritual, but rather the beginning of a commitment not to mix their worship of Yahweh with the practice of other religions, dilute their faith by intermarriage (Nehemiah 10:3), and neglect of the Sabbath (Nehemiah 10:4).

What follows is a recital of Israel's own history, their blessing, their sin, and their punishment.

This month there has been public reading the Scripture on a number of occasions. The Levites have taken pains to help them understand. So by now they were well aware of both the requirements of the Law, as well as their own failures to obey the Law. Now they are ready to confess their sins and to take steps of repentance as a nation. Verse 2b is a general statement; verse 3 describes how they divide their time.

> "2b They stood in their places and confessed their sins and the wickedness of their fathers. 3 They stood where they were and read from the Book of the Law of the LORD their God for a quarter of the day, and spent another quarter in confession and in worshiping the LORD their God." (Nehemiah 9:2-3)

What are "the stairs" mentioned in verse 4? We're not sure. Perhaps they are stairs within the temple complex. But they could refer to the wooden platform mentioned in Nehemiah 8:4.

> "4 Standing on the stairs were the Levites ... who called with loud voices to the LORD their God. 5 And the [other] Levites ... said: 'Stand up and praise the LORD your God, who is from everlasting to everlasting.'" (Nehemiah 9:4-5)

One group of Levites seems to have called out to God on behalf of the people in distress and confession. The other group leads in praise. In the lists of verses 4 and 5, five of the names seem to be in common – why, we don't know.

The praise continues

> "5b Blessed be your glorious name, and may it be exalted above all blessing and praise. 6 You alone are the LORD. You made the heavens, even the highest heavens, and all their starry host, the earth and all that is on it, the seas and all that is in them. You give life to everything, and the multitudes of heaven worship you." (Nehemiah 9:5b-6)

A Summary of Israel's History (Nehemiah 9:7-35)

What follows is a brief summary of the history of Israel. We see something like this in the mouth of Stephen just before his martyrdom (Acts 7). This recital of their common history unites them and reminds them that God has shown them love and mercy again and again, when they haven't deserved it. I'll just outline it here, but I encourage you to read the entire chapter.

1. God makes a covenant with Abraham (verses 7-8).
2. God delivers Israel from Egypt (verses 9-11).
3. God's provides food, water, and the Law in the wilderness (verses 12-15).
4. Israel sins terribly, but God still forgives (verses 16-18).
5. God's compassion and grace are shown to Israel (verses 19-21).
6. Through God they possess the land of Canaan (verses 22-25).
7. Again Israel sins, but God does not forsake them (verses 26-31).
8. Our hardships are God's just punishments (verses 32-35).

This passage summarizes Israel's history as found in the Pentateuch, as well as Joshua, the Historical Books, and the Prophets. It is a sad history that shows how undeserving Israel is of God's mercy. These words sum it up:

"You have acted faithfully, while we did wrong." (Nehemiah 9:33b)

I know that when God recounts our personal history on Judgment Day (Revelation 20:12-15), we'll see the same demonstration – our weakness and unfaithfulness and His great mercy!

Yahweh, the Gracious and Compassionate God (Nehemiah 9:17)

Indeed, the recurring theme of this passage is of God's great grace. The Levites recount Israel's deep sin in creating a golden calf and worshipping it as god. Then the reflection:

"But you are a **forgiving God, gracious and compassionate, slow to anger and abounding in love**. Therefore you did not desert them...." (Nehemiah 9:17)

This characterization of God's character is first stated by Yahweh when he appears to Moses in the cleft of the rock.

"And he passed in front of Moses, proclaiming, "The LORD, the LORD, the compassionate and gracious God, slow to anger, abounding in love and faithfulness, maintaining love to thousands, and forgiving wickedness, rebellion and sin. Yet he does not leave the guilty unpunished...." (Exodus 34:6-7a)

It is repeated here in Nehemiah 9:17b and several more times, in one form or another, throughout the Old Testament.[253] If our God weren't compassionate and gracious, he never would have sent Jesus to redeem us. His steadfast love endures forever!

Through the remainder of the passage we see an appreciation of God's grace:

1. "Because of your **great compassion**…" (verse 19a).
2. "They reveled in your **great goodness**" (verse 25b).
3. "In your **great compassion** you gave them deliverers" (verses 27).
4. "In your **compassion** you delivered them time after time" (verse 28).
5. "But in your **great mercy** you did not put an end to them or abandon them, for you are a **gracious and merciful God**" (verse 31).
6. "Our God, the great, mighty and awesome God … keeps his **covenant of love**" (verse 32).
7. "You have acted **faithfully**, while we did wrong" (verse 33b).

Q2. (Nehemiah 9:7-35) Why is God's compassion emphasized so strongly in Israel's history? How can God's compassion be present even in times of tough discipline (Hebrews 12:7-11)? How does the compassionate God of the Old Testament relate to Jesus giving himself as a ransom for sinners (Mark 10:45)?
http://www.joyfulheart.com/forums/topic/1750-q2-the-compassionate-god/

We Are Slaves Today (Nehemiah 9:36-37)

The passage concludes with Judah's current situation.

> [36] "But see, we are slaves today, slaves in the land you gave our forefathers so they could eat its fruit and the other good things it produces. [37] Because of our sins, its abundant harvest goes to the kings you have placed over us. They rule over our bodies and our cattle as they please. We are in great distress." (Nehemiah 9:36-37)

The people of Judah are not slaves in the personal sense of forced labor. But they are slaves in the sense that the King of Persia rules over them and requires a tribute from all of them in the form of heavy taxation. Though Nehemiah has been a kind governor on behalf of Persia, the taxes are still a heavy burden. "We are in great distress" (verse 37b) describes them well and explains their willingness to repent and covenant with God.

---

[253] Deuteronomy 5:9-10; Psalm 86:15; 103:8-10; Joel 2:13.

The Agreement of the People (Nehemiah 9:38-10:39)

> "In view of all this, we are making[254] a binding agreement,[255] putting it in writing, and our leaders, our Levites and our priests are affixing their seals to it." (Nehemiah 9:38)

What follows is a list of all the leaders of the people who seal this covenant beginning with "Nehemiah the governor, the son of Hacaliah," then the priests, the Levites, followed by the nobles, the leaders of various clans and cities (Nehemiah 10:27).

The leaders who are men of stature "sign" the document using their signets. The others, including their wives and sons and daughters, join those who sign and

> "... bind themselves with a curse and an oath to follow the Law of God given through Moses the servant of God and to obey carefully all the commands, regulations and decrees of the LORD our Lord." (10:29)

The agreement doesn't specify all the laws contained in the Pentateuch, but highlights those that have been seriously neglected.

1. No intermarriage with non-Jews (verse 30; Exodus 34:12-16).
2. No buying or selling on the Sabbath (verse 31a).
3. Letting the land lie fallow in the seventh year (verse 31b, Exodus 23:11; Leviticus 25:4-7, 20-22).
4. Cancelling all debts in the seventh year (verse 31c).
5. Giving a 1/3 shekel tax to maintain the temple and its services (verses 32-33, Exodus 30:11-16).
6. Staffing the temple with priests and Levites, as determined by lot (verse 34a).
7. Bringing wood for the altar, as determined by lot (verse 34b).
8. Bringing firstfruits of crops and fruit trees to the temple (verses 35, 37a).
9. Redeeming firstborn sons, and sacrificing the firstborn of livestock (verse 36).
10. Tithing 1/10th of crops to the Levites to support the Levites and the priesthood (verses 37b-38; Numbers 18:26).

---

[254] The verb translated "make" is *kārat*, "to cut," sometimes used in making a covenant, or "cutting" a covenant. A covenant must be cut because the slaughter of animals was a part of the covenant ritual (Genesis 15:18; Jeremiah 34:18). Cutting up the animals also represents a kind of curse against those who break a covenant (Elmer B. Smick, TWOT #1048).

[255] "Binding agreement" (NIV), "agreement" (NRSV), "firm covenant" (ESV), "sure covenant" (KJV) use one Hebrew word: *'amānâ*, "settled provision, support" from the verb *'āman*, "confirm, be faithful." Holladay (*Hebrew Lexicon*, p. 20) defines the word here as "agreement" and in Nehemiah 11:23 as "royal prescription."

The agreement concludes with the summary: "We will not neglect the house of our God" (verse 39).

The New Residents of Jerusalem (Nehemiah 11:1-24)

As noted previously, Jerusalem had been sparsely populated.

> "Now the city was large and spacious, but there were few people in it, and the houses had not yet been rebuilt." (Nehemiah 7:4)

Now that its walls were secure, however, it is important to increase the city population to maintain security, as well as to reestablish Jerusalem as the capital city of the province of Judah and the center of the Jewish faith; Nehemiah calls it "the holy city" (Nehemiah 11:1).

> "[1] Now the leaders of the people settled in Jerusalem, and the rest of the people cast lots to bring one out of every ten to live in Jerusalem, the holy city, while the remaining nine were to stay in their own towns. [2] The people commended all the men who volunteered to live in Jerusalem." (Nehemiah 11:1-2)

First, the leaders agree to living in Jerusalem. Next, Nehemiah first asks for volunteers. Then he institutes a kind of lottery to draft 10% of the people in the province to live within the city.

What follows is a list of names of tribes and leaders, with totals of the men selected to live within the city. Of course, they are joined by their wives, children, and households.

- Judah, 468 (verses 4-6)
- Benjamin, 928 men (verses 7-8)
- Priests, 1,192 (verses 10-14)
- Levites, 284 (verses 15-18)
- Gatekeepers, 172 (verse 19)

These total 3,044.

In addition, verse 23 notes that some of the temple singers, specifically provided for by King David's regulations, live within the city. Verse 24 seems to indicate that Pethahiah is the representative of Judah in the court of the King of Persia (see Ezra 10:23; Nehemiah 3:4).

Jewish Towns and Lists of Priests (Nehemiah 11:25-12:26)

Now the various towns where the Jews live are listed: First, the tribe of Judah (verses 25-30). Many of these towns are well known from the history of Israel. Members of the tribe of Judah are located in their ancestral cities to the south of Jerusalem.

"So they were living all the way from Beersheba to the Valley of Hinnom." (Nehemiah 11:30)

Benjamin, a smaller tribe, are settled north and west of Jerusalem, along with some of the Levites who had traditionally lived in Judean towns (verses 31-36).

Nehemiah 12:1-26 includes various lists of high priests and priestly and Levitical families. Though they have historical interest, there are few lessons for us here.

Preparing and Purifying the Singers, Instrumentalists, and Priests (Nehemiah 12:27-30)

The walls are complete, a spiritual revival is going on in Judah, but now it is time to cap it all off with a great ceremony to celebrate the completion of the wall – carefully planned and orchestrated. Levite musicians are identified from the various Jewish villages and brought into the city to practice for the big day.

"At the dedication[256] of the wall of Jerusalem, the Levites were sought out from where they lived and were brought to Jerusalem to celebrate joyfully[257] the dedication with songs of thanksgiving[258] and with the music[259] of cymbals, harps and lyres." (Nehemiah 12:27)

The joyful singing needs instruments for accompaniment. Three of these instruments are listed here – cymbals,[260] harps,[261] and lyres.[262]

---

[256] "Dedication" is ḥanukkâ, "dedication," from ḥānak, "dedicate, inaugurate.... Although usually rendered 'dedicate' a more accurate translation is 'begin' or 'initiate'" (Victor P. Hamilton, TWOT #693b). The Feast of Hanukkah celebrates the rededication of the temple in 165 BC after it had been desecrated by Antiochus Epiphanes in 167 BC. This feast is mentioned in John 10:22.

[257] The phrases, "celebrate joyfully" (NIV), "celebrate with gladness" (NRSV, ESV), "keep with gladness" (KJV) translate two words as we saw in Nehemiah 9:12: the infinitive construct of the verb ʿāśâ, "do, make" and the noun śimḥâ, "joy, mirth," from the verb "being glad or joyful with the whole disposition" (Bruce K. Waltke, TWOT #2268b).

[258] "Songs of thanksgiving" (NIV), "hymns of thanksgiving" (NRSV), or more literally, "with thanksgivings and with singing" (ESV), "both with thanksgivings and with singing" (KJV) is two words, tôdâ, "confession, praise, thanks, thanksgiving" (which we see in verse 31, TWOT #847b) and shîr, "song," from shîr, "to sing" (TWOT #2378a).

[259] "Music of" (NIV), "songs to the accompaniment of" (NRSV, NJB), "singing with" (ESV, KJV), is shîr, "song."

[260] "Cymbals" have been found in various Near Eastern sites from the 14th to the 8th centuries BC. Mesiltayim, "pair of cymbals," similar to ṣelṣelîm (from ṣll, "to ring, tremble") (TWOT #1919f). These are

Next, special teams of skilled singers are recruited from villages of singers near Jerusalem (Nehemiah 12:28-29).

At the same time, the priests and Levites make preparations for the great day with rites of cleansing.

> "When the priests and Levites had purified themselves ceremonially, they purified the people, the gates and the wall." (Nehemiah 22:30)

In Leviticus 8, when Aaron and his sons purify the newly-constructed tabernacle, the priests are purified first, then the tabernacle. In the same way, now the priests and Levites, first purify[263] themselves (verse 30a), and then "the people, the gates, and the wall" (verse 30b).

Grand Processions on the Wall (Nehemiah 12:31-43)

> "I had the leaders of Judah go up on top of the wall. I also assigned two large choirs[264] to give thanks." (Nehemiah 12:31)

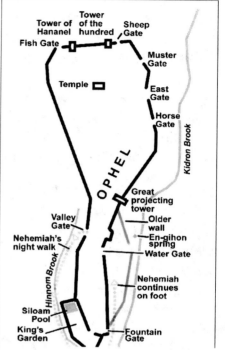

---

generally bronze round flat plates, 4 to 6 inches (10 to 15 cm.) in diameter, with central bowl-like depressions and fitted with iron finger rings (Daniel A. Foxvog and Anne D. Kilmer, "Music," ISBE 3:436-449).

[261] "Harps" (NIV, NRSV, ESV), "psalteries"(KJV) refer to an instrument of as many as 12 strings, plucked with the fingers (Louis Goldberg, *nēbel*, TWOT 1284b; Josephus, *Antiquities* 7.12).

[262] "Lyres" (NIV, NRSV, ESV), "harps" (KJV) which is smaller, and considered to have a "sweet" tone (Psalm 81:2), commonly associated with joy and gladness. The *kinnor* is the most often mentioned Old Testament stringed instrument, and the term itself was used widely throughout the ancient Near East. Its accompaniment was common in feasts, and was sometimes played by dancing girls (Isaiah 23:16). This is David's "harp," although it is now generally considered to be a type of lyre. It was the main instrument in the second temple orchestra (Foxvog and Kilmer, pp. 440-442; John N. Oswalt, *kinnor*, TWOT #1004a).

[263] "Purified," used twice in verse 30, is *ṭāhēr*, "be pure, be clean." Regarding the priests and Levites it appears with the Hithpael stem, "purify oneself"; regarding the people, gates, and walls it has the Piel stem, causative, "declare clean" (Holladay, *Hebrew Lexicon*, p. 122).

[264] The word "choirs" isn't in the text rather it is literally "great thanksgivings," or as the NRSV margin puts it "two great thanksgiving choirs." "Choirs to give thanks" (NIV, ESV), "choirs" (NRSV), "thanksgiving choirs" (NRSV margin), *"companies of* them that gave thanks" (KJV), is probably best "thanksgivings," using the plural noun *tôdâ*, "confession, praise, sacrifice of praise, thanks, thanksgiving, thank-offering."

Now Nehemiah describes two groups. Each great company has various leaders assigned, as well as singers, musicians playing cymbals, harps, and lyres, along with trumpeters.

When each completes its half-circuit of the city along the top of the wall, they come down and take their assigned places in the temple courts. Trumpets sound.

We are not told the starting points, but perhaps they start at the Valley Gate on the west side of the city (as had Nehemiah on his nocturnal reconnaissance, Nehemiah 2:12).

- **Ezra's company goes counter-clockwise** along the southern and then the eastern wall towards the temple with the musicians.
- **Nehemiah's company goes clockwise**, towards and along the north wall with the singers.

The exact routes of each company are specified in verses 31-39, but it is difficult to completely reconstruct them today, especially where they go down from the wall to proceed to the temple courts. Since all of the marchers have a personal stake in "their" section of the repaired wall, they all looked appreciatively at their handiwork.

Rejoicing in the Temple (Nehemiah 12:40-43)

"[40] The two choirs that gave thanks then took their places in the house of God; so did I, together with half the officials, [41] as well as the priests ... with their trumpets.... The choirs sang under the direction of Jezrahiah. [43] And on that day they offered great sacrifices, rejoicing because God had given them great joy. The women and children also rejoiced. The sound of rejoicing in Jerusalem could be heard far away." (Nehemiah 12:40-43)

Often accounts of great festivals tell in detail how many animals and of what variety were sacrificed. But here we read only that they "offered great sacrifices." The emphasis is on the joy, the singing, the trumpets, and the praise.

When the temple foundation had been dedicated years before, we read:

"No one could distinguish the sound of the shouts of joy from the sound of weeping, because the people made so much noise. And the sound was heard far away." (Ezra 3:13)

This time, the sound of rejoicing can be heard far from Jerusalem also, but now the people's rejoicing is not divided, but united – clear, loud, and joyful.

Tôdâ "basically means 'confession,' either of sin or of God's character and works," from *yādâ*, "confess, praise, give thanks, thank" (Ralph H. Alexander, TWOT #847b).

"The sound of rejoicing in Jerusalem could be heard far away." (Nehemiah 12:43b)

Appointing Storeroom Superintendents (Nehemiah 12:44-47)

Now Nehemiah appoints individuals to be responsible for the storerooms in the temple building. Verses 44-47 seem like an historical note, but the author includes it here to explain how a great sin came about after Nehemiah completed his first governorship. The writer is rightly proud that Judah is willingly supporting the priests and Levites who keep the temple services going according the Law. Sadly, this is to change, as we'll see in Nehemiah 13.

The Collapse of a Genuine Revival (Nehemiah 13)

The final chapter of Nehemiah is discouraging. The book has seen Nehemiah's vision of a restored Jerusalem, his diligence to rebuild the wall, and the spiritual revival that follows through the reading of the Law. These are all genuine works of the Holy Spirit.

But alas, without consistent leadership, many of the temple reforms fall into disuse. We read in verses 6 and 7:

> "While all this was going on, I was not in Jerusalem, for in the thirty-second year of Artaxerxes king of Babylon I had returned to the king. Some time later I asked his permission and came back to Jerusalem." (Nehemiah 13:6-7a)

Nehemiah had promised Artaxerxes that he would return to the palace in Susa, presumably to resume his duties as cupbearer (Nehemiah 2:6). His first term as governor of Judah is from 445 to 433 BC. Now he is obligated to return. In his absence, however, much of the fruit of the spiritual revival seems to dissipate. When he returns, an unspecified number of years later, things seem to have seriously fallen apart. He comes once more as governor of the province and doesn't hesitate to use his authority to set things in order without wasting much time.

Let's look at Nehemiah's reforms during his second term as governor.

The High Priest's Unfaithfulness (Nehemiah 13:1-5, 7b-9)

To set the scene of this spiritual decline, the author reminds us that the public reading of "the Book of Moses" under Ezra had informed the people that non-Jews should not be allowed in the temple, especially Ammonites and Moabites, Israel's historic enemies (Deuteronomy 23:3-5). At that time, the people obey this command and "they excluded from Israel all who were of foreign descent" (Nehemiah 13:3b).

We also know that during Nehemiah's first governorship, Eliashib serves as high priest, and seems to provide adequate leadership for the temple and the priests who serve under him (Nehemiah 3:1, 20-21). As high priest, he supervises those who had been appointed as storeroom supervisors (Nehemiah 12:44-47). But when Nehemiah leaves, Eliashib's sins become manifest.

> "4 Before this, Eliashib the priest had been put in charge of the storerooms of the house of our God. He was closely associated with Tobiah, 5 and he had provided him with a large room formerly used to store the grain offerings and incense and temple articles, and also the tithes of grain, new wine and oil prescribed for the Levites, singers and gatekeepers, as well as the contributions for the priests." (Nehemiah 13:4-5)

It turns out that Eliashib has retained close ties with Tobiah, one of Judah's arch-enemies, who had tried on several occasions to stop construction of the wall (Nehemiah 4 and 6). Tobiah is an Ammonite (Nehemiah 4:3), one of the peoples who were prohibited from entering the temple according to Mosaic Law (Deuteronomy 23:3-5).

You will recall that even as the wall was being constructed to keep out the enemy, some of the leading families of Judah were corresponding with the enemy (Nehemiah 6:17-19). Apparently, the high priest himself is one of those who maintains alliances with the enemy. After Nehemiah returns to Susa, the high priest's grandson marries the daughter of Sanballat, Judah's other arch enemy, so now it becomes clear that the high priest has ties with *both* chief enemies.

> "One of the sons of Joiada son of Eliashib the high priest was son-in-law to Sanballat the Horonite. And I drove him away from me." (Nehemiah 13:28)

Perhaps Eliashib thinks that keeping ties with Tobiah and Sanballat, leaders of adjoining provinces, is just good politics. But flirting with temptation leads him into both treason against his people and sin against Yahweh. Upon Nehemiah's return to Jerusalem he is appalled to find what the high priest has done.

> "7b I learned about the evil thing Eliashib had done in providing Tobiah a room in the courts of the house of God. 8 I was greatly displeased and threw all Tobiah's household goods out of the room. 9 I gave orders to purify the rooms, and then I put back into them the equipment of the house of God, with the grain offerings and the incense." (Nehemiah 13:7b-9)

Giving Tobiah his own personal room in the temple of God, formerly a storeroom, says to all of Jerusalem that the enemy Tobiah the Ammonite now has influence at the highest levels of government. The enemy who couldn't enter Jerusalem because of its rebuilt walls and gates, has now been invited by the high priest into the temple itself – the very place where an Ammonite was not allowed to enter by divine law!

Allowing the Enemy into the Center of our Lives

As I think about this incident, it reminds me of our own personal battle with sin. We can successfully fight Satan through the powerful spiritual weapons given to us believers – the Name of Jesus, truth, Christ's righteousness, the Word of God, assurance of our salvation, a readiness to run with the Good News, faith, prayer, etc. (Ephesians 6:10-18).

But so long as we nurse a desire for sin, our defenses are worthless.

> "Each one is tempted when, by his own evil desire, he is dragged away and enticed. Then, after desire has conceived, it gives birth to sin; and sin, when it is full-grown, gives birth to death." (James 1:14-15)

Heart repentance is necessary. Paul tells us to consider our old selves dead. We are told to "crucify" the flesh and its desires (Galatians 5:24; cf. 2:20; 6:14). We must keep constant vigilance, or our old selves will come back to reclaim their control of us. Even Paul feels the need to keep watch and discipline himself (1 Corinthians 9:26-27).

We're all subject to the attacks of the tempter. Peter exhorts us:

> "Be self-controlled and alert. Your enemy the devil prowls around like a roaring lion looking for someone to devour. Resist him, standing firm in the faith, because you know that your brothers throughout the world are undergoing the same kind of sufferings." (1 Peter 5:8-9)

My dear friend, if you've let the enemy back into the center of your life where he doesn't belong, repent and call upon Jesus to kick him out and give you strength. With the help of your brothers and sisters – and the Spirit of God – you can see victory in your life. Thank God that he is gracious and compassionate!

Q3. (Nehemiah 13:1-5, 7-9) Does God set higher standards for leaders than for others? If so, why? What results in the people when leaders become corrupt? How can you keep this from happening to you? If God shows you corruption within, how can you recover from it?
http://www.joyfulheart.com/forums/topic/1751-q3-leader-integrity/

Failure to Support God's House and Its Services (Nehemiah 13:10-14)

You'll remember the "binding agreement" signed by all of Judah's leaders (Nehemiah 9:38-10:39), and all the others who bound themselves "with a curse and an oath." It contained specific elements to provide for the temple workers, and concluded with the pledge: "We will not neglect the house of our God." (Nehemiah 10:39b).

While Nehemiah has been gone, the agreement has been ignored. There is no financial support for the temple workers, so they have gone back to their villages to earn a living from the soil. Temple worship is in shambles.

> "I also learned that the portions assigned to the Levites had not been given to them, and that all the Levites and singers responsible for the service had gone back to their own fields." (Nehemiah 13:10)

Nehemiah calls the officials to account:

> "[11] So I rebuked the officials and asked them, 'Why is the house of God neglected?' Then I called them together and stationed them at their posts. [12] All Judah brought the tithes of grain, new wine and oil into the storerooms." (Nehemiah 13:11-12)

Then Nehemiah fires the old leaders and appoints new leaders who will get the job done.

> "[13] I put Shelemiah the priest, Zadok the scribe, and a Levite named Pedaiah in charge of the storerooms and made Hanan son of Zaccur, the son of Mattaniah, their assistant, because these men were considered trustworthy. They were made responsible for distributing the supplies to their brothers. [14] Remember me for this, O my God, and do not blot out what I have so faithfully done for the house of my God and its services." (Nehemiah 13:13-14)

Why was the house of God neglected? A failure of leadership, pure and simple. After Nehemiah leaves, those he had appointed don't do their jobs. They slough off. They became functionaries in title only, but with no zeal for God's house. They are only going through the motions.

We know that Eliashib the high priest is corrupt. During this period, Ezra seems to have died. And Nehemiah's successor as governor probably isn't a spiritual man. Nor does he seem to have the influence and force of will to keep the people in line with God's word. Due to the lack of strong leadership, Satan regains a place in the temple.

Dear friends, when I read this sad account, my mind goes to our churches. Many of our churches have officers who serve almost as an "hereditary leader" – as treasurer or moderator or head of the deacons or trustees or vestry or session or board, whatever name your church has for them. They are uninspired, just going through the motions. No wonder our churches tend to be in decline.

What needs to happen is to fire those leaders in our churches who refuse to get "fired up" about the Lord and his work. That's what Nehemiah did. Of course, he had the authority of the king of Persia behind him.

If a new pastor comes to your church, with the authority of Christ Jesus behind him, and begins to clean up the church leadership, you know what happens. He or she is quickly crucified and fired so that the status quo can prevail.

Dear friends, we need to fast and pray and call out to God for our churches, that true revival from God will come and blow in with the refreshing Wind of the Spirit. I think of the chorus of the song, "Fall Afresh," that Jeremy Riddle has written as a prayer.

"Awaken, my soul, come awake
To hunger, to seek, to thirst.
Awaken, first love, come awake,
And do as you did at first.

Spirit of the Living God
Come, fall afresh on me.
Come wake me from my sleep.
Blow through the caverns of my soul,
Pour in me to overflow.

Come and fill this place!
Let your glory now invade!"[265]

"Fall Afresh" is written as a prayer for individual revival. But perhaps we ought to change the "me" and "my" to "us" and "our," and sing it as a corporate prayer. Our churches need what Jerusalem needed: a powerful spiritual revival that will fuel reforms of heart and will and lifestyle. God help us! Man can't revive our churches. We are utterly dependent upon the Holy Spirit to deliver us.

Desecrating the Sabbath (Nehemiah 13:15)

Another part of the "binding agreement" had specified:

"When the neighboring peoples bring merchandise or grain to sell on the Sabbath, we will not buy from them on the Sabbath or on any holy day." (Nehemiah 10:31a)

---

[265] "Fall Afresh," words and music by Jeremy Riddle (©2011 Mercy/Vineyard Publishing).

When Nehemiah returns he sees Sabbath laws completely disregarded, desecrated, profaned.[266]

> "In those days I saw men in Judah treading winepresses on the Sabbath and bringing in grain and loading it on donkeys, together with wine, grapes, figs and all other kinds of loads. And they were bringing all this into Jerusalem on the Sabbath." (Nehemiah 13:15a)

Nehemiah rebukes the leaders:

> "17b What is this wicked thing you are doing – desecrating the Sabbath day? 18 Didn't your forefathers do the same things, so that our God brought all this calamity upon us and upon this city? Now you are stirring up more wrath against Israel by desecrating the Sabbath." (Nehemiah 13:17b-18)

Nehemiah deals with the offense by commanding that Jerusalem's gates be shut for the entire Sabbath. This works for the short-term, but it doesn't change men's hearts or remove the greed that drives Sabbath-breaking. Later he makes guarding the city gates on the Sabbath a job of the Levites, not just secular guards (Nehemiah 13:19-22).

Intermarriage with Non-Jews (Nehemiah 13:23-29)

Now we come again to a recurring problem – intermarriage with non-Jews. Under Ezra some years before, men had agreed to put away their non-Jewish wives and families (Ezra 9:1-2; 10). Ezra is no longer on the scene, since he never would have allowed this recurrence of intermarriage.

> "23 Moreover, in those days I saw men of Judah who had married women from Ashdod, Ammon and Moab. 24 Half of their children spoke the language of Ashdod or the language of one of the other peoples, and did not know how to speak the language of Judah. 25 I rebuked them and called curses down on them. I beat some of the men and pulled out their hair." (Nehemiah 13:23-25)

When Nehemiah sees the return of intermarriage, he is beside himself. He starts beating up the offenders physically. The problem goes to the very top leadership, to the son of Eliashib the high priest.

> "One of the sons of Joiada son of Eliashib the high priest was son-in-law to Sanballat the Horonite. And I drove him away from me." (Nehemiah 13:28)

---

[266] "Desecrating" (NIV), "profaning" (NRSV, ESV, KJV) is *ḥālal*, "profane, defile, pollute, desecrate." The word is used 83 times in the Old Testament, often associated with uncleanness, breaking the covenant, defiling the temple, and personal defilement (Donald J. Wiseman, TWOT #661).

Nehemiah reminds them that intermarriage was the fall of Solomon himself and forces people to take an oath not to allow their sons or daughters to intermarry (Nehemiah 13:25-27). I can't help but think about the "binding agreement" that they signed and swore to a few years prior:

> "We promise not to give our daughters in marriage to the peoples around us or take their daughters for our sons." (Nehemiah 10:30)

What makes us think they'll keep this oath any more rigorously than they did the first?

The Covenant of the Priesthood (Nehemiah 13:29)

Nehemiah prays in resignation:

> "Remember them, O my God, because they defiled the priestly office and the covenant of the priesthood and of the Levites." (Nehemiah 13:29)

The "priestly office" or "priesthood"[267] is a holy institution, one that was instituted by the Mosaic Covenant. "Covenant" is berît, a formal and solemn agreement or treaty between nations or individuals, which includes both benefits and obligations. There are sometimes rituals of "cutting" a covenant, such as sacrifices, anointing, setting up a stone, etc.[268] In the case of the priests, the covenant is made between a superior (Yahweh) and his inferiors who answer directly to him – the priests, Aaron and his descendants.

The priests enter into the covenant with an elaborate ceremony of purification and ordination spelled out in the Mosaic Law (Exodus 29; Leviticus 8-9). This gives them the right (and obligation) to enter holy places and minister in God's presence. They enjoy a special "nearness" to God himself (Numbers 16:10). According to this covenant, they are not allowed to own land, but may live in Levitical towns among the other tribes. Their privileges include having their family's food supplied from the firstfruits offerings, tithes, and sacrifices of the people of Israel.

Malachi also talks about this special "covenant with Levi," a special "covenant of life and peace" (Malachi 2:4-5). The priest Phinehas and his descendants are given a special "covenant of peace" and a "covenant of lasting priesthood" with Yahweh because of Phinehas's zeal for the Lord's holiness (Numbers 25:12-13). Being a priest is a profound privilege, a privilege lost by Eli and his sons (1 Samuel 2:30-36; 1 Kings 2:27).

---

[267] "Priestly office" (NIV), "priesthood" (NRSV, ESV, KJV) is kehunnâ, "priesthood," from kāhan, "minister in a priest's office, act as priest." A related noun is kōhen, "principal officer or chief ruler, priest" (TWOT #959b) This word appears in Jewish communities today as Cohen.

[268] Elmer B. Smick, berit, TWOT #282a.

I realize that all Christians are included in a "priesthood of believers" (1 Peter 2:5). But I also believe that pastors and elders have special spiritual privileges before God – a God-given authority, a higher standard, and obligations of faithfulness (1 Timothy 5:17-20; James 3:1; Luke 12:47-48; 1 Corinthians 4:2; Hebrews 13:17). We have the privilege of searching the deep things of God so we can communicate them to others and lead them in the paths we have found to draw near to God. In a similar way, deacons who serve faithfully "gain an excellent standing" (1 Timothy 3:13).

Nehemiah's Disappointment (Nehemiah 13:30-31)

The book of Nehemiah concludes with Nehemiah reporting on how he has corrected the most recent offenses.

> "30 So I purified the priests and the Levites of everything foreign, and assigned them duties, each to his own task. 31 I also made provision for contributions of wood at designated times, and for the firstfruits." (Nehemiah 13:30-31a)

He cleans up the messes that have occurred in his absence and sets them right again. Then he prays.

> "Remember me with favor, O my God." (Nehemiah 13:31b)

Nehemiah has tried his hardest. But he has failed to change the hearts of the people. He has seen a Holy Spirit revival, but its effects are rapidly diminishing. He prays, "Remember, O God, that I tried." How sad a way to end the book of Nehemiah.

In Nehemiah's day, of course, only a few prophets were filled with the Holy Spirit. In our day, all believers taste of the Spirit (Romans 8:10). But it is one thing to have a glimmer of spiritual life in you because of the Spirit; it is quite another to walk daily in willing submission to the Spirit (Galatians 5:16-25). Many believers haven't grown to the place that they are firmly on the path of discipleship.

The Apostle Paul experienced something akin to Nehemiah's frustration when he addresses believers whom he had brought to faith, but have failed to grow, to mature. To the Corinthians he says,

> "Brothers, I could not address you as spiritual but as worldly – mere infants in Christ. I gave you milk, not solid food, for you were not yet ready for it. Indeed, you are still not ready. You are still worldly…." (1 Corinthians 3:1-3a)

To the Galatian believers he sighs….

> "My dear children, for whom I am again in the pains of childbirth until Christ is formed in you." (Galatians 4:19)

Jesus, too, experienced frustration. When he hears that his disciples have failed to deliver a demon-afflicted boy, Jesus says:

> "O faithless and twisted generation, how long am I to be with you? How long am I to bear with you? Bring him here to me." (Matthew 17:17, ESV)

What are leaders to do? Nehemiah is discouraged that he still had to clean up the messes created in his absence. Paul is discouraged at the sluggish pace of spiritual growth in some of his churches. Jesus' disciples don't seem to learn quickly. Nevertheless, we leaders must not give up. We patiently feed milk, if that is what is needed. We love. We are patient. We put up with each other (Ephesians 4:1-3). That is what Jesus does with his disciples. That is what Paul does with the Thessalonian believers:

> "For you know that we dealt with each of you as a father deals with his own children, encouraging, comforting and urging you to live lives worthy of God, who calls you into his kingdom and glory." (1 Thessalonians 2:11-12)

Paul exhorts Timothy:

> "Preach the Word; be prepared in season and out of season; correct, rebuke and encourage – with great patience and careful instruction." (2 Timothy 4:2)

Nehemiah shows patience in the face of discouragement. And that's what I encourage you, my friend, to continue in. Patiently do what God has called you to do, until he calls you home.

Ministry not Monuments

I can empathize with Nehemiah's discouragement to see the work he had so diligently set up, fall apart when he leaves. I saw this happen with my first church; I also had to close a church plant after more than a decade of its life – one of the hardest things I've ever had to do.

God taught me through this that he doesn't call us to build monuments to our achievements, so we can point to something and say, "I did that." That's pride.

Church leaders don't "own" the church they lead; God does. Rather, our job is one of a servant. We serve God at a particular point in time. We seek to listen to him and do our best. We care for the people he sends us and seek to teach them to serve Jesus as disciples. To be a faithful servant – that is enough. We do our part and leave the results in God's hands.

Our identity isn't identical to what we have labored to build. Our identity is found in God himself, who calls us, loves us, and cares for us. Nevertheless, I do understand Nehemiah's final prayer:

"Remember me with favor, O my God." (Nehemiah 13:31b)

Q4. (Nehemiah 13:30-31) How should you respond when the people you are ministering to disappoint you? How must you treat them? What must you do to sustain your own faith and spiritual momentum in times of discouragement?
http://www.joyfulheart.com/forums/topic/1752-q4-disappointment/

Discipleship Lessons

There are many spiritual lessons in these chapters.

1. Scripture reading – while communicating understanding of what is read – can be effective in bringing personal and corporate revival (Nehemiah 7:73b-8:18).
2. Scripture can cause grief and sorrow that leads to repentance (Nehemiah 7:9).
3. The joy of the Lord is an indicator of our faith in and love for Jesus – and thus is our strength (Nehemiah 8:9-11).
4. God's grace and compassion allow us to exist before him. These flow from his essential character revealed to Moses – "the compassionate and gracious God, slow to anger, abounding in love and faithfulness, maintaining love to thousands, and forgiving wickedness, rebellion and sin" (Exodus 34:6b-7a; Nehemiah 9:17).
5. Signing a covenant can deepen the impression of our decision in us – though the Israelites don't long enforce and keep the covenants they had sworn to (Nehemiah 9:38-10:39).
6. Grand celebrations, like the celebration at the completion of the wall, remind us of God's faithfulness (Nehemiah 12:31-43).
7. Leaders like Nehemiah can expect to be disappointed. Unless it is continually reinforced and led forward, a corporate body can atrophy and begin to decline (Nehemiah 13). One of the great challenges of church leaders today is to look forward, not back, to find the new great thing God has for the congregation.

8. God sets a higher standard for leaders, for people use them as a sort of standard of what is expected of them. When leaders like Eliashib the high priest are corrupt, they destroy the standard of holiness for the entire people (Nehemiah 13:1-5, 7b-9).

9. Failure to support the temple through tithes and offerings results in a drastic reduction of ministry (Nehemiah 13:10-14). The same is true of the church.

10. The priesthood is a core part of God's covenant with his people. To be a priest or Levite is a high calling. Today, it is a high calling to be a pastor, elder, deacon – whatever you call them in your congregation. The church leadership, like the priesthood, needs to be purified from everything "foreign" (Nehemiah 13:29-31).

Prayer

Father, I know the discouragement that Nehemiah must have felt when he returned to find that much of his work had fallen into disrepair. You brought him genuine revival, but it didn't last. I pray that you'd help us to seek you and not neglect our relationship with you, so that interior revival might be the "new normal." Help us to so lead our congregations with integrity that your work might not dissipate, but grow. In Jesus' name, I pray. Amen.

Key Verses

"… Ezra the priest brought the Law before the assembly, which was made up of men and women and all who were able to understand. He read it aloud from daybreak till noon as he faced the square before the Water Gate in the presence of the men, women and others who could understand. And all the people listened attentively to the Book of the Law." (Nehemiah 8:2b-3, NIV)

"The Levites … instructed the people in the Law while the people were standing there. They read from the Book of the Law of God, making it clear and giving the meaning so that the people could understand what was being read." (Nehemiah 8:7-8, NIV)

"Then Nehemiah the governor, Ezra the priest and scribe, and the Levites who were instructing the people said to them all, 'This day is sacred to the LORD your God. Do not mourn or weep.' For all the people had been weeping as they listened to the words of the Law. Nehemiah said, 'Go and enjoy choice food and sweet drinks, and send some to those who have nothing prepared. This day is sacred to our Lord. Do not grieve, for the joy of the LORD is your strength.'" (Nehemiah 8:9-10, NIV)

"... The Israelites gathered together, fasting and wearing sackcloth and having dust on their heads. Those of Israelite descent had separated themselves from all foreigners. They stood in their places and confessed their sins and the wickedness of their fathers. They stood where they were and read from the Book of the Law of the LORD their God for a quarter of the day, and spent another quarter in confession and in worshiping the LORD their God." (Nehemiah 9:1-3, NIV)

"So I rebuked the officials and asked them, 'Why is the house of God neglected?' Then I called them together and stationed them at their posts." (Nehemiah 13:11, NIV)

"So I purified the priests and the Levites of everything foreign, and assigned them duties, each to his own task." (Nehemiah 13:30, NIV)

9. Love, Worship, and Marriage (Malachi 1-2)

Ezra and Nehemiah (active from 458 to about 430 BC) have worked hard to secure Jerusalem from its enemies, purify the priesthood, establish support for temple worship, and deal with ethical issues that plagued the returned exiles. Ezra approaches it from the standpoint of a priest scribe – through the Word of God. Nehemiah approaches it from the standpoint of a godly administrator – through covenants, laws, and procedures. But God also sends Malachi, who approaches these problems from the standpoint of a prophet – through pointed words from God designed to reveal the heart and urge God's people to godly living.

James J. Tissot, detail from 'Malachi' (1898-1902), gouache on board, The Jewish Museum, New York.

We're not sure exactly when Malachi was written, since it doesn't include any historical mentions that might help us place it in an historical timeline. But the problems Malachi addresses are consistent with exiles who have become complacent. Some date it in the period from 500 to 475 BC, prior to Ezra's coming, though many place it a bit later, perhaps 450 to 430 BC, contemporaneous with the ministry of Ezra and Nehemiah.

Malachi seems to be divided into six oracles or prophecies. We'll cover three in this lesson and three in Lesson 10. Malachi's style is to set up a kind of "disputation." He asks rhetorical questions that might be in the mouths of his hearers. And then proceeds to answer them with words spoken directly from Yahweh. The effect is similar to the reasoned and forceful argumentation typical of a courtroom setting.[269]

Malachi's name means "messenger." Some have wondered if this is his real name. I think so; a number of prophets and kings in the Old Testament have meaningful names. I have a friend who calls him "the Italian prophet" by mispronouncing his name with

---

[269] Andrew E. Hill, "Malachi, Book of," Mark J. Boda and J. Gordon McConville (eds.), *Dictionary of the Old Testament Prophets*, pp. 525-533.

the "ch" sound rather than the hard "k" sound – ma-LA-chee vs. MAL-a-kai vs. (It's a joke, friends.)

Let's turn now to the various oracles or prophecies by which Yahweh seeks to renew his people.

Oracle 1. Jacob Loved, Esau Hated (Malachi 1:1-5)

"An oracle: The word of the LORD to Israel through Malachi." (Malachi 1:1)

The word translated "oracle" (NIV, NRSV, ESV), "burden" (KJV) is a heavy prophetic "pronouncement" accompanied by strong warnings. [270]

> "² 'I have loved you,' says the LORD.
>
> But you ask, "How have you loved us?"
>
> 'Was not Esau Jacob's brother?' the LORD says. 'Yet I have loved Jacob, ³ but Esau I have hated, and I have turned his mountains into a wasteland and left his inheritance to the desert jackals.'" (Malachi 1:2-3)

It's easy to over-translate these words "love" and "hate" to make them seem extreme polar opposites. The Hebrew word "love" (*ʾâhêb*) can cover anything from intense personal affection to preference for a specific food.[271] In the same way "hate" (*śānēʾ*) can range from deeply detesting something to a desire to avoid.[272] But it's fair to say that God is at least saying that he strongly prefers Jacob over Esau.

These verses are what we might think of as a kind "backhanded compliment." God is saying that Israel can see his love for them by comparing their reasonably good situation to the terrible judgment he has wreaked upon Edom, the traditional territory of Esau. Though Edom rebuilds, God promises that he will destroy them again.

---

[270] "Oracle" (NIV, NRSV, ESV), "burden" (KJV) is *maśśāʾ*, "burden, oracle," from *nāśāʾ*, "to lift, carry, take." Normally *maśśāʾ* refers to a burden, "imposed by a master, a despot, or a deity on subjects, beasts, men, or things." But when used in the context of prophecy (24 times in the Old Testament), *maśśāʾ* is a technical term, "a burden imposed on...." introducing the theme of a prophecy. Most modern translations render it as "oracle," though the term still contains the ideas of compulsion, urgency, dread. Holladay (*Hebrew Lexicon*, p. 217) renders it "pronouncement." See Baldwin, *Haggai, Zechariah, Malachi*, pp. 162-163; P.A.H. de Boer, *An Inquiry into the Meaning of the Term* Maśśāʾ (Brill: Leiden, 1948); Walter C. Kaiser, TWOT #1421e.

[271] "Loved" is *ʾâhêb*, "love," with meanings that can vary from God's intense affection for his people to someone who "loves" chocolate. Context must determine what the word denotes (Robert L. Alden, *ʾâhêb*, TWOT #29).

[272] "Hated" is *śānēʾ*, "hate, to be hateful." It expresses an emotional attitude toward persons and things which are opposed, detested, despised and with which one wishes to have no contact or relationship (Gerard Van Groenigen, *śānēʾ*, TWOT #2272).

Originally, of course, Jacob (Israel) and Esau are brothers. But, of the two, Jacob seeks God, while Esau doesn't seem to have much interest in his birthright or in God's promises. All this had taken place 1,500 years or so before Malachi's time. The results of those original ancestors' affections – and God's gracious and faithful love to Jacob – were that a remnant of Jacob's descendants followed Yahweh (sometimes only nominally), while Esau's descendants worshipped fertility gods and goddesses.

At this point, Yahweh considers Edom "the Wicked Land,[273] a people always under the wrath of the LORD" (Malachi 1:4b).

> "You will see it with your own eyes and say, 'Great is the LORD – even beyond the borders of Israel!'" (Malachi 1:5)

God promises that Israel will see the judgment upon Edom and attribute it to God's greatness as the universal God, not just the parochial, national God of Israel only.

Paul picks up this passage in Romans 9:10-15 to illustrate that God's election is entirely dependent upon His will, not upon the strivings of men.

You and I suffer various problems. But when we look at the blessings we experience from following the Lord, compared to the personal lives of those who have turned their backs on God, we can see what God has protected us from. Praise the Lord.

Oracle 2. Sincere Worship (Malachi 1:6-14)

The prophet has laid a foundation of assuring Israel of God's love. Now he asks: If I am a Father who loves you, why don't you treat me with respect?

> "'A son honors[274] his father, and a servant his master. If I am a father, where is the honor[275] due me? If I am a master, where is the respect[276] due me?' says the LORD Almighty." (Malachi 1:6)

---

[273] "Wicked" is *rish'â*, "guilt, wickedness," denoting the kind of life that is opposite to God's character (G. Herbert Livingston, TWOT #2222c). "Land" (NIV, NRSV, ESV), "border" (KJV) is *gebûl*, "border," also used in verse 5. The noun is used to designate either a geographical boundary or the territory as a whole. Here it refers to "the territory of wickedness." (Victor P. Hamilton, TWOT #307a).

[274] "Honors" is the Piel stem of *kābēd*, "honor" (Holladay, *Hebrew Lexicon*, p. 150). In the Psalms this word is often translated "glorify" (e.g. Psalm 50:15). This is the same root from which we get the noun *kābôd*, "glory."

[275] "Honor " is *kābôd*, "distinction, respect, mark of honor"(Holladay, *Hebrew Lexicon*, p. 151). When used to describe God the word is translated "glory."

[276] "Respect" (NIV, NRSV), literally, "fear" (ESV, KJV), *môrā'*, "fear," from *yārē*, "fear, be afraid, revere" (TWOT #907c).

I can almost hear the famous line from American stand-up comedian Rodney Dangerfield (1921-2004) – "I don't get no respect at all!"

When we treat holy things casually, we show that we don't respect God. I hope I don't offend you deeply in saying this, but when we put other things in front of gathering to worship God weekly, we disrespect God. Weekly worship must not be dependent upon the "quality" of the churches available in our community or our busyness. Worship is about God – our respect for him and our love for him.

Showing Contempt for God (Malachi 1:6-10)

God's strongest indictment concerning disrespect, however, doesn't focus on the people's general disrespect only, but on the priests who should know better and allow the disrespect in the first place.

> "It is you, O priests, who show contempt[277] for my name.[278]
>
> But you ask, 'How have we shown contempt for your name?'
>
> 7 You place defiled[279] food[280] on my altar. [281]
>
> But you ask, "How have we defiled you?"
>
> By saying that the LORD's table[282] is contemptible.[283] 8 When you bring blind animals for sacrifice, is that not wrong? When you sacrifice crippled or diseased ani-

---

[277] "Show contempt" (NIV), "despise" (NRSV, ESV, KJV) is *bāzâ*, "to despise, disdain, hold in contempt." The basic meaning of the root is "to accord little worth to something." While this action may or may not include overt feelings of contempt or scorn, the biblical usage indicates that the very act of undervaluing something or someone implies contempt. The use of *bāzâ* shows that disobedience to the Lord is based on "contempt, despising" of him. Thus David's adultery with Bathsheba is equated with contempt for the Lord (2 Samuel 12:10, 19) and his word (Bruce K. Waltke, TWOT #224).

[278] "Name" is *shēm*, "The concept of personal names in the Old Testament often included existence, character, and reputation" (Walter C. Kaiser, TWOT #2405).

[279] "Defiled" (NIV), "polluted" (NRSV, ESV, KJV) is *gā'al*, "defile, pollute," used 12 times in the Old Testament. A similar root is found in Aramaic meaning, "abhor, loathe." It is used in Malachi 1:7, 12 to refer to "ceremonial pollution of imperfect sacrifices" (R. Laird Harris, TWOT #301a).

[280] "Food" (NIV, NRSV, ESV) is literally "bread" (KJV), *leḥem*.

[281] "Altar" is *mizbēah*, a place of sacrifice, from *zābah*, "to sacrifice, slaughter" (TWOT #525b). "Altar" is used in parallel with "table," *shulḥān*, "table," originally an animal skin, later "table" or "place of eating" (Hermann J. Austel, TWOT #2395a).

[282] Notice the phrase "the Lord's table" in verses 7 and 12. The altar is "the Lord's table." (See also Ezekiel 41:22; 1 Corinthians 10:21). Some Protestant groups have downplayed a physical communion table as an "altar," but the connection between an altar of sacrifice and the Lord's Table is founded in Scripture.

[283] "Is contemptible" (NIV, KJV), "is to be despised" (NRSV), "may be despised" (ESV) is the Niphal stem of *bāzâ*, "despise, distain, hold in contempt" (TWOT #224).

mals, is that not wrong? Try offering them to your governor! Would he be pleased with you? Would he accept you?' says the LORD Almighty." (Nehemiah 1:6-8)

What's going on is that people are taking the attitude: So long as I bring some kind of sacrifice, that's all I need to do. And why should I bring my best animal to sacrifice, an animal I can get top dollar for in the market? Instead, I'll bring animals of lesser value to the temple, animals that have defects such as blindness or injured limbs or various diseases. That way I can get rid of the poorest of my flock and still perform my religious duties.

You can see the deep disrespect for God inherent in such thinking. And the Mosaic Law is very clear about this.

> "If an animal has a defect, is lame or blind, or has any serious flaw, you must not sacrifice it to the LORD your God." (Deuteronomy 15:21)

Again and again you see the phrase "without blemish" or "without defect" (Deuteronomy 17:1).

The priests know the Law – or are supposed to. But they accept inferior sacrifices nevertheless. Why? Perhaps they are getting paid under the table to do so. Or perhaps they don't care. Or perhaps they feel that something is better than nothing. Whatever the reason, the people who bring the sacrifices demonstrate deep disrespect towards God – and the priests even more, because they know better.

How will the nation – and their neighbors around them – understand the greatness of God when his own people and priests treat him disrespectfully?

> "'My name will be great among the nations, from the rising to the setting of the sun. In every place incense and pure offerings will be brought to my name, because my name will be great among the nations,' says the LORD Almighty." (Malachi 2:11)

Attacking God's Reputation (Malachi 1:12-13)

Now the prophet goes back to the priests' attitude that profanes Yahweh's name and reputation.

> "[12] 'But you profane it by saying of the Lord's table, "It is defiled," and of its food, "It is contemptible." [13] And you say, "What a burden!" and you sniff at it contemptuously,'" says the LORD Almighty. 'When you bring injured,[284] crippled or dis-

---

[284] "Injured" (NIV), "taken by robbery" (NASB), "taken by violence" (NRSV, ESV), "that which was torn" (KJV) is *gāzal*, "seize, tear off, pull off, take away by force, rob" (TWOT #337). Perhaps people were stealing animals that they would then offer in the temple.

eased animals and offer them as sacrifices, should I accept them from your hands?' says the LORD." (Malachi 1:12-13)

The priests probably don't actually utter the words, "The altar is defiled," and "These sacrifices are worthless." They say all the prescribed words of the ritual, but their actions speak louder than words of their disregard of God and his commandments. The priests see their ministry as a tiresome burden[285] rather than a privilege to bring reconciliation between man and God.

This casual attitude towards sacrifices "profanes" the Lord's name. The Hebrew word is *ḥālal*, "profane, defile, pollute, desecrate," with the idea of doing acts of "violence to the established law of God, breaking the covenant, or the divine statutes."[286]

When we treat worship as meaningless and not worthy of our full participation, we are saying to the world, our God isn't worth honoring with our very best. Though we say we are followers of Christ, those are just words. We don't really care!

A Curse on Those Who Cheat God (Malachi 1:14)

Now Malachi utters a curse on Yahweh's behalf.

"'Cursed[287] is the cheat who has an acceptable male in his flock and vows to give it, but then sacrifices a blemished animal to the Lord. For I am a great king,' says the LORD Almighty, 'and my name is to be feared among the nations.'" (Malachi 1:14)

The prophet has admonished and cursed the priests for accepting flawed sacrifices. Now he curses the people who bring flawed animals for sacrifice, while they keep the better animals for themselves. He calls them "cheats," from a verb that means to "act cleverly, cunningly, deceitfully."[288] These shrewd people think they're so smart in bringing defective sacrifices, but in doing so they bring on themselves God's curse and the punishments that come with it.

Instead of congratulating themselves for their cleverness, these cheats should call out to God for mercy.

---

[285] "What a burden" (NIV), "How tiresome" (NASB), "What a weariness" (NRSV, ESV, KJV) uses the noun *telā'â*, "toil, hardship" (TWOT #1066a).

[286] Donald J. Wiseman, *ḥālal*, TWOT #661.

[287] "Cursed" is *'ārar*, "cursed," often used in the declaration of punishments, and the utterance of threats (Victor P. Hamilton, TWOT #168).

[288] Holladay, *Hebrew Lexicon*, p. 238. "Cheat" (NIV, ESV, NRSV), "deceiver" (KJV) is the Qal stem of *nākal*, "be crafty, deceitful, knavish" (TWOT #366).

"⁹ 'Now implore God to be gracious to us. With such offerings from your hands, will he accept you?'[289] – says the LORD Almighty. ¹⁰ 'Oh, that one of you would shut the temple doors, so that you would not light useless fires[290] on my altar! I am not pleased[291] with you,' says the LORD Almighty, 'and I will accept[292] no offering from your hands.'" (Malachi 1:9-10)

You think that God doesn't see your terrible attitude? Of course he does, and he doesn't accept your sacrifices for forgiveness of sins. Which means that you are still in your sins before the Righteous and Living God, our God who is a "consuming fire" (Hebrews 12:9). Don't even bother to come to the temple, God says. Don't bother to light "useless fires" on the altar. Unless you come with repentance before a God whom you honor, it is better that you don't come at all.

I recall two other occasions when God's prophet denounces the corruption of temple worship. First, Eli allows his sons to steal the worshippers' portion of the sacrifices they are bringing to the temple.

"The sin of the young men was very great in the sight of the LORD, for the men treated the offering of the LORD with contempt."[293] (1 Samuel 2:17, ESV)

And the punishment is severe, affecting their father, and generations after them.

"I am about to punish [Eli's] house forever, for the iniquity that he knew, because his sons were blaspheming God, and he did not restrain them." (1 Samuel 3:12b-13)

The most familiar occasion, of course, is Jesus overturning the tables of the money changers and driving sheep and cattle out of the temple.

"He said to them, 'It is written, "My house shall be called a house of prayer," but you make it a den of robbers.'" (Matthew 21:13)

---

[289] "Accept" (NIV), "show favor" (NRSV, ESV), "regard your persons" (KJV) is literally, "lift up his face/countenance" as an indication of a good conscience, confidence, or acceptance (Walter C. Kaiser, nāśā', TWOT #1421). We see this construction in the Aaronic blessing, "The LORD lift up his countenance upon thee," or, as the NIV puts it, "turn his face toward you" (Numbers 6:26).

[290] "Light useless fires" (NIV) "kindle fire in vain" (NRSV, ESV), "kindle fire for naught" (KJV), uses the word ḥinnām, "freely, for nothing, unjustly, without cause, in vain." (TWOT #694b). Ironically, this word is derived from ḥānan, "be gracious, show pity" and related to ḥēn, "favor, grace."

[291] "Not pleased" (NIV, NRSV), "have no pleasure" (ESV, KJV) is the negative with ḥēpes, "delight" (TWOT #712b).

[292] "Accept" is rāsâ, "be pleased with, be favorable to" (TWOT #2207).

[293] "Treat with contempt" (NIV, NRSV, ESV), "abhorred" (KJV) is nā'as, "despise, abhor," an action or attitude whereby the former recipient of favorable disposition and/or services is consciously viewed and/or treated with disdain (Leonard J. Coppes, TWOT #1274).

This was a powerful rebuke on the high priest's family who received a profit from sales of sacrifices and money changing within the temple. The punishment was severe: the temple was utterly destroyed in 70 AD.

> **Q1. (Malachi 1:6-14) How were the people and priests disrespecting God with regard to offering sacrifices? In what ways do we today disrespect God in our attitudes toward worship, in giving to God, and in regard to holy things? What is God saying to you personally as you ponder this?**
> http://www.joyfulheart.com/forums/topic/1753-q1-respectful-worship/

Admonition for the Priests (Malachi 2:1-9)

Chapter 2:1-9 seems to be a continuation of Oracle 2, but now directed to the priests. Malachi has rebuked concerning laxity in offering blemished animals; now he warns the priests what will happen if they don't give "honor" (*kâbôd*) to Yahweh's name.

> "1 'And now this admonition is for you, O priests. 2 If you do not listen, and if you do not set your heart to honor my name,' says the LORD Almighty, 'I will send a curse upon you, and I will curse your blessings. Yes, I have already cursed them, because you have not set your heart to honor me.'" (Malachi 2:1-2)

They have dishonored Yahweh by accepting and then offering sick and blemished animals on the Lord's altar (Malachi 1:6-7). The curse probably involves withholding the blessings that he has promised his people if they're obedient. We saw in Haggai 1:10-11 a drought that severely affects both crops and cattle. When we get to Malachi 3:9-12 the curse for not bringing the whole tithe is small crops. The blessing is the removal of obstacles. God promises to send rain, prevent pests from ruining crops, and to help vines bear full clusters of grapes. The prophet continues.

> "Because of you I will rebuke your descendants; I will spread on your faces the offal from your festival sacrifices, and you will be carried off with it." (Malachi 2:3)

The rebuke will extend to the next generations as well. "Offal" (NIV) or "dung" (ESV) from the sacrifices is the feces of the sacrifices after they are killed. To spread animal feces on one's face is a particularly strong rebuke.

Our God is the Great God who fashioned the Universe and beyond. He must not be treated casually or with disrespect. His worship must be sincere.

"Ascribe to the LORD the glory due his name;
bring an offering,
and come into his courts!
Worship the LORD in the splendor of holiness;
tremble before him, all the earth!" (Psalm 96:8-9)

In the Old Testament the sacrifice was an animal. In the New Testament the sacrifice is our own bodies (Romans 12:1-2) and our praise (Hebrews 13:15).

The Covenant with Levi (Malachi 2:4-8)

Now Malachi contrasts the priests' dishonoring Yahweh to God's original intention, a covenant with the tribe of Levi, which we discussed in Lesson 8 in some detail.

"Remember them, O my God, because they defiled the priestly office and the covenant of the priesthood and of the Levites." (Nehemiah 13:29)

In this passage, Malachi points to several additional elements of this covenant.

"⁴ And you will know that I have sent you this admonition so that **my covenant** with Levi may continue," says the LORD Almighty. ⁵ **My covenant** was with him, a **covenant of life and peace**, and I gave them to him; this called for reverence and he revered me and stood in awe of my name." (Malachi 2:4-5)

This covenant with the priests results in "life and peace," that is, forgiveness and peace with God for those who present a sacrifice for their sins. But such a covenant must not be taken for granted. It calls for "reverence" (NIV, NRSV), "fear" (ESV, KJV). We are not to be terrified of God. But we must have great respect for him, and not abuse the intimacy he gives us with holy things.

"This called for reverence (*môwrâ'*) and [Levi] revered (*yārē'*) me and stood in awe (*ḥātat*) of my name." (Malachi 2:5b)

Three separate words in verse 5 communicate this idea – reverence (fear),[294] revered (feared),[295] and stood in awe (was afraid).[296]

---

[294] "Reverence" (NIV, NRSV), "fear" (ESV, KJV) is the noun *môwrâ'*, "fear," from the root *yārē'* which appears a word or two later (TWOT #907c). Probably the translation "reverence" catches the sense, with its opposite discussed previously disrespect, profane, disregard. The covenant is based on respect.

[295] "Revered" (NIV, NRSV), "feared" (ESV, KJV) is the Qal stem of the verb *yārē'*, discussed above: "fear, be afraid, revere."

[296] "Stood in awe" (NIV, NRSV, ESV), "was afraid" (KJV) is the Niphal stem of *ḥātat*, "be afraid, dismayed." The root idea of *ḥātat* is "to be broken." The word is used here in the abstract sense of being shattered, demoralized, or in terror before God's awesome might (Andrew Bowling, TWOT #784).

There is a strong tendency in certain Christian circles to soft-pedal any idea of fear and terror in the Bible. I think it is a reaction to the overdone theme of fire and brimstone that preachers used to scare their listeners into converting. Instead, people today quote to us a New Testament verse:

> "There is no fear in love. But perfect love drives out fear, because fear has to do with punishment. The one who fears is not made perfect in love." (1 John 4:18)

John rightly explains that faith based in fear isn't mature. Mature love for God moves from fear to love, so that actions are no longer motivated by fear of God's punishment but love for God himself. How very true!

Having said that, the New and Old Testaments are filled with incidents designed to create fear that brings respect for a Living and Awesome God. Many examples can be found in Jesus' teaching (Luke 12:5; Matthew 8:12; 13:42, 50; 22:13; 24:51; 25:30), Ananias and Sapphira (Acts 5:5), the fearsome visions of the Book of Revelation, Paul's writings (2 Corinthians 5:10-11; 1 Timothy 5:20) the warnings of Peter (2 Peter 2:4-22; 3:10-14), and of the writer of Hebrews (Hebrews 12:27-30).

In Defense of Fearing God

Most of us live in cultures that can hardly be called God-fearing. Rather, the culture prides itself on its irreverence and secularism. While politically-correct minds are loathe to make fun of Islam or Judaism, Christianity is fair play, and the characterization of God, Christians, and the Christian faith in the media is cheap, stereotyped, and merciless.

If you and I want to return to a biblical Christianity, we need to have a healthy fear of displeasing God – and a fear of punishment and strong Fatherly discipline if we get out of line. Until we have a healthy respect for our Heavenly Father's wrath, we're just kidding ourselves if we purport to love him.

Two things have helped me understand this. First, I lived in Los Angeles for about twenty years where the traffic is notorious. I learned that if I wanted to turn left in downtown Los Angeles, I couldn't just wait for traffic to clear – it never did. Rather, I learned to edge the nose of my car slightly into the lane of opposing traffic – not enough to get hit, but enough to make drivers think I might pull out in front of them. It was essentially a game of "chicken." Once I learned this, I was able to navigate the city streets well enough. However, I made two exceptions: trucks and buses. Never play chicken with trucks and buses, because if they hit you, you'll be crushed. It's one thing to show disrespect for human beings; it's quite another to disrespect the Living God, whose wrath is well-known towards the rebellious, and only becomes mercy when we repent.

Second, is an experience I had while in college. I roomed with a fellow Christian. And over time we began to joke about the church, and holy things such as the Lord's Supper and anything else. Nothing was sacred to our so-called humor. One night during a marathon study, I went to the restroom down the hall to rinse out my coffee cup. Somehow, it slipped off the shelf above the sink, broke *on the way down,* deeply slicing my left thumb as I tried to catch it, and then shattered when it hit the sink. I wrapped my thumb in paper towels and walked up the hill to the college infirmary, where a nurse cleaned the wound and put a couple of butterfly-bandages on it to keep the sides of the wound together. On my way back to the dormitory, I asked the Lord why that had happened. He spoke to me very clearly, "Don't joke about holy things!" I immediately stopped joking, though my roommate didn't understand and thought I was being way too sanctimonious. But I learned. And every once-in-a-while I look at the scar on my left thumb and remember.

My dear friend, we must fear God's wrath and discipline enough to obey him, before we can move to a mature love for him.

> **Q2. (Malachi 2:5; 1 John 4:18) What does it mean to "fear God" in Old Testament days? Should we "fear God" now, as Christian believers? How does fear of God interface with our love for God? How does our love change the fear?**
> **http://www.joyfulheart.com/forums/topic/1754-q2-fearing-god/**

Teaching Priests (Malachi 2:6)

Malachi has been talking about the covenant of the priesthood.

> "True instruction was in his mouth and nothing false was found on his lips. He walked with me in peace and uprightness, and turned many from sin." (Malachi 2:6)

I think Malachi is pointing to an ideal priest, not any single person. Especially, not Aaron, who in his early ministry enables the people to set up a golden calf to worship! (Exodus 32:1-6). The Pentateuch suggests that a primary role for the priests and Levites is to teach the people:

"[Levi] teaches your precepts to Jacob and your law to Israel...." (Deuteronomy 33:10)

"Act according to the law they teach you and the decisions they give you. Do not turn aside from what they tell you, to the right or to the left." (Deuteronomy 17:11)

"... Be very careful to do exactly as the priests, who are Levites, instruct you. You must follow carefully what I have commanded them." (Deuteronomy 24:8)

Though this priestly teaching ministry was often neglected, it occurs occasionally throughout the Old Testament.

"For a long time Israel was without the true God, without a priest to teach and without the law." (2 Chronicles 15:3; see also 2 Chronicles 35:3a)

"They taught throughout Judah, taking with them the Book of the Law of the LORD; they went around to all the towns of Judah and taught the people." (2 Chronicles 17:9)

Ezra, of course, is one of these teaching priests, and during his time,

"The Levites ... instructed the people in the Law while the people were standing there. They read from the Book of the Law of God, making it clear and giving the meaning so that the people could understand what was being read." (Nehemiah 8:7-8)

The Ideal Priest (Malachi 2:6-8)

With that background on God's plan for a teaching priesthood, let's read Malachi's entire prophecy on teaching priests and then seek to understand his message.

"[6] True instruction was in his mouth and nothing false was found on his lips. He walked with me in peace and uprightness, and turned many from sin. [7] 'For the lips of a priest ought to preserve knowledge, and from his mouth men should seek instruction – because he is the messenger of the LORD Almighty. [8] But you have turned from the way and by your teaching have caused many to stumble; you have violated the covenant with Levi,' says the LORD Almighty." (Malachi 2:6-8)

In a former passage (Malachi 1:6-14) Malachi has indicted the priests for failings in their ministry of atonement via animal sacrifice. Now he indicts them for their failings in their teaching responsibilities. Malachi is obviously contrasting the priesthood in his time with the covenant priesthood that God had envisioned. As I read this passage, I see many of the same requirements that are necessary for pastors today, who, like priests, function as mediators, ambassadors, relational links, to bring men to God. I see five elements of this priestly ministry in this passage.

1. Offering true instruction (verse 6a, 7b).
2. Walking with God in peace and uprightness (verse 6b).
3. Turning many from sin (verse 6c).
4. Serving as messengers of Yahweh (verse 7b).
5. Preserving and guarding knowledge (verse 7a).

Let's look at them one by one.

1. Offering true instruction (verses 6a, 7b). Priests and pastors must offer "true instruction," in contrast to something "false ... found upon his lips." "True instruction" (NIV, NRSV, ESV) or "law of truth" is two words: *tôrâ*, "law, instruction,"[297] and *'emet*, "firmness, truth, verity," carrying an underlying sense of certainty, dependability.[298]

"True instruction" (verse 6) that a priest should bring is contrasted with that which is "false" (NIV), "wrong" (NRSV, ESV), "iniquity" (KJV). The word is *'avlâh*, "injustice, unrighteousness," acts or deeds that are contrary to what is right and righteous.[299] Priests are to be the judges and interpreters of the Torah. They are to decide cases brought to them, but in Malachi's time the priests themselves are both allowing and sometimes advocating that which is contrary to the law. Later, Malachi brings a powerful word from God against those who are unrighteous and unjust (Malachi 3:5)

In our own day, we hear lots of "feel good" messages that pass for "true instruction," but fail to deliver actual instruction that can change lives. In some instances, preachers are even declaring a false or incomplete gospel in the guise of Christianity. Fellow pastors and elders, we are responsible to God for what we teach.

2. Walking with God in peace and uprightness (verse 6b). In both Old and New Testaments, "walk" is used figuratively to describe one's habit of life. Enoch "walked with God" (Genesis 5:22-24), Ahaziah, an evil king of Judah, "walked in the way of the house of Ahab" (2 Kings 8:27). Paul points to the "sins in which you once walked, when you followed the ways of the world..." (Ephesians 2:1b-2a). He exhorts believers to

---

[297] *Tôrâ* in verses 6, 7, and 8 is "law, instruction" (from which we get the English transliteration, "Torah"). Hartley, notes, "Teaching is the special task of the wisdom school as seen especially through the book of Proverbs and of the priesthood." The word *tôrâ* means basically "teaching" whether it is the wise man instructing his son or God instructing Israel.... The book of Deuteronomy itself shows that the law has a broad meaning to encompass history, regulations and their interpretation, and exhortations (John E. Hartley, *tôrâ*, TWOT #910d).

[298] Jack B. Scott, *'emet*, TWOT #116k.

[299] G. Herbert Livingston, *'avlâh*, TWOT #1580b.

"walk by the Spirit" (Galatians 5:16), "walk not according to the flesh, but according to the Spirit" (Romans 8:4).

In fact, walking with Jesus is the quintessential act of a disciple. Jesus calls men and women, "Come, follow me." Walking is following, that's why I've named my Bible studies, the JesusWalk Bible Study Series.

When my family camps in state and national parks, we enjoy the scheduled Ranger Walks that help explain the wonders of nature. I've observed that on such walks, some people (usually children) run on ahead, some cluster around the ranger, listening and asking questions. Then behind, people are strung out for 50 or 100 feet or more. When the ranger stops to explain something, the people at the back have hardly caught up by the time the ranger is ready to go on. It's one thing to go on a Ranger Walk; it is quite another to walk with the ranger. Priests and pastors must walk with the Ranger.

Two words characterize this fellowship – "in peace and uprightness." Peace (*shalom*) can refer generally to a state of blessing and wholeness. But here I think it points to a relationship of peace, a state of peace, between us and God, the opposite of a state of war that might exist because of rebelliousness. Paul declares concerning believers, "We have peace with God through our Lord Jesus Christ" (Romans 5:1). "Uprightness" or "equity"[300] refers particularly to justice in judging and deciding the cases brought to them. As the priests serve as judges (Deuteronomy 17:9; Ezekiel 44:24), they need to be just and honest, rather than showing favoritism or taking bribes to sway their decision. A lack of justice is one of the reasons God has punished the priests.

> "So I have caused you to be despised and humiliated before all the people, because you have not followed my ways but have shown partiality in matters of the law." (Malachi 2:9)

3. Turning many from sin (verse 6c). "Turned" occurs more than 1,000 times in the Old Testament, usually literally, but often figuratively in the sense of repentance.[301] The Hiphil stem here suggests causation, "cause to turn, cause to repent." A true priest or pastor turns many from sin. But the corrupt priests of Malachi's day, do the opposite.

---

[300] "Uprightness" (NIV, NRSV, ESV), "equity" (KJV) is *mîshôr*, "level place," figuratively, "uprightness," from the root *yāshar*, "be level, straight." The verb means literally "to go straight or direct in the way." Ethically it refers to uprightness in your manner of life. The verb *mîshôr*, in particular, refers to "uprightness, straightness (in government), justice," judging with equity rather than partiality (Donald J. Wiseman, *mîshôr*, TWOT #930f).

[301] Victor P. Hamilton, *shûb*, TWOT #2340.

"But you have turned[302] from the way and by your teaching have caused many to stumble."[303] (Malachi 2:8)

Jesus speaks harshly of those who cause others to sin.

"If anyone causes one of these little ones who believe in me to sin, it would be better for him to be thrown into the sea with a large millstone tied around his neck." (Mark 9:42)

How do priests and pastors cause people to turn away from sin – or cause people to sin? In two ways:

a. Example. Though people often complain about their leaders, they tend to pattern their lives after them, and after others in places of authority or the public eye. "If the President can do it, I guess it's okay for me." We know that in the time of Ezra, Nehemiah, and Malachi, the high priest and his family were sinning deeply, marrying non-Jewish women, and failing to condemn marriage to foreign wives (Nehemiah 13:28-29). If a leader sets an upright, faithful example, he or she encourages others to do the same. That's why sports heroes often act as role models for their young, impressionable followers. Our children watch our lives and more often than not end up emulating us, for better or for worse. Thus Paul can say,

"Follow my example, as I follow the example of Christ." (1 Corinthians 11:1)

b. Teaching. In the teaching of priests and pastors, we can (1) accurately reflect the teaching of the Word, or we can (2) focus on our own interpretations. We can say what people want to hear. Love, of course, is the central theme of the New Testament, but if love is taught stand-alone, without reference to repentance and faith, it becomes a corrupt gospel. Sometimes we preachers feel that God's word is too harsh or runs counter to the times, so we soften it or explain it away. When we do that we can be responsible for causing people to sin. God holds us responsible for what we teach.

4. Serving as messengers of Yahweh. Malachi refers to a faithful priest as "the messenger[304] of the LORD Almighty" (Malachi 2:7). As we observed earlier, *mal'āk*, "messenger," is the core of Malachi's own name – "my messenger."

---

[302] "Turned away" (NIV), "turned aside" (NRSV, ESV), "departed" (KJV) is the Qal stem of *sûr*, "turn aside, depart, withdraw" (TWOT #1480).

[303] "Stumble" in verse 9 is *kāshal*, "stumble, totter, stagger," usually from weakness or weariness, or in flight from attackers, or figuratively in the sense of failing or ruin. Rarely – and verse 9 is an example of this – the word is used in the sense of the New Testament *skandalidzō*, "cause one to fall into sin" (R. Laird Harris, TWOT #1050). Other examples are Jeremiah 18:15 and Proverbs 4:16.

To be a "messenger" of Yahweh is an awesome responsibility! Jesus tells his disciples something similar.

> "He who listens to you listens to me; he who rejects you rejects me; but he who rejects me rejects him who sent me." (Luke 10:16, cf. Matthew 10:40)

> "I tell you the truth, whoever accepts anyone I send accepts me; and whoever accepts me accepts the one who sent me." (John 13:20)

Paul writes,

> "He has committed to us the message of reconciliation. We are therefore Christ's ambassadors, as though God were making his appeal through us." (2 Corinthians 5:19-20)

We are weak; we are prone to misspeaking and mistakes. And yet, in spite of all that, we are entrusted with his message of life, we are "messengers of the Lord Almighty," a high and holy calling.

5. Preserving and guarding knowledge. Finally, the priest and pastor must "preserve knowledge," that is, guard knowledge with care."[305] Malachi is speaking both of the *relational* knowing of God as a Person, as well as knowing the content of the written record of God's words, the Scriptures.[306]

Priests and pastors must be students of the Word. They must know and teach the Scriptures. The prophet Amos says that God will send a famine, not for food or water, but "a famine of hearing the words of the LORD" (Amos 8:11). I live in California where secularism has a strong hold. Sermons are topical and relevant to needs, but Scripture often goes untaught, with the result that most younger Christians are truly biblically

---

[304] "Messenger" (NIV) is *mal'āk*, "messenger, representative, courtier." The word can also refer to an "angel," a divine messenger. Bowling notes that "messenger" is an inadequate term for the range of tasks carried out by the Hebrew word *mal'āk*. These were a) to carry a message, b) to perform some other specific commission, and c) to represent more or less officially the one sending him (Andrew Bowling, *mal'āk*, TWOT #1068a).

[305] "Preserve" (NIV), "guard" (NRSV, ESV), "keep" (KJV) translate the Qal stem of *shāmar*, "keep, guard, observe, give heed," with the basic idea of "to exercise great care over" (TWOT #2414). The NRSV, ESV translation reflects the connotation of "take care of, guard," involving keeping or tending to things. The NIV translation reflects the connotation of "preserving, storing up." It's difficult to know here which connotation Malachi intended originally, as both fit the context. Whatever the exact idea, this is clearly a defensive action.

[306] "Knowledge" is the noun *da'at*, "knowledge" from the common verb *yāda'*, "to know." *Da'at* is a general term for knowledge, particularly that which is of a personal, experimental nature, and includes the knowledge of God (Paul R. Gilchrist, TWOT #848c).

illiterate. I can see this as a famine. It is a pastor's job to preserve and guard God's word, even in times and places where it is unpopular.

These are the core positive characteristics of the ideal priest that Malachi pictures. But the priests in his time have also committed serious sins (verses 8):

1. "Turned from the way."
2. "Caused many to stumble."
3. "Violated the covenant with Levi."
4. "Not followed my ways."
5. "Shown partiality in matters of the law."

As a result,

> "I have caused you to be despised and humiliated before all the people." (Malachi 2:8)

What a sad epitaph on what an important, influential, and promising calling.

> **Q3. (Malachi 2:1-9) In what ways do church pastors and teachers fall heir to the role of "teaching priests"? Which of the roles of teaching priests do you see as most vital in your situation?**
> **http://www.joyfulheart.com/forums/topic/1755-q3-teaching-priests/**

Oracle 3. Judah Unfaithful in Marriage Vows (Malachi 2:10-16)

Now Malachi turns from an indictment of the priesthood, to unfaithfulness in marriage, a sin that affects both priest and layperson alike. In Malachi's day, this unfaithfulness has two aspects in particular: (1) marrying non-Jews, and (2) divorcing wives.

Breaking God's Covenant (Malachi 2:10)

Malachi begins by establishing that Jews are part of one family, a family with covenant obligations.

> "Have we not all one father?[307] Did not one God create us? Why do we profane the covenant of our fathers by breaking faith with one another?" (Malachi 2:10)

---

[307] The NIV and ESV capitalize "Father." The NRSV and KJV do not. There is a dispute about which father is the subject. One argument is that the first two clauses of verse 10 are employing Hebrew synoptic parallelism; they both refer to the people's responsibility to God. Another argument sees "father" in the first clause as referring to one of the patriarchs – Abraham or Jacob, since the third clause refers to "our

Malachi's point is that all the people of the nation have covenant obligations to God. And to allow anyone in the nation to flagrantly break any of these covenant obligations puts the whole nation at risk of punishment.

These returnees from Exile have learned the hard way what the punishment is for repeated disobedience and rebellion against God. Memories of the destruction of Jerusalem and years in Babylonian Captivity are still part of the national memory, even though Malachi's hearers are several generations later than the original group that returned from Babylon in 537 BC.

Malachi asks rhetorically:

> "Why do we profane[308] the covenant of our fathers by breaking faith with one another?" (Malachi 2:10)

To allow some people to disobey covenant obligations breaks faith with the whole people, since it puts them all at risk and subjects the nation to God's wrath. The expression "breaking faith" (NIV), "are faithless" (NRSV, ESV), "deal treacherously (KJV) is the verb *bāgad*, "deal or act treacherously, deal deceitfully, (deal) unfaithfully, offend."[309] Some have broken the covenant, breaking faith both with God as well as with their own countrymen.

Marriage with Non-Jewish Women (Malachi 2:11-12)

> "Judah has broken faith. A detestable thing has been committed in Israel and in Jerusalem: Judah has desecrated the sanctuary the LORD loves, by marrying the daughter of a foreign god." (Malachi 2:11)

What is the "detestable thing," the "abomination"?[310] Marrying women who are non-Jewish, "the daughter of a foreign god."[311] This intermarriage with pagans in surround-

---

fathers," our ancestors. What did Malachi intend? I don't think we can know for sure – and it doesn't make too much difference.

[308] "Profane" is the Piel stem of *ḥālal*, "profane, defile, pollute, desecrate" (Donald J. Wiseman, TWOT #661). The root *ḥll* is used to mark the act of doing violence to the established law of God, breaking the covenant or the divine statutes.

[309] Louis Goldberg, *bāgad*, TWOT #198. The root in South Arabic means "to deceive." The verb is often used of unfaithfulness to marriage vows, and by analogy, being unfaithful to the Lord. In addition it is used to refer to unfaithfulness to property rights, and failing in one's responsibility to a king.

[310] "Detestable thing" (NIV), "abomination" (NRSV, ESV, KJV) is *tô'ēbâ*, "abominable (custom, thing)." The basic meanings of the Piel stem of the verb *tā'ab* are "abhor, loathe" in a physical sense and "detest, exclude" for ritual or ethical reasons (Ronald F. Youngblood, TWOT #2530a).

[311] "Daughter of" is a Hebraic expression that means "to 'bear the character of' a deity whose ethos was diametrically opposed to the righteousness of Israel's God" (Baldwin, *Haggai, Zechariah, Malachi*, p. 238).

ing villages had plagued Israel for a thousand years, ever since the time of the Judges. But the Covenant is crystal clear: "Do not intermarry with them" (Deuteronomy 7:3-4).

This isn't some kind of racial purity law. It has to do with faith. The "mixed multitude" that came out of Egypt with the Israelites were incorporated into the people (Exodus 12:38). When proselytes to Judaism accept circumcision, they are included within the covenant and treated just like natural-born Israelites (Exodus 12:48-49; Ezekiel 44:9; 47:22-23).

It seems strange that we see the problem of intermarriage in Malachi, since we've seen it twice before in our study: Ezra 9-10 and Nehemiah 13:23-30. Does Malachi prophesy directly to either of these separate incidents? We don't know, since it is impossible to date Malachi exactly.

Malachi's prescription, however, seems somewhat different than those offered by Ezra and Nehemiah.

> "As for the man who does this, whoever he may be,[312] may the LORD cut him off from the tents of Jacob – even though he brings offerings to the LORD Almighty." (Malachi 2:12)

The priests "bring offerings" before God, but they are not exempt. Offenders will be punished "whoever he may be." Malachi prays down a curse on offenders, that God will "cut him off from the tents of Jacob." "Cut off" is *karat*, literally, "cut off," metaphorically, "to root out, eliminate, remove, excommunicate or destroy by a violent act of man or nature."[313] The verse is hard to interpret exactly, since it includes a Hebrew idiom we don't understand, but the idea is that Yahweh's punishment will surely fall on offenders, on anyone "whoever he may be" (NIV). Offenders won't escape God's wrath.

Breaking the Marriage Covenant by Divorce (Malachi 2:13-16)

Malachi indicts the people for marrying pagan women. But he also condemns them for breaking the marriage covenant by divorcing "the wife of your youth."

---

[312] ESV suggests that the punishment shall fall on "any descendant of the man who does this" – in other words that they shall be without any offspring. The Hebrew text includes an idiom, "any to witness or answer" (NRSV), but we're not sure exactly what it means. "The master and the scholar" (KJV) is one attempt at translating this incomprehensible phrase.

[313] Elmer B. Smick, *karat*, TWOT #1048. This is the same word that is sometimes used in relation to making a covenant, "to cut" a covenant. Smick notes, "It is sometimes difficult in a given context to know whether the person(s) who is "cut off" is to be killed or only excommunicated."

> "¹³ Another thing you do: You flood the LORD's altar with tears. You weep and wail because he no longer pays attention to your offerings or accepts them with pleasure from your hands. ¹⁴ You ask, 'Why?'" (Malachi 2:13-14a)

You are very upset that the Lord doesn't seem to hear your prayers, says Malachi. Here's the reason:

> "It is because the LORD is acting as the witness between you and the wife of your youth, because you have broken faith with her, though she is your partner, the wife of your marriage covenant." (Malachi 2:14b)

The situation seems to be that middle aged men are divorcing "the wife of their youth," women they married when they were young. This isn't a divorce immediately after marriage because of a bride's supposed unfaithfulness prior to marriage. Rather this is men who see their wives getting older and losing their beauty, and want to discard them for someone younger. It was possible for women to initiate divorce proceedings under Jewish law,[314] but historically, such situations were rare and require very good cause.[315] Though our passage relates to men divorcing, the principles apply to both husbands and wives.

When you dig into these verses you begin to see more clearly a number of truths about marriage.

1. Marriage is a covenant (Malachi 2:14d). Verse 14 uses the term *berît*, essentially an agreement, here between individuals, that is witnessed by others and sealed by an oath. David and Jonathan had covenanted with each other "before the Lord" (1 Samuel 18:3; 20:8; 22:8; 23:18), that is, both parties agreed that God is witness to their agreement, so if either breaks it, he has to answer to God. Marriage is such a covenant between two individuals.

Though the words "covenant" and "contract" are used nearly synonymously in America, from a scriptural standpoint there is a difference. In Western law, a contract is an agreement between two parties that is enforceable by law. This is similar to a covenant, except that, while a contract is a purely secular agreement with no appeal to God, a covenant includes divine sanctions for breaching its terms.

---

[314] *m.Ket.5.5-8.*

[315] See David Instone-Brewer, *Divorce and Remarriage in the Church: Biblical Solutions for Pastoral Realities* (InterVarsity Press, 2006) and *Divorce and Remarriage in the Bible: The Social and Literary Context* (Eerdmans, 2002). Instone-Brewer sees Exodus 21:10-11 as the duties that the Jews assumed men must fulfill, and believes they underlie New Testament marriage and divorce passages.

2. God is Witness to the marriage covenant (Malachi 2:14a). You know the familiar words that begin a marriage ceremony:

> "Beloved, we are gathered here in the sight of God and of these witnesses...."

God is a Witness, one who can bring proceedings against offenders. However, he is more than that; he is the One who designs and orders the relationship, as we'll see in a moment.

3. Divorce is a "breaking faith" with your spouse (Malachi 2:14b, 15d, 16d). "The expression "broken faith" (NIV), "been faithless" (NRSV, ESV), "dealt treacherously (KJV) in verses 14 and 15 is the verb *bāgad* (which we see above in verses 10 and 11) "deal(act) treacherously, deal deceitfully, (deal) unfaithfully, offend." The person who acts this way "does not honor an agreement.[316]

Divorce is the legal breaking of an agreement. Of course, agreements can be rendered void, when either party fails to abide by the terms of the agreement – another way of "dealing treacherously." Jesus acknowledges that adultery is cause to break the marriage covenant (Matthew 5:32; 19:9) – though even then, the parties may (and often do) decide to reconcile and stay in the relationship.

The problem that Malachi is speaking against, however, is not men breaking marriage covenants because their wives are adulterous. In Jesus' day, there was a very low bar for cause for divorce (for men, anyway). It came down to how one interpreted the Law's provision for divorce.

> "If a man marries a woman who becomes displeasing to him because he finds something indecent[317] about her, and he writes her a certificate of divorce, gives it to her and sends her from his house." (Deuteronomy 24:1)

In Jesus' day, the School of Hillel understood the passage to mean that a man could divorce his wife for any cause, even burning his toast.[318] This kind of sloppy Bible interpretation to justify one's sin is going on in Malachi's day also. Thus divorcing your spouse just because you didn't like her or she has lost her beauty, is, according to Yahweh, "breaking faith" or "acting treacherously" with regard to a solemn covenant.

4. We are God's property by creation (Malachi 2:15a)

---

[316] Louis Goldberg, *bāgad*, TWOT #198.

[317] The phrase "something indecent" (NIV), "something objectionable" (NRSV), "some indecency" (ESV), "some uncleanness" (KJV) are two words, *dābār*, "word, speaking, thing," and *'erwâ*, "nakedness, shame." Jesus interpreted this as sexual unfaithfulness, Greek *porneia*, "unlawful sexual intercourse, prostitution, unchastity, fornication" (BDAG 854, 1).

[318] *m. Gittin* 9:10; *Sipre Deut.* 269.1.1.

"Has not [the LORD] made them one? In flesh and spirit they are his." (Malachi 2:15a)

God owns us because he created us. Rebellion against God, claiming we are agnostics or atheists, doesn't change the fact that we belong to God. To say that breaking a marriage is "nobody's business but our own," leaves out the fact that you and your spouse belong to God. He invents marriage. He is Witness to your covenant. It is indeed his business.

5. God makes husband and wife one in body and spirit (Malachi 2:15a). The "oneness" of marriage is not just a physical joining in sexual intercourse, but spiritual also (1 Corinthians 6:16-17).

6. God's interest in marriage is raising godly offspring (Malachi 2:15b).

"And why one? Because he was seeking godly offspring." (Malachi 2:15b)

In many countries, marriages are governed by civil law, which represents society's interest in a just society where wives and children are cared for, and do not have to rely on welfare to support them. God cares about these things too. His particular interest, according to verse 15b is "godly offspring" (NIV, NRSV, ESV), "godly seed" (KJV).[319] The implication is that the best opportunity for boys and girls to grow up as godly and knowing God is to be raised by both parents. Can this happen when they are raised by one parent? Of course, but it is more difficult. Malachi indicates that God's institution of marriage is intended to accomplish his purposes.

7. God hates to see divorce (Malachi 2:16a).

"'I hate divorce,' says the LORD God of Israel." (Malachi 2:16a)

My dear friend, please don't read this to think that God hates people who have been divorced. He doesn't. It means that his heart is broken when he sees divorce, since it is contrary to his purposes in marriage. Sometimes it is necessary, but it still breaks his heart, and ours. The church needs to love divorced people, not judge them or fear them. We all are broken people, whether divorced or not, needing the healing power of God and the love of his people to become whole.

8. God abhors marital violence (Malachi 2:16b).

"'I hate divorce,' says the LORD God of Israel, 'and I hate a man's covering himself with violence as well as with his garment,' says the LORD Almighty." (Malachi 2:16)

---

[319] "Godly" here is 'elōhîm. "Offspring" (NIV, NRSV, ESV), "seed" (KJV) is zera', "seed, offspring." The word literally means "seed, semen," and then metaphorically to the product of what is sown (TWOT #582a).

In parallel with God hating divorce, Malachi uses a common analogy of putting on violence and therefore covering oneself with violence in the same way as one puts on and covers oneself with clothing.[320] The term "violence" is almost always used in the Old Testament as sinful violence.[321] In connection with marriage, the implication seems to me to include physical abuse: beatings and the like. In other words, God not only hates breaking the marriage covenant, but also violence against one's spouse within that covenant relationship. Violence is completely contrary to the spirit of a mutual covenant,[322] and the opposite of a spirit of agape love.

9. The desire for divorce is a spiritual problem (Malachi 2:15c, 16d). Twice, Malachi warns men to guard against an attitude that would lead to divorce.

> "So guard yourself in your spirit, and do not break faith with the wife of your youth." (verse 15c)

> "So guard yourself in your spirit, and do not break faith." (verse 16d)

The basic idea of the verb "guard" (NIV, ESV), "look to" (NRSV), "take heed" (KJV) is "to exercise great care over" your spirit. The word is sometimes used regarding tending a garden or flock, guarding a city, etc. We're told, "He who guards his lips guards his life" (Proverbs 13:3a), and, with a close synonym, "Keep your heart with all vigilance" (Proverbs 4:23a).[323] In the Malachi passage we're exhorted to watch over our spirit, so that this desire to divorce or beat our wives doesn't take hold of us.

10. Divorce and marital violence hinder our prayers (Malachi 2:13). This matter about divorce came up in the first place in response to a rhetorical question: Why doesn't Yahweh answer our prayers? (verse 13). The answer is: God doesn't answer your prayers because you are sinning by divorcing and abusing your wives. We read something similar in 1 Peter:

---

[320] You often see this analogy of "putting on clothing" in Paul's epistles (Colossians 3:9-10; etc.).

[321] "Violence" is *ḥāmās*, "violence, wrong," from the verb *ḥāmas*, "wrong, do violence to, treat violently." The Arabic cognate means to be hard, strict, severe. In the Old Testament *ḥāmās* is almost always used in connection with sinful violence, not to natural disasters or doing justice. It is often a name for extreme wickedness (R. Laird Harris, *ḥāmas*, TWOT #678a). Note that the terrorist organization Hamas traces its name from an Arabic word meaning, "courage, zeal," not this word.

[322] Baldwin sees this as "a figurative expression of all kinds of gross injustice, which like the blood of a murdered victim, leave their mark for all to see" (*Haggai, Zechariah, Malachi*, p. 241).

[323] "Guard yourselves" (NIV, ESV), "look to" and "take heed" to yourselves" (NRSV, cf. KJV) is the Niphal stem of *shāmar*, "keep, guard, give heed." The basic idea of the root is "to exercise great care over" (TWOT #2414). We're told, "He who guards (*nāṣar*) his lips guards (*shāmar*) his life" (Proverbs 13:3a). A close synonym, *nāṣar*, is used in a similar saying, "Keep your heart with all vigilance" (Proverbs 4:23a).

"Husbands, in the same way be considerate as you live with your wives, and treat them with respect as the weaker partner and as heirs with you of the gracious gift of life, so that nothing will hinder your prayers." (1 Peter 3:7)

God won't hear us if we treat our spouses with disrespect, because our spouse is a "joint heir" in the same covenant that is designed to bring life. In the same way, Peter says, God won't hear you if are drunk and out of control (1 Peter 4:7). If we want God to answer our prayers, we must make a sincere effort to obey him – and this very much includes our marriage relationships. We can't do violence to a covenant to which God is party and expect no consequences to our relationship with Him.

> **Q4. (Malachi 2:13-16). What does Malachi teach us about marriage in this passage? Which two or three of these truths do you think would most help improve Christian marriages if applied today?**
> **http://www.joyfulheart.com/forums/topic/1756-q4-marriage-covenant/**

Lessons for Disciples

There are many nuggets of truth for disciples in this passage, though some are difficult for us to digest.

1. God loves us, even though we sometimes experience his discipline. Malachi points to how God has blessed Jacob (whom he "loves"), compared to Esau (whom he "hates"). The blessings of God protect us from a great deal that we aren't even aware of (Malachi 1:1-5).

2. We owe God our respect – which shows in the sincerity by which we worship him (Malachi 1:6-14). To neglect sincere worship actually shows contempt for God.

3. The issue in Malachi's day was offering diseased or crippled animals on the altar, rather than animals without blemish. Perhaps for us the application is that we must not offer God our second-best. Only our best will do for serving God (Malachi 1:6-14).

4. If we can't worship God with truth and sincerity, then it's better to close the church and not even go through the motions of worship (Malachi 1:9-10)

5. Offering our second-best is an offense to God. He is the Great King, not someone we can offend without risk of his curse, and the withholding of his blessings (Malachi 1:14).

6. God has made a covenant with Levi, that is, the priests and Levites have a prominent place in his Covenant, with responsibilities and privileges (Malachi 2:4-5). In our day, pastors and church leaders fill this role.

7. We are required to fear God, that is, to revere him, and be afraid to offend him (Malachi 2:5).

8. The pastors and church leaders of the New Covenant, are heirs of the "teaching priests" of the Old Covenant. We are called to offer true instruction, walk sincerely with God, turn people from sin, serve as messengers of God, and preserve knowledge (Malachi 2:6-7).

9. God expects us to honor marriage by not marrying unbelievers, which he considers breaking faith with God's covenant (Malachi 2:10-11).

10. From the passage on divorce we learn a number of things about marriage (Malachi 2:14-16).

    a. Marriage is a covenant (14d).
    b. God is Witness to this covenant (14a).
    c. Divorce is "breaking faith" with the covenant you make with your spouse when you marry (14-16).
    d. We are God's property by creation – so he sets the rules of marriage (15a).
    e. God makes husband and wife one in body and spirit (15a).
    f. God desires us to have godly offspring (15b).
    g. God hates to see divorce (16a).
    h. God abhors marital violence (16b).
    i. The desire for divorce is a spiritual problem (15c, 16d).
    j. Divorce and marital violence hinder our prayers (13).

Prayer

Father, thank you for your love and mercy. Without that we would have already been consumed. Help us to fear you in appropriate ways, to offer to you sincere worship, and to include you in our marriages. We fall so short sometimes. Help us when we fail, and forgive us. In Jesus' name, we pray. Amen.

Key Verses

"'A son honors his father, and a servant his master. If I am a father, where is the honor due me? If I am a master, where is the respect due me?' says the LORD Almighty. 'It is you, O priests, who show contempt for my name. But you ask, "How have we shown contempt for your name?"'" (Malachi 1:6, NIV)

"'When you bring blind animals for sacrifice, is that not wrong? When you sacrifice crippled or diseased animals, is that not wrong? Try offering them to your governor! Would he be pleased with you? Would he accept you?' says the LORD Almighty." (Malachi 1:8, NIV)

"My covenant was with [Levi], a covenant of life and peace, and I gave them to him; this called for reverence and he revered me and stood in awe of my name. True instruction was in his mouth and nothing false was found on his lips. He walked with me in peace and uprightness, and turned many from sin. For the lips of a priest ought to preserve knowledge, and from his mouth men should seek instruction – because he is the messenger of the LORD Almighty." (Malachi 2:5-7, NIV)

"'The LORD is acting as the witness between you and the wife of your youth, because you have broken faith with her, though she is your partner, the wife of your marriage covenant. Has not [the LORD] made them one? In flesh and spirit they are his. And why one? Because he was seeking godly offspring. So guard yourself in your spirit, and do not break faith with the wife of your youth. I hate divorce,' says the LORD God of Israel, 'and I hate a man's covering himself with violence as well as with his garment,' says the LORD Almighty. 'So guard yourself in your spirit, and do not break faith.'" (Malachi 2:14-16 , NIV)

10. Justice, Tithing, Purifying, and Judgment (Malachi 3-4)

How much force does it take to drive a nail into hardwood? How many hammer blows does it take? Malachi, the Lord's prophet, has brought prophecy after prophecy, hitting hard at the shell of religion and self-serving practice that prevents priests and people from enjoying the full and joyous presence of their God. That prevents them from knowing him as he is. And so Malachi brings another word from God, hopeful that this time people will listen, that this time God's hammer will break their tough exterior – *our* tough exterior. He brings a message of judgment.

"He will be like a refiner's fire or a launderer's soap. He will sit as a refiner and purifier of silver; he will purify the Levites and refine them like gold and silver." (Malachi 3:2-3)

Oracle 4. Refining, Purifying, and Judgment (Malachi 2:17-3:6)

Day of Judgment (Malachi 2:17-3:6)

Scoffers in Malachi's day seek to undermine belief in God's holiness and justice.

"[17] You have wearied the LORD with your words. 'How have we wearied him?' you ask. By saying, 'All who do evil are good in the eyes of the LORD, and he is pleased with them' or 'Where is the God of justice?'" (Malachi 2:17)

God is wearied.[324] He is so tired of hearing his people's foolish and perverted questions and excuses and unbelief. We see the same theme in Isaiah:

"You have burdened me with your sins
and wearied me with your offenses." (Isaiah 43:24)

"You were wearied by all your ways...." (Isaiah 57:10)

They said:

---

[324] "Wearied" is *yāga'*, "toil, labor, grow or be weary." The primary meaning is "to work until one is tired and exhausted" (Ralph H. Alexander, TWOT #842).

1. God is pleased with you whether or not you obey him.

> "All who do evil are good in the eyes of the LORD, and he is pleased with them." (Malachi 2:17b)

This isn't too far from the kind of cheap grace in our day that claims, "God loves you no matter what you do." It's true but misleading. People do their best to rationalize their sins by perverting the nature of God into a soft cuddly bundle of love who spoils you like a doting uncle or saying that sin doesn't matter. It doesn't matter what you do.

God's holiness as revealed in the Bible scares us. But woe to us if we pretend God is someone who he is not in order for us feel better about our sin!

2. God isn't just.

> "Where is the God of justice?" (Malachi 2:17c)

Another heresy is the claim that God won't punish sin – a second affront to God's holiness. This attitude of unbelief is noted throughout the Bible.

> "God has forgotten; he covers his face and never sees." (Psalm 10:11b)

> "The LORD does not see us; the LORD has forsaken the land." (Ezekiel 8:12b)

> "The LORD will do nothing, either good or bad." (Zephaniah 1:12)

> "You must understand that in the last days scoffers will come, scoffing and following their own evil desires. They will say, 'Where is this "coming" he promised? Ever since our fathers died, everything goes on as it has since the beginning of creation.'" (2 Peter 3:3-4)

The Two Messengers (Malachi 3:1)

The prophet's answer to the people's cynicism and unbelief is a declaration that the Lord is indeed coming in judgment.

> "'See, I will send **my messenger**,[325] who will prepare the way before me. Then suddenly the Lord you are seeking will come to his temple; **the messenger of the covenant**, whom you desire, will come,' says the LORD Almighty." (Malachi 3:1)

Observe that there are two different messengers mentioned:

1. The messenger who prepares the way.
2. The messenger of the covenant.

---

[325] "My messenger" in verse 1 is *mal'ākî*, transliterated, "Malachi." However, the prophet isn't speaking of himself, but a future messenger of Yahweh, "who will prepare the way before me."

1. The messenger who prepares the way. The first messenger gets ready or prepares[326] for the second. The New Testament clearly identifies this messenger with John the Baptist, quoting our passage in Malachi (Matthew 11:10). Malachi mentions this messenger who prepares the way again near the end of the book.

> "See, I will send you the prophet Elijah before that great and dreadful day of the LORD comes." (Malachi 4:5)

John the Baptist's father, Zechariah, prophesied this preparatory role.

> "And you, my child, will be called a prophet of the Most High;
> for you will go on before the Lord to prepare the way for him." (Luke 1:76)

Jesus acknowledges that this indeed refers to John the Baptist's ministry (Matthew 11:14; 17:10-13).

John the Baptist identifies Isaiah's prophecy as referring to himself (Matthew 3:1-3; John 1:23):

> "A voice of one calling:
> 'In the desert prepare the way for the LORD;
> make straight in the wilderness a highway for our God.
> Every valley shall be raised up,
> every mountain and hill made low;
> the rough ground shall become level,
> the rugged places a plain.
> And the glory of the LORD will be revealed,
> and all mankind together will see it.
> For the mouth of the LORD has spoken.'" (Isaiah 40:3-5)

What a clear image major road work to prepare the King's highway – straightening the curves, as well as cutting and filling so that the road might be level and easy to travel upon. Major roadwork – that's what's ahead for us would-be disciples on this journey with Jesus.

2. The messenger of the covenant. The second messenger mentioned in verse 1 is the messenger of the covenant.

---

[326] "Prepare" is the Piel stem of *pānâ*, "turn." However, in the Piel stem means, "get rid of, clear up." Here and in Isaiah 40:3; 57:14; 62:10 with the noun "way, road" (*derek*) it means, "clear (the way)" (Holladay, *Hebrew Lexicon*, p. 293). In verse 1a there is a wordplay: *pannû* ("clear") with *pânîym* (literally, "before my face").

"Then suddenly the Lord you are seeking will come to his temple;
the messenger of the covenant, whom you desire, will come,'
says the LORD Almighty." (Malachi 3:1b)

When I read this verse my mind goes to the bass recitative in Handel's "Messiah," followed by the bass air and chorus putting these powerful verses to music, with the question: "Who shall stand when he appeareth? .... For He is like a Refiner's Fire."

In Malachi 3:1, the Lord whom the people claim to be seeking will suddenly[327] come to his temple. When I was in the army, we often had advance notice of company inspections so we could get ready for them. But woe to us if the officer entered the barracks suddenly, without warning.

Malachi 3:1b is an important Messianic prophecy that seems to have been fulfilled when Jesus comes to the temple following his Triumphal Entry (Mark 11:15-18). Handel's Messiah puts Malachi's prophecy of the Lord's sudden appearance in the temple alongside Haggai's prophecy that we considered in Lesson 2.

"I will shake all nations,
and the desired of all nations will come,
and I will fill this house with glory,' says the LORD Almighty." (Haggai 2:7)

In what sense is Jesus the "messenger of the covenant"? Malachi has a particular interest in the covenant. We read about:

- "My covenant with Levi" (Malachi 2:4, 5, 8).
- "Profaning the covenant of our fathers," by breaking faith (Malachi 2:10).
- "She is your wife by covenant" (Malachi 2:14).

The people have broken God's covenant with them, counting it as nothing. Now the Messenger of the Covenant will come suddenly to call them to account. John the Baptist called for repentance. Now Jesus comes proclaiming, "The time is come. The kingdom of God is at hand. Repent and believe the gospel" (Mark 1:15). Repentance is John's message. Repentance is Jesus' message. Dear friends, without repentance there is no forgiveness, no grace. Repentance is the first step to restoration.

Malachi tells us about the judgment this Messenger will bring – which we'll look at in a moment. What he doesn't tell us, we learn from the New Testament. At the Last Supper, Jesus said:

---

[327] Pit'ōm means "suddenly, surprisingly." Of the 25 uses of this word in the prophets and writings only once does it refer to a pleasant event. Elsewhere it is connected with disaster or judgment (Victor P. Hamilton, TWOT #1859a).

"He took bread, gave thanks and broke it, and gave it to them, saying, 'This is my body given for you; do this in remembrance of me.' In the same way, after the supper he took the cup, saying, 'This cup is the **new covenant in my blood**, which is poured out for you.'" (Luke 22:19-20)

Time and time again, God's people have broken the Mosaic Covenant – and have been judged for it. Jesus is the Mediator of a New Covenant, the covenant with new promises prophesied by Jeremiah (Jeremiah 31:31-34). Jesus dies as a ransom for many to set them free from the guilt and power of sin (Hebrews 9:15; Mark 10:45). And so the Messenger of the Covenant fulfills the terms of the Covenant in his own body.

Refiner's Fire and Fullers' Soap (Malachi 3:2-5a)

Malachi says with deep irony that the people "desire" this Messenger of the Covenant. But when he comes, he will bring judgment. As John the Baptist says,

"His winnowing fork is in his hand,
and he will clear his threshing floor
and gather his wheat into the barn,
but the chaff he will burn with unquenchable fire." (Matthew 3:12)

Woe to the chaff! But it is the chaff Malachi is addressing in this passage. Malachi asks,

"Who can endure the day of his coming?
Who can stand when he appears?" (Malachi 3:2a)

The implied answer is that no one will remain standing when he appears in judgment. Then Malachi introduces two analogies to help his hearers envision the intensity of the judgment that is coming:

"For he will be like a refiner's fire or a launderer's soap." (Malachi 3:2b)

A regular fire that you might cook with is hot enough. But Malachi speaks of a "refiner's fire"[328] used for smelting metals. Such a fire is made extra hot through the use of bellows (Jeremiah 6:29) to the point that it melts the ore in a crucible, allowing lighter impurities to separate and rise to the surface to be skimmed off, while the heavier metals – iron, gold, silver, etc. – will fall to the bottom. Refiner's fire is unbearably hot.

The second analogy is "launderer's soap" or "fullers' soap."[329] "To full," in ancient times, means to make clothing clean and soft by treading, kneading, and beating them in

---

[328] "Refiner's fire" is "fire" (ʾēsh) with a participle of ṣārap, "smelt, refine, test" (TWOT #1972).

[329] "Launderer's soap" (NIV) or "fullers' soap" (NRSV, ESV, KJV) is "soap" (bōrît) and the Piel participle of kābas, "wash, be washed, perform the work of a fuller" (John N. Oswalt, TWOT #946).

cold water. The soap is a caustic alkali, the process a continual pounding. God's judgment is relentless and painful.

Who can "abide" (KJV) or "endure" (NIV, NRSV, ESV) such judgment? I recall the African American spiritual inspired by the punishments described in the Book of Revelation:

> "O sinner man, where you gonna run to?
> O sinner man, where you gonna run to?
> O sinner man, where you gonna run to
> All on that day?

> Run to the rock, the rock was a'melting,
> Run to the sea, the sea was a'boiling,
> Run to the moon, moon was a'bleeding
> All on that day."

The judgment here focuses on the priests and Levites who are corrupt:

> "3 He will sit as a refiner[330] and purifier[331] of silver; he will purify the Levites and refine[332] them like gold and silver. Then the LORD will have men who will bring offerings in righteousness, 4 and the offerings of Judah and Jerusalem will be acceptable to the LORD, as in days gone by, as in former years. So I will come near[333] to you for judgment."[334] (Malachi 3:3-5a)

Notice that Yahweh doesn't want to destroy the Levites, but to refine them so they can serve acceptably. The process will be exceedingly painful, but the fruit will be sweet.

Q1. (Malachi 3:1-5) For what purpose is the Messenger sent to prepare the way? What will the Messenger of the Covenant do? Why do God's people need refining and deep cleaning? How do you sense God wants to refine and cleanse you?
http://www.joyfulheart.com/forums/topic/1757-q1-deep-cleaning/

---

[330] "Refiner" in verse 3a is uses the verb ṣārap, "smelt, refine, test" (TWOT #1972).

[331] "Purifier/purify" in verse 3a and 3b uses the verb ṭāhēr, "be pure, clean" (TWOT #792).

[332] "Refine" in verse 4b is zāqaq, "refine, purify." The basic idea is of making something pure (Leon J. Wood, TWOT #576).

[333] "Come near" (NIV), "draw near" (NRSV, ESV, KJV) is qārab, "come near, approach, enter into." Basically our root denotes being or coming into the most near and intimate proximity of the object (or subject). A secondary meaning entails actual contact with the object (Leonard J. Coppes, TWOT #2065).

[334] "Judgment" is mishpāṭ, in the sense of deciding a case of litigation brought before a civil magistrate (Robert D. Culver, TWOT #2443c).

A Witness against Injustice (Malachi 3:5b)

Now Malachi turns from the priests and Levites to others among God's covenant people who are committing gross sin and injustice.

> "'I will be quick to testify against sorcerers, adulterers and perjurers, against those who defraud laborers of their wages, who oppress the widows and the fatherless, and deprive aliens of justice, but do not fear me,' says the LORD Almighty." (Malachi 3:5b)

Notice that Yahweh will testify – that is, speak what he personally knows to be true[335] – before the Court on Judgment Day. He is quick to do so. He hastens, he is eager[336] to do it. The time has come!

Malachi gives a short list of the sinners whom Yahweh is singling out for punishment, though all sinners will be judged on that Day:

- **Sorcerers**[337] are those who use witchcraft and occult arts to influence events. Sorcery is strictly forbidden to Jews (Deuteronomy 18:10-12; Exodus 22:18), though it was practiced by King Manasseh (2 Chronicles 33:6), the "witch of Endor" (1 Samuel 28:3-25), and others. In our day the occult includes use of tarot cards, Ouija boards (or "talking boards"), astrology, fortune tellers, spirit mediums, channeling, as well as practices of Wicca, among others.
- **Adulterers**, those who "commit adultery," specifically, "sexual intercourse with the wife or betrothed of another man."[338] The prohibition against adultery is found, of course, in the Ten Commandments (Exodus 20:14). Jesus extends the spirit of adultery to looking at a woman lustfully (Matthew 5:27-28). In our day, the spirit of adultery would extend to looking at pornography.

The next group of sins relate to crimes committed to subvert justice and the rights of the weak and powerless in society. Of course, it begins by making false statements in court (and, in our day, on government forms)

- **"Perjurers"** (NIV), **"those who swear falsely"** (NRSV, ESV), "false swearers" (KJV) refers specifically to those who make false statements in court under oath,

---

[335] "Testify against" (NIV), "bear witness against" (NRSV), "be a swift witness against" (ESV, KJV) is words, *ʿēd*, "witness." A witness is a person who has firsthand knowledge of an event or one who can testify on the basis of a report which he has heard. (Carl Schultz, TWOT #1576b). See Jeremiah 29:23, ESV.

[336] Piel stem of *māhar*, "hasten" is used of wicked men who are eager to shed blood and practice evil (Proverbs 1:16, 6:18; Isaiah 59:7), but also of God who will come to bear prompt or swift witness against their sins (Walter C. Kaiser, TWOT #1152).

[337] "Sorcerers" is a participle of *kāshap*, "use witchcraft" (TWOT #1051).

[338] Leonard J. Coppes, *nāʾap*, TWOT #1273.

as prohibited in the Ten Commandments (Exodus 20:16). Swearing falsely is one way of oppressing others by using the legal system. Then Malachi goes on to two other forms of oppression.

The key word in the next phrase is translated "defraud" or "oppress" – 'āshaq, "oppress, get deceitfully, defraud, do violence," involving acts of abuse of power or authority, the burdening, trampling, and crushing of those lower in station. Those most likely to be mistreated and oppressed were those without adequate defense of their rights, i.e. the widow, the orphan, the sojourner and the poor. Such oppression is a breach of faith against Yahweh himself.[339]

- **"Those who defraud laborers of their wages"** (NIV), "oppress the hired workers in their wages" (NRSV, ESV), "oppress the hireling in his wages" (KJV), are those who cheat day laborers out of their full pay because they have little recourse in the courts. This has been going on for thousands of years. The poor fear losing their jobs if they complain.

- **[Who oppress] the widows and the fatherless.** Widows were often cheated out of their husband's family property because they didn't understand the law and weren't represented in court – or the judges were bribed. As a kinsman-redeemer, Boaz protects his kinswoman Naomi and her daughter-in-law Ruth, both widows (Book of Ruth), though widows without such protectors were often cheated (Luke 18:1-8).

- **"Deprive aliens of justice"** (NIV), "thrust aside the alien/sojourner" (NRSV, ESV), "turn aside the stranger from his right" (KJV). It is common in America, for example, for contractors to hire illegal aliens as day laborers at substandard wages "under the table," that is, without reporting it to the government, and thus avoiding social security and worker's comprehensive insurance payments. If the employer doesn't pay what he promises, the illegal alien can't take him to court or he risks being deported. It has been common in our world for stronger societies to deprive weaker societies of their rights. For example, the US government repeatedly disregarded Native American treaties in the nineteenth century.

The Scripture often speaks on this subject, since it is so common.[340]

> "Cursed be anyone who perverts the justice due to the sojourner, the fatherless, and the widow.' And all the people shall say, 'Amen.'" (Deuteronomy 27:19)

---

[339] Ronald B. Allen, 'āshaq, TWOT #1713.
[340] See, for example, Isaiah 1:17, 23; Psalm 82:3-4; Proverbs 31:9; Jeremiah 22:3.

Many of the urban reform movements that have taken place in the last two hundred years, have been motivated, at least in part, by Christians taking seriously God's demand for justice to the poor. Such movements include: the abolition of the slave trade, child labor laws, labor legislation and unions, social welfare, urban health clinics, human sex trafficking, etc. How well a society cares for the rights of the poor is one indicator of how much that society is pleasing to God.

As I write this, there has been an outcry against massive immigration to Europe, along with increased prejudice against aliens of all kinds. In America, we've seen increased anti-alien rhetoric. There is fear in immigrant communities of government deportation of *illegal* aliens – as well as safety concerns for *legal* aliens. We Christians are challenged to seek God how to respond as he would have us do.

The root problem, of course, is one of personal belief in and respect for God. In our passage, Malachi gives a list of various kinds of sinners and concludes with those **"who do not fear me."** "Fear" is *yārē'*, "fear, be afraid, revere," which we discussed in depth in Lesson 9 under Malachi 2:5.[341] God doesn't want us to live in abject terror. But he wants us to have a healthy respect for his discipline, if we chose to rebel against him. A healthy fear of God is a helpful deterrent to sin.

The Immutable, Unchanging God (Malachi 3:6)

This section concludes with this sentence:

"I the LORD do not change.[342]
So you, O descendants of Jacob, are not destroyed."[343] (Malachi 3:6)

In other words, God is saying, if I didn't act with faithfulness to the promises I made to Abraham, Isaac, and Jacob, you would have already been destroyed for your sins – in the modern vernacular, "you would be toast."

This passage is one of the clearest statements in Scripture about the unchangeableness of God. The hymn "Great Is Thy Faithfulness" expresses this well.

---

[341] *Yārē'*, TWOT #907.

[342] "Change" is *shānâ*, here, the intransitive of "to change" (Holladay, *Hebrew Lexicon*, p. 378; TWOT #2419).

[343] "Are not destroyed" (NIV), "have not perished" (NRSV), "are not consumed" (ESV, KJV) is the negative with the Qal stem of *kālâ*, which can be translated variously "accomplish, cease, consume, determine, end, fail, finish," depending upon the context. The basic idea of this root is "to bring a process to completion." On the negative side something which is "used up, vanished, spent, consumed" The idea of being consumed is most commonly applied to violent destruction, often by war (John N. Oswalt, TWOT #982).

"Great is thy faithfulness, O God our Father,
There is no shadow of turning with Thee.[344]
Thou changest not, thy compassions they fail not.
As Thou hast been, Thou forever shalt be."[345]

Wayne Grudem states the Doctrine of Immutability or Unchangeableness of God in this way:

"God is unchanging in his being, perfections, purposes, and promises, yet God does act and feel emotions, and he acts and feels differently in response to different situations."[346]

In addition to many passages that speak of God's eternal nature, these deal specifically with his unchangeableness:

"But you remain the same,
and your years will never end." (Psalm 102:27)

"Every good and perfect gift is from above,
coming down from the Father of the heavenly lights,
who does not change like shifting shadows." (James 1:17)

God's Faithfulness to His Promises

You're fortunate that I don't change, says God in our passage, or you would be destroyed. It is important for us sinners to understand that God's restraint towards us is not because we are righteous, but because of his promises. To the people of Israel, Yahweh says:

"It is not because of your righteousness or your integrity that you are going in to take possession of their land; but on account of the wickedness of these nations, the LORD your God will drive them out before you, to accomplish what he swore to your fathers, to Abraham, Isaac and Jacob." (Deuteronomy 9:5)

Paul wrote to Timothy:

"Here is a trustworthy saying…
if we are faithless,

---

[344] This phrase comes from the KJV translation of James 1:17 – "With whom is no variableness, neither shadow of turning," which the NIV renders as "shifting shadows."

[345] "Great Is Thy Faithfulness," words by Thomas O. Chisolm (1923), music by William M. Runyan (1923), © 1923, Hope Publishing Company.

[346] Wayne Grudem, *Systematic Theology* (Zondervan, 1994), p. 162.

he will remain faithful,
  for he cannot disown himself." (2 Timothy 2:11, 13)

God's character and faithfulness to his promises never changes. Hallelujah!

> **Q2. (Malachi 3:6) Why should we rejoice that God doesn't change? We know that God's *character* doesn't change But if he is immutable, unchangeable, how can he answer our *prayers*? Does prayer have any effect?**
> **http://www.joyfulheart.com/forums/topic/1758-q2-immutable-god/**

Oracle 5. Repent of Robbing God in Tithes and Offerings (Malachi 3:7-12)

Repent of Your Laxity and Drifting! (Malachi 3:7)

The prophet's next oracle accuses the people of turning away from God in the area of tithing and bringing offerings.

> "⁷ 'Ever since the time of your forefathers you have turned away from my decrees and have not kept them. Return to me, and I will return to you,' says the LORD Almighty." (Malachi 3:7)

When we neglect to do something our faith requires of us, we don't see it as rebellion. We view it as an excusable laxity that we'll get around to correcting one of these days. But as we've seen in Malachi's previous prophecies, laxity is really a form of passive rebellion, of cynicism towards God, a kind of unbelief. The word use here is *śûr*, "turn aside, depart,"[347] a word often used to refer to Israel's apostasy.

What God requires of us, when we recognize our drifting away is to "turn" or "re-turn" (*shûb*), a word often used of returning to God in repentance.[348] Where we are casual about our sins of laxity, Jesus the great Discipler, calls us to repent and follow him, so as not to miss out on the blessings that accompany obedience.

---

[347] "Turned away" (NIV), "turned aside" (NRSV, ESV), "gone away" (KJV) is *śûr*, "turn aside, depart." The root is often used of Israel's apostasy. In many cases it is translated "turn aside/away" (TWOT #1480).

[348] "Return," used three times in verse 7b, is *shûb*, "(re)turn." The most important theological use of *shûb* in the Qal is in passages dealing with the covenant community's return to God (in the sense of repentance), or turning away from evil, in the sense of renouncing and disowning sin, or turning away from God, in the sense of becoming apostate (Victor P. Hamilton, TWOT #2340).

Robbing God in Tithes and Offerings (Malachi 3:7b-9)

The people wonder what Malachi is talking about? What do you mean, Malachi?

> 7b But you ask, 'How are we to return?' 8 "Will a man rob God? Yet you rob me. "But you ask, 'How do we rob you?' "In tithes and offerings. 9 You are under a curse – the whole nation of you – because you are robbing me." (Malachi 3:7b-9)

You are robbing me, because you aren't bringing to me the tithes and offerings that belong to me according to the Covenant we have agreed to.

The word "rob"[349] is shocking. None of us would "rob" the church office, or strip the church sanctuary of its beautiful objects. To do so would be a desecration. The kind of people who would do something like this would have no fear of God in them at all! But failing to bring what belongs to God, is just as surely robbing him as is violently taking something from his house.

The prophet mentions two things they have neglected: tithes and offerings. The tithe ("tenth") refers to an offering of 10% of their income to support the temple and God's work.[350] Offerings, on the other hand, is a general term for various sacrifices and offerings brought to the temple.[351]

> "Bring the whole tithe into the storehouse, that there may be food in my house." (Malachi 3:10a)

The prophet specifies the "whole," "full" or "all" the tithe, as opposed to only a portion.[352] Essentially the people are cheating God. Yes, they bring some of what the Covenant requires, especially when it is convenient, but often they just don't.

The "storehouse" refers to literal storeroom within the temple buildings where the tithes of the people are kept.[353] Often, these temple storerooms are filled with actual

---

[349] "Rob" (used three times in verse 8, and once in verse 9) is *qāba'*. The meaning is uncertain, as it is rare in the Old Testament, perhaps "rob." Used only here and in Proverbs 22:23. The word is well established in Talmudic literature, meaning, "to take forcibly" (Baldwin, *Haggai, Zechariah, Malachi*, p. 246). "Deceive," or perhaps "rob" (Holladay, *Hebrew Lexicon*, p. 311), achieved by transposing the consonants.

[350] "Tithe" is *ma'ăśēr*, "tithe," related to the word for "ten." The Egyptians and Mesopotamians tithed to gods or temples (Ronald B. Allen, TWOT #1711h).

[351] "Offerings" (NIV, NRSV, KJV), "contributions" (ESV) is *terûmâ*, "contribution," from the verb *rûm*, "be high; lofty; rise up." Used both as a general cultic term for various offerings and as a term for those parts of the offerings designated especially for the officiating priest (Andrew Bowling, TWOT #2133i).

[352] "Whole" (NIV), "full" (NRSV, ESV), "all" (KJV) is *kōl*, "totality" *Kōl* before a determinate noun expresses unity, e.g., "the whole earth" (Genesis 9:19) (Holladay, *Hebrew Lexicon*, pp. 156-157).

[353] "Storehouse" is two words, *bayit*, "house, household, home, temple," and *'ôṣār*, "treasure, treasury, storehouse," from *'āṣar*, "to store up, lay up" (TWOT #154a). *Bayit* is used later in the verse to refer to "my house," that is, the temple.

food[354] to feed the priests and Levites who serve in the temple, brought by the people as part of their regular tithe. When there is food available, priests and Levites are able to come to the temple to serve according to a regular schedule; when there isn't food, they have to stay home and work their fields and care for their flocks, so their families don't starve. As a result, the temple ministry has to work with a skeleton crew and things rapidly fall into disrepair.

You sometimes hear teaching advocating "storehouse tithing," that all of one's tithe should be given to the local church (the "storehouse"), rather than the giver distributing his or her tithe among worthy ministries. This teaching, however, requires substituting the word "local congregation" for "Jerusalem temple" – which can't really be justified. Yes, there are comparison points, but centralized temple worship and local church ministry are vastly different. And in our day many para-church organizations exist to carry out the work of the church, a situation that didn't exist in Bible times.

A Brief History of the Tithe

It is tempting to try to give a comprehensive summary of what the Old and New Testaments teach us about giving to God, but I'll try to restrain myself. Nevertheless, it is important that we understand what the tithe is and what is required by the Mosaic Law.

Tithing predates the patriarchs. Israel is merely one among many ancient Near Eastern peoples that tithe, that is, contribute 10% of their property, produce, or currency for religious purposes. Tithing to support temples and priests is often seen in Mesopotamia and Egypt. Among the patriarchs, Abraham tithes the plunder of a successful raid to Melchizedek, king of Salem (Jerusalem; Genesis 14:20). Jacob promises to tithe to Yahweh after seeing a vision at Bethel (Genesis 28:22).

In the Mosaic Law, the tabernacle/temple is considered Yahweh's palace and courtyard, placed in the center of the encampment of his people. The priests and Levites are assigned to care for the tabernacle, and later the temple, and to offer the sacrifices to atone for sin.

The tribe of Levi is specifically excluded from the tribal division of land under Joshua. Rather, they are given certain towns and surrounding pastureland within lands assigned to other of the 12 tribes (Numbers 35:1-5). According to a schedule attributed to

---

[354] "Food" (NIV, NRSV, ESV), "meat" (KJV) is *ṭerep*, "prey, food, leaf," from the verb *ṭārap*, "to seize a creature with predaciousness, tear the flesh, and consume it" (TWOT #827b).

David, priests and Levites are assigned "shifts," when they come to Jerusalem to serve in the temple for an appointed period of time, and then return to their homes.

To support the priests and Levites, the Mosaic Law provides that the priests are entitled to a specific portion from most of the animal and grain sacrifices to provide food for them and their families (for example, Numbers 18:8-20).

In addition, a tithe of 10% of the people's income is assigned to provide for the Levites (members of the tribe of Levi who serve at the tabernacle/temple), and 10% of that (a tithe of the tithe) goes to support the priests who perform the actual sacrifices and ministry inside the tabernacle/temple (Nehemiah 10:37-39).

It appears that, in at least some periods, the tithe is not brought to the temple, but every three years distributed to the Levites and the poor living in one's region (Deuteronomy 14:22-29). How the temple services are supported those years isn't clear.

Throughout the history of Israel following the Exodus, when the nation's faith is strong, the tithe is available to support the ministry, but when it is weak, the temple is neglected. There isn't food or money to support priestly functions, and revival is necessary to restore the practice of tithing (2 Chronicles 31:12-15).

You may recall from earlier lessons, that support of the temple and priesthood are issues following the Exile. During Nehemiah's first term as governor, the system is functioning well and there is support for the priests and Levites (Nehemiah 12:47), but then he returns to Susa and things seem to fall apart. On Nehemiah's second term as governor, he records:

> "10 I also learned that the portions assigned to the Levites had not been given to them, and that all the Levites and singers responsible for the service had gone back to their own fields. 11 So I rebuked the officials and asked them, 'Why is the house of God neglected?' Then I called them together and stationed them at their posts. 12 All Judah brought the tithes of grain, new wine and oil into the storerooms." (Nehemiah 13:10-12)

You also see tithing mentioned in the Gospels. I'm sure that, as a good Jew, Jesus and his parents tithe, though we're not told so explicitly. By one of his backhanded compliments to the Pharisees, you can see that he approves of the principle of tithing, if not the Pharisees' particular practice.

> "Woe to you Pharisees, because you give God a tenth of your mint, rue and all other kinds of garden herbs, but you neglect justice and the love of God. You should have practiced the latter without leaving the former undone." (Luke 11:42)

The Pharisees are over-scrupulous about tithing, but clueless about practicing God's justice and mercy.

After we finish this passage in Malachi, we'll consider how the early church seems to apply the principles, and how we might apply them today. But first, let's continue with Malachi.

An Invitation to Test Yahweh by Tithing (Malachi 3:10b)

"'Test me in this,' says the LORD Almighty…." (Malachi 3:10b)

I can't recall any other place in Scripture where God invites us to test[355] him, to see if he will fulfill his promise of blessing. It's a rather remarkable challenge. You tithe and see how I'll bless you. The blessings mentioned fall into three categories.

1. Positive – God will provide an abundant blessing.

"'See if I will not throw open the floodgates of heaven
and pour out so much blessing
that you will not have room enough for it." (Malachi 3:10b)

He uses the analogy of opening the "windows" or "sluices" of heaven,[356] in the way that a downpour[357] might cause a flash flood – so much blessing[358] that you can't contain it all.[359] Along these lines, Jesus promised a "good measure, pressed down, shaken together and running over" (Luke 6:38). We'll look at this passage further in a moment.

2. Negative – God will prevent destruction of what they have.

---

[355] "Test" (NIV), "put to the test" (NRSV, KJV), "prove" (KJV) is *bāḥan*, "to examine, try, prove," denoting, "examining to determine essential qualities, especially integrity" (John N. Oswalt, TWOT #230).

[356] "Floodgates" (NIV), "windows" (NRSV, ESV, KJV) is *'arubbâ*, "window, chimney, sluice" (TWOT #156d). "Window, chimney" (Holladay, *Hebrew Lexicon*, p. 26).

[357] "Pour out" (NIV, KJV), "pour down" (NRSV, ESVI) is the Hiphil stem of *rîq*, "make empty," Hiphil, "empty out," used a few times literally of emptying vessels, sacks, etc. (William White, TWOT #2161). "Empty out, pour out" (Holladay, *Hebrew Lexicon*, p. 339).

[358] "Blessing" is *berākâ*, "blessing," Either the verbal enduement with good things or a collective expression for the good things themselves (John N. Oswalt, TWOT #285b).

[359] "So much" (NIV), "overflowing" (NRSV), "until" (ESV) is "until, up to, upon," here, expresses degree or measure, "to an overwhelming degree" (Malachi 3:10; Holladay, *Hebrew Lexicon*, pp. 264-265). "Not room enough" (NIV, KJV), "overflowing" (NRSV), "no more need" (ESV) is simply *day*, "sufficiency, necessary supply, enough." Here, negatively, "until there is no more necessity, sufficient" (Malachi 3:10; Holladay, *Hebrew Lexicon*, p. 70).

"'I will prevent[360] pests from devouring[361] your crops,
and the vines[362] in your fields will not cast their fruit,'[363]
says the LORD Almighty." (Malachi 3:11)

Unless God protects us from unforeseen problems, all our resources can easily disappear. That was the case when the returned exiles put off rebuilding the temple in favor of building their own homes. Haggai explains to them that their disobedience has brought God's curse of scarcity.

"'You have planted much, but have harvested little.
You eat, but never have enough.
You drink, but never have your fill.
You put on clothes, but are not warm.
You earn wages, only to put them in a purse with holes in it....
You expected much, but see, it turned out to be little.
What you brought home, I blew away.

Why?' declares the LORD Almighty.
'Because of my house, which remains a ruin,
while each of you is busy with his own house.
Therefore, because of you the heavens have withheld their dew
and the earth its crops.
I called for a drought on the fields and the mountains,
on the grain, the new wine, the oil and whatever the ground produces,
on men and cattle, and on the labor of your hands.'" (Haggai 1:6, 9-11)

3. A reputation of being blessed.

"'Then all the nations will call you blessed,[364]
for yours will be a delightful land,'[365]
says the LORD Almighty." (Malachi 3:12)

---

[360] "Prevent" (NIV), "rebuke" (NRSV, ESV, KJV) is *gā'ar*, "rebuke, reprove," indicating a check applied to a person or peoples through strong admonitions or actions (Harold G. Stigers, TWOT #370).

[361] "Pests from devouring" (NIV), "the locust" (NRSV), "the devourer" (ESV, KJV) is a participle of the verb, *'ākal*, "eat, consume, devour," with the primary meaning of "to consume" (Jack B. Scott, TWOT #85). The ESV footnote says, "probably a name for a crop-consuming pest or pests."

[362] "Vine," *gepen*, indicates a grape vine of whatever species (Harold G. Sitgers, TWOT #372a).

[363] "Cast their fruit" (NIV, KJV), "be barren" (NRSV), "fail to bear" (ESV) is the Piel stem of *shākal*, "be bereaved, make childless, miscarry" (TWOT #2385).

[364] "Call blessed" (NIV, ESV, KJV), "count happy" (NRSV), here and in verse 15 is the Piel stem of the verb *'āshar*. In the Qal stem it means "walk in the way of understanding." In the Piel stem, as in our verse, it

When we're serving God in obedience, we're triply blessed. (1) He blesses our endeavors, (2) prevents those events that diminish that blessing, and (3) others see our blessing and honor our God.

Principles of Stewardship

Stewardship as taught in the Bible is based on several principles. They aren't taught here in Malachi, but I think it is useful to recount them in this context.

1. Everything belongs to God (Psalm 24:1). The tithe *belongs* to the Lord according to the Mosaic Law. It is his, not theirs. Thus, when the Jews do not give the tithe to the Lord, they are guilty of robbing God, since they are keeping back what belongs to him. As a result they experience a curse for robbery.

2. We are stewards, caretakers of what belongs to God (Genesis 2:15; Luke 19:11-29).

3. Tithing is a form of proportional giving. In the tithe, the rich and the poor give the same percentage of their income. The poor give a little, the rich give a lot. 1 Corinthians 16:2 teaches something similar, to give as God has prospered you.[366]

4. There is a law of spiritual causality in operation. In other words, there is often an underlying cause for our relative degree of blessing from God or non-blessing (2 Corinthians 9:6). In both Haggai 1 and Malachi 3, the people are experiencing scarcity because of their lack of giving, whereas they can experience God's blessing if they obey. I don't think the promises of blessing are given only in response to giving money. The

---

means something like, "to bless, called blessed." A more commonly used synonym is *bārak*. Of the two words only *bārak* is used by God or towards God. To be blessed ('*āshar*) a man has to do something. To be blessed (*bārak*), one only has to trust in God. *Bārak* is a benediction; '*āshar* more of a congratulation. Asher is one of the tribes of Israel, the name meaning, "happy, fortunate one" (Victor P. Hamilton, TWOT #183).

[365] "Delightful land" (NIV), "land of delight" (NRSV, ESV), "delightsome land" (KJV) is two words: the noun is '*eres*, "earth, land." The adjective is *hēpes*, "delight, pleasure," where it speaks of the pleasure which the land gives. It is formed from the verb *hāpēs*, "take delight in, be pleased with, desire," the basic meaning being to feel great favor towards something, suggesting a definite emotional involvement. The word can also be used in reference to that in which God finds delight (Leonard J. Wood, TWOT #712b).

[366] *Euodoō*, BDAG 410. Danker translates the phrase, "save as much as he gains." But Fee notes that the Christian community contained a number of slaves who might have no income at all. He sees the verb as "intentionally ambiguous, and does not mean that each should lay aside all his or her 'profits,' which a literal translation of the Greek text would allow, but that in accordance with 'whatever success or prosperity may have come their way that week,' each should set aside something for this collection. There is no hint of a tithe or proportional giving; the gift is simply to be related to their ability from week to week as they have been prospered by God" (Gordon D. Fee, *The First Epistle to the Corinthians* (New International Commentary; Eerdmans, 1987), p. 814). The NRSV's translation "whatever extra you earn," misses the sense of it, I think.

promises of blessing are conditional upon obedience to God in general; giving money is a subset of obedience.

5. You can't outgive God. When your heart is right before God, I don't believe you can outgive him, for his ability to bless you is far beyond your ability to give. Jesus said,

> "Give, and it will be given to you. A good measure, pressed down, shaken together and running over, will be poured into your lap. For with the measure you use, it will be measured to you." (Luke 6:38)

When Jesus talks about the measure you use, he means: If you give with a big scoop or a cup completely full, then you'll receive with the same big scoop and full cup. If you give with a tiny scoop or just a pinch, you'll receive just a tiny blessing. This truth has been distorted by some Prosperity Teachers who motivate people to give to God as a means of getting wealthy. Their motivation for giving isn't worship, but greed and selfishness.

How Should We Apply the Principle of Tithing Today?

To be direct, you don't see tithing taught in the New Testament church. You might argue that it wasn't mentioned because it was assumed, but that's an argument from silence. You might argue that we are the New Israel, but the New Testament is clear that we aren't under the Mosaic Law (Romans 6:14; 7:4-11; Galatians 3:23; 5:18).

Rather than tithing, I see two practices taught in the New Testament:

1. Generosity towards the poor. You can see this in Paul's organizing the churches he plants to prepare gifts to bring to the poor in Jerusalem. Regular giving for this big gift is the context of the great stewardship passages of 2 Corinthians 8-9, for example.

2. Support for Christian leaders. It is clear that Paul defends the right of apostles to be supported (1 Corinthians 9:5-12a), while at the same time waiving that right with regard to himself (1 Corinthians 9:12b-18). He also supports the right of local leaders to receive financial support from the church (1 Timothy 5:17-18). In fact, Paul implies that what is owed to the priests under the Old Covenant is now transferred in some sense to Christian pastors, evangelists, and teachers.[367]

> "Don't you know that those who work in the temple get their food from the temple, and those who serve at the altar share in what is offered on the altar? In the same way, the Lord has commanded that those who preach the gospel should receive their living from the gospel." (1 Corinthians 9:13-14)

---

[367] You can see this spelled out much more fully in my article, "Does Your Church Run a Spiritual Sweatshop?" http://joyfulheart.com/church/sweatshop.htm

The legal requirement of tithing does not apply to Christian believers who are not Jews. Once the temple is finally destroyed in 70 AD, the tithing regulations for Jews become moot.

So how do we apply the principles in our day.

1. **Use the tithe as a guideline, not a law.** My seminary professor, Dr. George Eldon Ladd used to say, "To give less under grace than under law is a *dis*grace." If the Jews were expected to give 10%, how can we feel a lesser amount is appropriate for us? It is not a law, but a guideline.

2. **The blessings of the tithe are blessings for obedience.** Our obedience is not to the Mosaic law, but to Jesus and his Spirit. But the blessings can be just as abundant. As you give in faith from a life that seeks to be obedient to Jesus, your blessings can be just as great as those promised in Malachi 3 – both materially and spiritually.

3. **Our giving reflects our love for God.** Jesus said, "Where your treasure is, there will your heart be also" (Matthew 6:21). In general, a person who gives little to God and his work reflects a heart that loves God little (Luke 7:47).

4. **Our giving should support Christian workers as well as the poor.** Giving to them is the same as giving to God himself, for they are his servants. For many in organized churches, this means giving to the church, allowing the church to pay the pastoral staff.

5. **Cheerful giving is the standard** (2 Corinthians 9:7). I've heard some sermons that use "fear of the curse" as a motivator. Others employ motivations such as greed, a love of monetary blessings, to get people to tithe. But the best motivator for the mature believer is love. We love giving, because giving to the One we love makes us happy.

There's a lot more that can be said, but these are the principles.

Note: People differ on whether they believe that Christians are required to obey the Old Testament law of tithing. Feel free to disagree, but on the online forum be gentle, loving. Remember, we are brothers and sisters.

Q3. (Malachi 3:8-11) In our passage, why does God call people who neglect to tithe "robbers"? Why does he withhold blessing from those who don't fully tithe? Does the Old Testament law of the tithe obligate Christian believers to tithe? What

principles of stewardship can we learn from this passage?
http://www.joyfulheart.com/forums/topic/1759-q3-tithing/

Oracle 6. Judgment of the Righteous and the Wicked (Malachi 3:13-4:6)

Now we see a dialog and more rhetorical questions that signal a new direction for the prophet. This oracle seems to provide a climax to the previous indictments of God's people and priests – judgment for the wicked and vindication for the righteous.

Cynicism of Unbelievers towards God (Malachi 3:13-15)

The prophet speaks now to those unbelievers who say that it just doesn't pay to serve the Lord.[368]

> "13 'You have said harsh things against me,' says the LORD. 'Yet you ask, "What have we said against you?" 14 'You have said, "It is futile to serve God. What did we gain by carrying out his requirements and going about like mourners before the LORD Almighty? 15 But now we call the arrogant blessed. Certainly the evildoers prosper, and even those who challenge God escape."'" (Malachi 3:13-15)

Yahweh, speaking through Malachi, calls unbelievers to account for their insulting words about him. He says, literally, "You are hard against me."[369] Here are their accusations. Many of them seem familiar in our day, as well.

1. **Serving God is pointless.** "Futile" or "vain" means "empty, worthless."[370] In other words, these cynics are saying that serving God is a waste of time. They characterize religion as consisting of rule-keeping and repentance, rather than anything meaningful.

---

[368] Baldwin (*Haggai, Zechariah, Malachi*, p. 248) notes that some think Malachi is speaking to the discouraged believers here as in Psalm 73:2-15, but I think the attitudes expressed in Malachi 3:13-15 clearly reflect the mindset of the wicked, the unbeliever.

[369] The idea of speaking words is implied, not stated. "Harsh" (NIV, NRSV), "hard" (ESV), "stout" (KJV) is *ḥāzaq*, "be(come) strong, strengthen, prevail, harden, be courageous, be sore" (meaning "be severe"). This can include the ideas of being severe, and hardening of the heart (TWOT #636). The same word is used elsewhere in the Old Testament to refer to hardened hearts.

[370] "Futile" (NIV), "vain" (NRSV, ESV, KJV) is the noun *sihāw'*, "emptiness, vanity, falsehood." The primary meaning of *shāw'* is "emptiness, vanity." It designates anything that is unsubstantial, unreal, worthless, either materially or morally (Victor P. Hamilton, TWOT #2338a).

2. **Serving God doesn't get me ahead**. Here the emphasis is on "me." If something doesn't bring me personal "gain" or "profit," then I shouldn't do it. The connotation of the Hebrew word is "unjust gain, covetousness."[371]

3. **The proud are those who should be admired or considered happy.**[372] The self-confident, those who are arrogant, even presumptuous and rebellious,[373] are the real winners here on earth. Remember Jesus' words in the Beatitudes that the meek shall inherit the earth (Matthew 5:5)? This is the exact opposite.

4. **Law-breakers[374] come out better[375] than the righteous.** This is saying that criminals do better in the end than upright people.

5. **Those who defy God[376] aren't punished.** You can get away with anything. The Psalmist recognized this attitude in his day: "God has forgotten; he covers his face and never sees" (Psalm 10:11). There will be no accounting for sin.

As I consider this unbelief and self-centeredness in Malachi's time, it sounds just like the glorification of Success in our society. Those who are wealthy and influential are the ones to be congratulated, even though the ways they became wealthy may be unrighteous. It is too easy for us Christians to get caught up in a pursuit of Success, rather than continue on the humble path of following our Master. The Apostle John said:

"**Do not love the world** or anything in the world.

If anyone loves the world,

the love of the Father is not in him.

For everything in the world –

---

[371] "Gain" (NIV), "profit" (NRSV, ESV, KJV) is *besa'*, "profit." The root idea is to cut off what is not one's own, or in the slang of our day, to take a "rip-off," thus to be greedy, covetous. So *besa'* is "profit, unjust gain, covetousness," personal advantage derived from some activity, usually in a negative sense (John N. Oswalt, TWOT #267a).

[372] "Blessed" (NIV, ESV), "happy" (NRSV, KJV) is *'ashar*, which we saw in Malachi 3:12.

[373] "Arrogant" (NIV, NRSV, ESV), "proud" (KJV) is *zed*, "proud, arrogant," from *zûd*, "boil, act proudly, presumptuously, rebelliously" (TWOT #547a).

[374] "Evildoers" (NIV, NRSV, ESV), "they that work wickedness" (KJV) is *rish'â*, "guilt, wickedness," mostly in the abstract sense of wickedness or act of wickedness. This word group is used as the opposite of righteousness (*sdq*). "In contrast to *sdq* it denotes the negative behavior of evil thoughts, words and deeds, a behavior not only contrary to God's character, but also hostile to the community and which at the same time betrays the inner disharmony and unrest of a man" (G. Herbert Livingston, TWOT #2222c).

[375] "Prosper" (NIV, NRSV, ESV), "are set up" (KJV) is the Niphal stem of *bānâ*, "build, rebuild" (TWOT #255).

[376] "Challenge" (NIV), "put to the test" (NRSV, ESV, KJV) is *bāhan*, "to examine, try, prove." In most cases, it is God testing man. But in three instances we see man challenging God to perform, once in the Psalms (Psalm 95:9) and twice here in Malachi (Malachi 3:10, 15).

> the **cravings of sinful man**,
> the **lust of his eyes** and
> the **boasting** of what he has and does –
> comes not from the Father but from the world.
> The world and its desires pass away,
> but the man who does the will of God lives forever." (1 John 2:15-17)

Our culture is vastly different from that of Malachi's day, but people are still the same in their unbelief. Still deceived. Still lost. Still pursuing things that will never satisfy. So needy for the salvation that Jesus offers so freely. And there for the great grace of God, we could be as well.

> "People need the Lord, people need the Lord
> At the end of broken dreams, He's the open door
> People need the Lord, people need the Lord
> When will we realize that we must give our lives?
> For people need the Lord, people need the Lord."[377]

Sadly, these are the people who are doomed to destruction on Judgment Day, unless they turn to the Lord for salvation.

Those Who Fear the Lord (Malachi 3:16-18)

Now the prophet turns to those who believe in the Lord and follow him.

> "Then those who feared the LORD talked with each other, and the LORD listened and heard." (Malachi 3:16a)

As we discussed in Lesson 9, on Malachi 2:5b, those who "fear the Lord," aren't the ones who shudder in abject terror of him, but those who fear him in the sense of revering him, who believe in him, who take him and what he says seriously. In verse 16a, they "talked/spoke with each other." The Hebrew uses an idiom something like, "a man speaks to his friend."[378] *The Message* paraphrases it this way:

> "Then those whose lives honored GOD got together and talked it over.
> GOD saw what they were doing and listened in."

---

[377] "People Need the Lord," words and Music by Greg Nelson and Phil McHugh (© 1983 River Oaks Music Co.).

[378] "One another" uses two words in an idiom, using *ish*, "man" to *rēa'*, "friend, companion, another person, neighbor, associate – close or occasional" (R. Laird Harris, TWOT #2186a).

In other words, the believers are evaluating among themselves the attitude of the unbelievers, and making sure that their lives continue to follow the Lord's path. God listens to their conversation approvingly – and rewards their faith.[379]

The Book of Remembrance (Malachi 3:16b)

Now we begin to see how God heeds the faith he sees in the believers. First, their names are written down in a special book.

> "A scroll[380] of remembrance[381] was written in his presence concerning those who feared the LORD and honored[382] his name." (Malachi 3:16b)

We see this mentioned elsewhere in Scripture. Moses refers to "the book you have written" (Genesis 32:32-33). The Psalmist speaks of "the book of life" where the names of the righteous are listed (Psalm 69:28; Philippians 4:3). Daniel refers to such a book containing the names of the righteous (Daniel 12:1). Jesus says that his disciples' names are "written in heaven" (Luke 10:20). In Revelation it is called "the Book of Life" and "the Lamb's Book of Life" (Revelation 13:18; 17:8; 21:27).

Yahweh's Precious People (Malachi 3:17)

Second, Yahweh sets his people apart from the rest on Judgment Day, just as Jesus taught in his Parables of the Sheep and the Goats (Matthew 25:31-46), the Wheat and Tares (Matthew 13:24-30), and the Fish Net (Matthew 13:47-50).

> "'They will be mine,' says the LORD Almighty, 'in the day when I make up my treasured possession. I will spare them, just as in compassion a man spares his son who serves him.'" (Malachi 3:17)

---

[379] "Listened and heard" (NIV), "took note and listened" (NRSV), "paid attention and heard" (ESV), "hearkened and heard" (KJV) are two nearly synonymous words: *qāshab*, "hear, be attentive, heed," and *shāmaʿ*, "hear, listen to, obey."

[380] "Scroll" (NIV), "book" (NRSV, ESV, KJV) is *sēper*, "writing, book" (TWOT #1540). In this era this would refer to a scroll, not a codex that has bound sheets.

[381] "Remembrance" is *zikkārôn*, "memorial, reminder, token, record." The *zikkārôn* is an object or act which brings something else to mind or which represents something else. As such it may be a "memorial," a "reminder," a historical "record," or a physical "token" which calls to mind a deity (Thomas E. McComiskey, TWOT #551b).

[382] "Honored" (NIV), "thought on" (NRSV, KJV), "esteemed" (ESV) is the Qal stem of *ḥāshab*, "think, plan, make a judgment, imagine, count." The main idea is "the employment of the mind in thinking activity." Here it probably has the idea of "running thoughts through the mind, meditating" (Leonard J. Wood, TWOT #767).

The prophet mentions "the day," no doubt referring to the Day of Judgment, which we'll discuss further at Malachi 4:1. Here, it is not just a day of punishment, but a day of vindication and reward.

I've pondered the curious expression translated in various ways:

"In the day when I make up my treasured possession." (NIV, ESV)

"My special possession on the day when I act." (NRSV)

"In that day when I make up my jewels." (KJV)

"On the day when I act, they will be my most prized possession." (NJB)

What does this mean? "Treasured possession" (NIV, ESV), "special possession" (NRSV), "jewels" (KJV), "my most prized possession" (NJB) is *segullâ*, "property, possession," with the basic meaning of "personal property."[383] We first see it in Exodus 19:5 as a reference to God's covenant people out of all nations (Deuteronomy 4:20; 7:6; 14:2; 26:18). In the New Testament, the followers of the Messiah, the New Israel, are heirs to this designation

"You are a chosen race, a royal priesthood, a holy nation, a people for his own possession...." (1 Peter 2:9a, ESV; cf. Titus 2:14)

The expression, "*make up* my treasured possession," is more difficult. The verb is *āśâ*, "do, fashion, accomplish," sometimes used of God's creative work.[384] Is this God sorting out and preparing his jewel collection for display? Perhaps the NRSV and NJB catch the feel of the sentence by making the verb refer to the act of judging on the Day of Judgment, rather than to preparing one's special possessions.

This much is crystal clear. God looks at those who love him with a special affection. "They are mine!" he says. We belong to him, not in just a general way, but as his own selected and prized personal property, those whom he has selected to be close to him always, those whom he has redeemed or bought back "with the precious blood of Christ, a lamb without blemish or defect" (1 Peter 1:19).

As a result of this special affection – "election," the New Testament calls it – he will spare us from punishment on Judgment Day.

---

[383] *Segullâ*, TWOT #1460.

[384] "Make up" (KJV, NIV, ESV), "day when I act" (NRSV, NJB) is *āśâ*, "do, fashion, accomplish." Used of God's creative work. (TWOT #1708).

> "I will spare them,
> just as in compassion
> a man spares his son who serves[385] him." (Malachi 3:17b)

The word "spare" (*hāmal*) can mean either, "spare" or "have compassion on."[386] The NIV includes both ideas in its translation. When difficulty or hardship comes, parents are quick to shield (spare) their children, because they love them.

The Distinction Will Be Clear (Malachi 3:18)

What follows is a transitional verse.

> "And you will again see the distinction between the righteous and the wicked, between those who serve God and those who do not." (Malachi 3:18)

The "distinction" or "difference"[387] between the way of the wicked and the way of the righteous will be manifestly clear on the Day when God brings justice. Right now it may appear that following Jesus doesn't pay, but on that Day it will be obvious. To the wicked it is a day of punishment, but to the righteous it will be a day of vindication and reward.

> **Q4. (Malachi 3:16-18) In what ways does it encourage us that God keeps a list of those who love him? That he considers us his own private and treasured posses-sion? Do we deserve this? What effect should that knowledge have on us? What does it teach us about grace?**
> **http://www.joyfulheart.com/forums/topic/1760-q4-gods-list/**

The Day of the Lord (Malachi 4:1)

Malachi has noted the cynicism of the unbelievers, and the special place that belongs to those who fear him. Now he turns to the day when judgment will occur – and in verse 2, the day when God's people will be set free in healing and victory.

---

[385] "Serves" is *ʿābad*, "work, serve" (TWOT #1553).

[386] Coppes says, "Basically, this root connotes that emotional response which results (or may result) in action to remove its object (and/or its subject) from impending difficulty" (Leonard J. Coppes, *hāmal*, TWOT #676).

[387] "See the distinction" (NIV, ESV), "see the difference" (NRSV), "discern" (KJV) is the Qal stem of *rāʾâ*, "see, look at, inspect" (TWOT #2095).

"'Surely the day is coming; it will burn like a furnace. All the arrogant and every evildoer will be stubble, and that day that is coming will set them on fire,' says the LORD Almighty. 'Not a root or a branch will be left to them.'" (Malachi 4:1)

The word "day" is shorthand for the "Day of the Judgment," which we'll consider in a moment. Malachi describes the punishment like the burning[388] of stubble,[389] what is left of the dry stalks of grain after the harvest. If you've ever watched dry grass burn, you know that it burns with great speed and generates great heat. But this is no ordinary fire. It is the fire of a furnace, a special oven designed to concentrate the heat for the baking of bread.[390] The fire of judgment is especially hot. It recalls the words of the Psalmist:

"At the time of your appearing you will make them like a fiery furnace.
In his wrath the LORD will swallow them up,
and his fire will consume them." (Psalm 21:9)

The objects of this punishment are the arrogant and "every evildoer." We met these people in Malachi 3:14-15 claiming that serving God doesn't pay. Now they and their philosophy of life is judged. They are utterly destroyed without "root or branch," that is, the entire plant (Job 18:16; Amos 2:9).

The Day of the Lord as a Major Theme of the Bible

The Day of the Lord is a theme that begins with the Old Testament prophets and carries through to the last book of the New Testament. It is a day of judgment upon the enemies of the people of God, and upon all unbelievers. In many references it is dark and negative, a time of terror and horror for the unbeliever. It is called by various names:

- **The Day of Judgment** (Matthew 10:15; 11:22, 24; 2 Peter 2:9; 3:7).
- **The Day of the Lord** (Amos 5:18-20; Zephaniah 1:14; 1 Thessalonians 5:2).
- **The Day of the Lord Jesus / Christ** (1 Corinthians 1:8; 2 Corinthians 1:14; Philippians 1:6, 10)
- **The Great Day** (Jude 6).
- **The Great and Dreadful Day of the Lord** (Joel 2:31; Malachi 4:5).

---

[388] "Burn/burning," "glowing" (NJB) is *bāʿar*, "to burn, consume, be kindled" (TWOT #263).

[389] "Stubble" is *qash*, "stubble, chaff." (TWOT #2091a).

[390] "Furnace" is *tannûr*, "furnace, oven." The word denotes basically the relatively small and sometimes portable stove or oven rather than the larger furnace. Constructed of clay and often sunk into the ground, they had a cylindrical or beehive shape and were two to three feet in diameter. Bread and other foods were baked in them (Roland F. Youngblood, TWOT #2526).

- **The Day or That Day** (Malachi 4:1; Romans 2:16; 1 Corinthians 3:13; 1 Thessalonians 5:4; Hebrews 10:25).
- **The Day of Wrath** (Zephaniah 1:15, 18; 2:2-3; Romans 2:5; Revelation 6:17; cf. 1 Thessalonians 1:10).

In a former generation, many sermons detailed the horrors of the Day of Judgment in an attempt to frighten listeners into repentance. Then there was a strong reaction to "fire and brimstone" preaching, so that in many churches today, very, very few sermons ever mention a Day of Judgment.

If you take an objective look at the preaching of John the Baptist and Jesus you see that God's judgment was a prominent theme.

- John the Baptist (Matthew 3:7-10).
- Jesus (Matthew 12:36; 13:24-50; 19:28; 24; 25:31-46; John 3:36).

When you add the teaching of the apostles and the Book of Revelation, you see many, many references to God's judgment, referring to this Day that Malachi mentions. If we are to accurately pass on the teachings of Jesus to our generation, we can't leave out our Master's clear teaching about the Day of Judgment.

The Son of Righteousness with Healing in His Wings (Malachi 4:2-3)

But it is wrong to look at the Day of Judgment in purely negative terms. For the unbeliever it will be a day of terror and horrible punishment. But for the believer, it will be a day of joy. You'll recall Jesus' Parable of the Sheep and the Goats (Matthew 25:31-46). The "goats" experience terrible punishment, excluded from his presence, cursed, thrown into "the eternal fire prepared for the devil and his angels." But the "sheep" experience the loving welcome of the Son of Man:

"Come, you who are blessed by my Father;
take your inheritance,
the kingdom prepared for you since the creation of the world." (Matthew 25:34b)

In the same way, Malachi declares the blessings of the believers:

"But for you who revere my name,
the sun of righteousness will rise
with healing in its wings." (Malachi 4:2a)

It's easy for English-speakers to confuse "son" with "sun," since these words are homonyms. But Malachi specifies the "Sun of Righteousness," who rises in God's sky with healing[391] in his rays or wings.[392] Apparently, Malachi is appropriating a symbol of a winged sun that was common in the ancient Near East and associated with divinity, royalty, and power. Hezekiah uses a winged sun as part of the seal of his kingdom.[393] Upon the righteous, God's sun will rise and bring to them healing and restoration from all they have suffered. Of course, this Sun of Righteousness is a title of Jesus the Messiah.

This idea is incorporated in Zechariah's prophecy concerning his son John the Baptist and Jesus the Messiah:

"... **The rising sun** will come to us from heaven
to shine on those living in darkness and in the shadow of death,
to guide our feet into the path of peace." (Luke 1:78b-79)

Then Malachi compares this experience of vindication to how calves act when they are released from confinement in a stall. In a kind of exaltation, they rush out and leap up in joy.

"And you will go out and leap like calves released from the stall." (Malachi 4:2b)

Whereas, the righteous had been oppressed by the wicked in the world system, now the roles will be reversed.

'"Then you will trample down the wicked;
they will be ashes under the soles of your feet
on the day when I do these things,'
says the LORD Almighty." (Malachi 4:3)

Finally, Malachi gives a reminder to continue to obey God's laws.

"Remember the law of my servant Moses,
the decrees and laws
I gave him at Horeb for all Israel." (Malachi 4:4)

---

[391] "Healing" is *marpē'*, "healing," from *rāpā'*, "heal, make healthful" (TWOT #2196c). In many of the occurrences, it is God who causes healing or afflicts with disease or catastrophes which cannot be healed but by divine intervention.

[392] "Wings" is *kānāp*, "wing, winged, border, corner, shirt." Malachi 4:2 speaks of the Sun of righteousness rising with healing in his wings. Evidently this is an appropriation of the winged sun disc symbol which is used throughout the ancient near east as a manifestation of the deity's protection (John N. Oswalt, TWOT #1003a).

[393] Meir Lubetski, "King Hezekiah's Seal Revisited," *Biblical Archaeology Review*, July/August 2001.

The Prophet Elijah – a Brief Reprieve (Malachi 4:5-6)

The Book of Malachi – and the Old Testament canon – concludes with a promise of hope to come. Judgment will not occur until the people hear a prophet seeking to turn them back to God.

> "See, I will send you the prophet Elijah before that great and dreadful day[394] of the LORD comes." (Malachi 4:5)

Elijah, as you may recall, was one of the archetypical Old Testament prophets who serves during a dark time in Israel's history. During the Intertestamental Period, the period after Malachi is written and Jesus' ministry, there is lots of interest and speculation about this Elijah who is to come, so when John the Baptist appears, he is asked if he is this Elijah. He denies it (John 1:21a), since he probably doesn't identify himself with Malachi's prophecy so much as Isaiah's Voice crying in the wilderness.

But he is indeed the prophet Elijah who was to come to prepare the people. He dresses like Elijah. Of Elijah, it was said, "He was a man with a garment of hair and with a leather belt around his waist" (2 Kings 1:8a). Matthew declares:

> "John's clothes were made of camel's hair,
> and he had a leather belt around his waist.
> His food was locusts and wild honey." (Matthew 3:4)

Like Elijah, John ministers in the wilderness and boldly rebukes the sins of the powerful (Luke 3:7-14; Mark 6:18). John the Baptist comes "in the power and energy with which Elijah rose up to lead back the ungodly generation of his own time to the God of the fathers."[395]

Jesus acknowledges that, indeed, John is this Elijah who was to come (Matthew 11:14; 17:10-13).

Turning the Hearts (Malachi 4:6)

Malachi gives a particular flavor to the ministry of this Elijah to come:

---

[394] "Great and dreadful day" (NIV, KJV), "great and terrible day" (NRSV), "great and awesome day" (ESV) is *gādôl*, "great" plus the Niphal stem of *yārē*, "fear, be afraid."

[395] C. F. Keil and Franz Delitzsch, *Commentary on the Old Testament*, in loc.

"He will turn[396] the hearts of the fathers to their children,
and the hearts of the children to their fathers;
or else I will come and strike the land with a curse." (Malachi 4:6)

What does this mean? Does he refer to a healing of the generation gap, or to something more? Malachi certainly speaks to the healing of frayed relations between parents and children, but it seems like this is a symbol of something even great. Or perhaps Malachi is speaking of a return to the true faith of our spiritual fathers, who would have been ashamed of their descendants' apostasy. The prophet brings the two together by restoring the children to repentance, without which there is only curse and judgment.[397]

The angel's prophecy to Zechariah concerning his son John the Baptist, echoes Malachi's words and interprets them in the sense of turning of hearts in repentance.

"And he will turn[398] many of the children of Israel to the Lord their God,
and he will go before him in the spirit and power of Elijah,
to turn the hearts of the fathers to the children,
and the disobedient to the wisdom of the just,
to make ready for the Lord a people prepared." (Luke 1:16-17, ESV)

This, too, indicates a ministry of repentance and restoration prior to judgment.

And so ends our study of the post-exilic books. In one sense it is a kind of abrupt way to end, but it does so by calling for repentance, and looking forward to God who will bring his people another chance to turn before the final judgment.

The abrupt end leaves us waiting for these Messengers who will come. It leaves us waiting for the New Covenant, God's answer to our lostness and sin. Thank you for the grace you have brought, Lord Jesus. Now come, we pray, for the final judgment and victory. Amen.

Lessons for Disciples

There are many lessons for disciples in this passage.

---

[396] "Turn" is the extremely common verb *shûb*, "turn, return," that we've encountered before. Sometimes it's used in the sense of repentance, but usually it lacks a theological connotation.

[397] This seems to be the approach of Keil and Delitzsch, *op. cit.*

[398] "Bring back" (NIV in vs. 16), "turn" (NRSV, ESV, KJV, and NIV in vs. 17) is *epistrephō*, "to turn to," here, "to cause a person to change belief or course of conduct, with focus on the thing to which one turns, turn," in a spiritual or moral sense (BDAG 382, 3).

1. People who scoff at God, with accusations that he doesn't care, doesn't see, doesn't exist, doesn't reward those who obey him, and doesn't punish evil, have been present for thousands of years (Malachi 2:17).

2. God's answer to the scoffers and unbelievers is to send two messengers: (a) the Messenger who prepares the way (John the Baptist), and (b) the Messenger of the Covenant (Jesus), who will suddenly come to his temple in judgment (Malachi 3:1).

3. The Messenger of the Covenant (Jesus) will come like white hot fire and strong caustic soap to refine his priests and Levites (Malachi 3:2-5).

4. On the Day of Judgment, God will judge all kinds of sinners: sorcerers, adulterers, liars, cheaters, and those who oppress the weak and helpless – all those who have no respect for Yahweh and his commands (Malachi 3:5).

5. God's character doesn't change, he is immutable. As a result, he keeps his promises to the Patriarchs by not destroying their descendants (Malachi 3:6).

6. God calls us to repent, to turn from our sins and turn back to him (Malachi 3:7).

7. God calls the Jews to stop robbing him by neglecting to offer the tithes and offerings to which he is due under the Covenant (Malachi 3:8-9).

8. God invites his people to test him by bringing the full tithe to the temple, and then observing the overwhelming blessings he will bring. These blessings are both positive (abundance) and negative (protection from destruction). (Malachi 3:10-11).

9. Principles of stewardship include:
   a. Everything belongs to God (Psalm 24:1).
   b. We are stewards of what belongs to God (Genesis 2:15; Luke 19:11-29).
   c. Tithing is a form of proportional giving.
   d. There is a law of spiritual causality in operation: blessings for obedience, curses for disobedience.
   e. You can't outgive God (Luke 6:38).

10. We apply the principle of tithing through (a) generosity towards the poor, and (b) support for Christian leaders.

11. We apply the principles today in this fashion:
    a. Use the tithe as a guideline, not a law.

      b. The blessings of the tithe are blessings for obedience.

      c. Our giving reflects our love for God (Matthew 6:21).

      d. Our giving should support Christian workers as well as the poor.

      e. Cheerful giving is the standard (2 Corinthians 9:7).

12. Malachi challenges the statements of cynics and unbelievers that serving God is pointless and unprofitable, that the proud should be admired, lawbreakers do better than the righteous, and that God doesn't punish the wicked (Malachi 3:13-15).

13. God keeps track of those who fear and love him in a "scroll of remembrance." They are his special personal possession that he treasures greatly (Malachi 3:16-17).

14. On Judgment Day the distinction between the righteous and wicked will be clear (Malachi 3:18).

15. Judgment Day, "the Day of the Lord," will bring fiery punishment for those who don't love God, but blessing and peace to those who trust him (Malachi 4:1-2).

16. God will send someone to come in the spirit of the Prophet Elijah (John the Baptist) before the Day of Judgment, to bring people to repentance and faith (Malachi 4:5-6).

Prayer

Father, we live in a world of skeptics and unbelievers, who scoff at the idea of a righteous God and make fun of people who follow Jesus. Help us not to get caught up in the spirit of the age, and so become subject to the judgment that will surely fall upon it. Thank you, that you write our names in heaven and consider us your very special beloved people. That's your grace, Lord, not our deserving anything. Thank you. Thank you for your mercy and undeserved grace that we experience in Jesus Christ our Lord. In his name, we pray. Amen.

Key Verses

"See, I will send my messenger, who will prepare the way before me. Then suddenly the Lord you are seeking will come to his temple; the messenger of the covenant, whom you desire, will come," says the LORD Almighty." (Malachi 3:1, NIV)

"But who can endure the day of his coming? Who can stand when he appears? For he will be like a refiner's fire or a launderer's soap. He will sit as a refiner and purifier of silver; he will purify the Levites and refine them like gold and silver...." (Malachi 3:2-3a, NIV)

"I the LORD do not change. So you, O descendants of Jacob, are not destroyed." (Malachi 3:6, NIV)

"'You are under a curse – the whole nation of you – because you are robbing me. Bring the whole tithe into the storehouse, that there may be food in my house. Test me in this,' says the LORD Almighty, 'and see if I will not throw open the floodgates of heaven and pour out so much blessing that you will not have room enough for it.'" (Malachi 3:9-10, NIV)

"'They will be mine,' says the LORD Almighty, 'in the day when I make up my treasured possession. I will spare them, just as in compassion a man spares his son who serves him.'" (Malachi 3:17, NIV)

"For you who revere my name, the sun of righteousness will rise with healing in its wings. And you will go out and leap like calves released from the stall." (Malachi 4:2, NIV)

"See, I will send you the prophet Elijah before that great and dreadful day of the LORD comes. He will turn the hearts of the fathers to their children, and the hearts of the children to their fathers; or else I will come and strike the land with a curse." (Malachi 4:5-6, NIV)

Appendix 1. Participant Handouts

If you are working with a class or small group, feel free to duplicate the following handouts at no additional charge. If you'd like to print 8-1/2" x 11" or A4 size pages, you can download the free Participant Guide handout sheets at:

www.jesuswalk.com/rebuild/rebuild-lesson-handouts.pdf

Discussion Questions

You'll typically find 4 or 5 questions for each lesson. Each question may include several sub-questions. These are designed to get group members engaged in discussion of the key points of the passage. If you're running short of time, feel free to skip questions or portions of questions.

Suggestions for Classes and Groups

Individuals who are studying online can probably complete one full lesson per week, though they'll need to be diligent to do so. But some of the chapters just have too much material for a one hour class discussion. Feel free to arrange the lessons any way that works best for your group.

Because of the length of these handouts – and to keep down the page count so we can keep the book price lower – they are being made available at no cost online.

www.jesuswalk.com/rebuild/rebuild-lesson-handouts.pdf

Appendix 2 – Chronology of the Post-Exilic Period

559 to 530 BC **Cyrus the Great** reigns, founds the Medo-Persian Empire.

539   **Babylon falls** to the Persians.

538   **Cyrus allows the first wave of Jews to return to Jerusalem** (Ezra 1:1-4).

537-520   **Temple rebuilt in Jerusalem** (Ezra 5:1; Haggai 2:18).

530-522   Cambyses, king of Persia (alluded to in Daniel 11:12).

520s to 518   **Haggai's prophecy** (to 520 BC), **Zechariah's prophecy** 520-518 BC)

521-486   Darius I Hystaspes, king of Persia (Ezra 5:5).

486-465   **Xerxes I (King Ahasuerus; Ezra 4:6). His second queen was Esther.**

464-424   **Artaxerxes I** Longimanus

458   **Ezra receives authorized by Artaxerxes to rebuild the Temple** (Ezra 7)

445   **Nehemiah goes to Jerusalem to repair its walls** (Nehemiah).

424-405   Darius II, king of Persia.

404-359   Artaxerxes II, king of Persia

338-336   Arses, king of Persia

336-331   Darius III, king of Persia

334-323   Alexander the Great conquers Persia, begins Greek Empire (Daniel 8:5, 21)

For dates see K.A. Kitchen, *On the Reliability of the Old Testament* (Eerdmans, 2003), pp. 70-79; E.M. Yamauchi, "Ezra and Nehemiah, Books of," in Bill T. Arnold and H.G.M. Williamson, *Dictionary of the Old Testament: Historical Books* (abbreviated DOTHB; InterVarsity Press, 2005), pp. 284-295.